THE UNIVERSAL SOLUTION

FOR NUMERICAL AND LITERAL EQUATIONS

BY WHICH

THE ROOTS OF EQUATIONS OF ALL DEGREES CAN BE EXPRESSED IN TERMS OF THEIR COEFFICIENTS

BY

M. A. McGINNIS

KANSAS CITY, MISSOURI
THE MATHEMATICAL BOOK COMPANY
1900

Norwood Press
J. S. Cushing & Co. — Berwick & Smith
Norwood Mass. U.S.A.

PREFACE.

THIS volume of the author's mathematical discoveries makes its appearance at the request of many able mathematicians, teachers, and scholars throughout the United States, among a few of whom are: J. M. Greenwood, Superintendent of Kansas City Schools and President of the National Association of Education; N. B. Newsom, Professor of Mathematics and Languages at the Kansas State University, Lawrence; R. P. Baker, Professor of Mathematics and Languages, Lamar, and J. C. Shelton, President of Scarritt College, Neosho, Missouri; F. C. Colburn, Principal of High School, Texarkana, Texas; and L. D. Harvey, State Superintendent of Wisconsin.

We feel confident that these discoveries and new methods for the solution of numerical equations will meet with the approval of all teachers and pupils; and especially do we feel that this volume will be food for new thought by all true students of mathematics, — at whose hands we expect a just criticism.

The symbols are such as have been used in prior mathematical works. The definitions are limited, and a few of them new and original.

The theorems are taken up in their order, and their application in the solution of numerical equations fully illustrated and demonstrated.

The formation of equations is fully treated, and the binomial theorem briefly stated.

The Absolute Theorems are of a nature so simple that

any pupil who understands the formation of equations and the nature of imaginaries will have no difficulty in grasping their full meaning.

The roots of quadratics are placed in a new light.

The General Theorem of Imaginary Quantities, in its demonstration and illustrations, fully accounts for such quantities, and gives them a true place and meaning (for the first time) in the history of mathematics,—thus demonstrating that imaginaries are intelligible expressions of quantity. We feel confident that the true student of mathematics will admit that we have forever settled the question of the interpretation of imaginary quantities by placing upon them the only true and correct interpretation.

Theorem 2 is the combined results of Theorems 1 and D, and its universal application in the solution of equations of all degrees is fully illustrated by numerous examples.

Theorems 3, 4, and 5 are taken up in their order, and their applications fully illustrated in the solution of equations of their class.

The application of the several theorems in determining the location, character (real or imaginary), and signs of the roots of an equation is fully illustrated; and the method is such that it will convince any impartial student that it is a great step beyond the Sturm Theorem; and that in the solution of equations of all degrees it greatly excels, in brevity, that of any known method.

Cubic equations are thoroughly treated, and all kinds and classes of such equations are given and solved by the new method.

Biquadratics are more thoroughly treated than in any prior work of this kind; and all kinds and classes of such equations are given and solved by the new method without removing the second term; and in the universal solution for biquadratics will be found the *first true general solution ever* offered for such equations. The mathematical world during a period of over two centuries has been struggling to offer a true general solution of the Fourth degree. Many able mathematicians laid claim to such discovery; and while it has been generally, if not universally, conceded that a general solution had been accomplished, the *New World* now challenges the *Old* in the birth of the *universal solution for biquadratics.*

Of Fifth degree equations all kinds and classes of such equations are given and solved by the new method; and for the first time in the history of mathematics is an algebraic solution given to equations of this class whose roots are all real: and for a further discussion of the Fifth, the reader is referred to the universal solution.

By application of the theorems, if an equation of the Fifth contains all real roots, but approximate, the sum of the plus roots and the sum of the minus roots in the formation of the equation can be determined; and when this is obtained, an algebraic solution lies, because the equation can then be separated into a quadratic and cubic, or the method reduces the Fifth to an equation of the Fourth. When all the roots of the Fifth are real, but have the same sign, the roots are determined without separating the equation. When the Fifth contains only one real root, but approximate, if its Natural cannot be discovered, we give a method for changing the Fifth to an equation of the Tenth. This method of changing the Fifth into an equation of the Tenth is worthy the attention and study of all students of mathematics, *for in this alone lies a solution of the Fifth by quadratics.* If the Fifth contains but one real root, the Tenth will contain two real roots, which will be the separate products of the imaginary roots. The Tenth will separate into two biquadratics whose roots are all imaginary and a quadratic whose roots are real; and the solution of the quadratic is the solution of the Fifth from which it is derived.

These discoveries open up a new field for thought and investigation in the solution of numerical equations; and, in the opinion of an able teacher, scholar, and mathematician, should be thoroughly mastered by every pupil who studies algebra or geometry.

The application of these theorems is almost limitless in the investigation of simple methods for the solution of numerical equations. The theorems are suggestive; that is, they call up in the mind new thoughts, which will be the thoughts of the student, *and this is the only true secret to a proper study of mathematics from the lower to the higher branches.*

Fifth degree equations are followed by W. M. H. Woodward's able discussion of the celebrated Wantzel Theorem. Mr. Woodward fully sets forth the fallacies of the Wantzel Theorem, which has, we believe, taken the place of Abel's demonstration of the impossibility of the solution by radicals of equations higher than the Fourth degree.

The universal solution offers a method by which general solutions can be obtained for equations as high as the Twelfth degree.

The general solutions offered here will be found to be great helps in the solution of equations of their class; and many equations requiring two or three days' labor to find the roots by the Horner method, can be solved in as many hours by the methods and general solutions which this volume contains.

In conclusion, we are deeply grateful to the many teachers and scholars, and especially to Professor J. M. Greenwood, for timely criticism and words of encouragement; and to W. H. Fleming and John V. Fleming for many acts of kindness, and for such valuable assistance that they have become interested in the publication of this volume. And while the work is entirely our own, we are thankful to those who lent assistance in whatever form.

M. A. McGINNIS.

NEOSHO, MISSOURI,
May 1, 1900.

CONTENTS.

SYMBOLS.

$\therefore$ therefore.	Q.E.D. as was to be proved.
$+$ plus.	$\square$ square of, or square.
$-$ minus.	$\boxed{s}$ squares.
$=$ is equal to.	diffs., differences.
$>$ is greater than.	Pure, Pure Imaginary.
$<$ is less than.	Real, Real Imaginary.
$\perp$ perpendicular.	$f(x)$ function x.
$\perp$s perpendiculars.	$F(x)$ Function x.
$\odot$ circle.	$\div$ divided by.
rt. $\angle$ right angle.	$\frac{a}{b}$ a divided by b.
$\triangle$ triangle.	
$\triangle$s triangles.	resp., respectively.
AB line or side AB.	p_1, sum of roots.

p_2, sum of products of roots taken two and two.

$p_3, p_4 \cdots$ sum of products of roots taken three and three $\cdots$.

$a \sim b$ the difference between a and b.

$\sim$ the difference between.

FUNCTIONS OF SQUARES.

DEFINITIONS.

1. A **Definition** is placing within a compass that which we are describing.

2. "**Algebra** is universal arithmetic," compassed by our knowledge of the science of geometry.

3. There can be no advancement in the science of algebra unless there be an advancement in the science of geometry by the discovery of new theorems; for all algebraic processes are established by the laws of geometrical reasoning — either consciously or unconsciously. When consciously, we know the reason and apply the law; when unconsciously, we apply the law in ignorance of its meaning.

4. An **Algebraic Process** is an abbreviated method of arithmetical computation, in which letters or characters are used to represent real quantities which we are to determine.

5. **Quantity** is anything that can be measured.

6. **Number,** as the term is used here, is meant to include one or more units; as 1, 5, 100.

7. An **Equation** is an algebraic expression of equality; as $5x = 10$; $x^3 - 2x = 15$; $x^2 - 5 = 0$.

8. Equations are **Determinate** and **Indeterminate.**

9. A **Determinate Equation** is an algebraic expression of equality in which the values of the unknown quantities are fixed. Thus, if $x + y = 11$ when $xy = 7$, x and y can have but one value.

10. An **Indeterminate Equation** is an algebraic expression of equality in which the values of the unknown quantities may be assumed. Thus, if $x + y = 7$, x and y may take an infinite number of values.

11. All determinate equations containing two or more unknown quantities may be condensed by using but one letter or character, and letting the numbers 1, 2, 3, 4, 5, ⋯, written above and to the left of the character or letter, represent the number of unknown quantities to be considered. Thus: x^1, x^2, x^3, x^4, ⋯, in which 1, 2, 3, 4, 5, ⋯, are called indices or powers, and indicate the number of values assigned to x.

12. The degree of an equation is the number of unknown quantities which the equation contains, and is always indicated by the highest exponent of the letter or character used to represent the number of unknown quantities.

13. An equation containing two values is an equation of the Second Degree, and is usually called a **Quadratic**; when three values are considered, we have an equation of the Third Degree, called a **Cubic**; when four values are considered, we have an equation of the Fourth Degree, called a **Biquadratic**; when five values are considered, we have an equation of the Fifth Degree, called the **Quintic**; and so on, without limit.

14. The coefficient of the unknown quantity is the character, letter, or numeral which stands before it, indicating the number of times the unknown quantity is to be taken. Thus, in $5x$, $dx^2 + nx + q = 0$, 5 is the coefficient of x, and shows that x is taken five times. d and n are the coefficients of x^2 and x respectively; while q may be considered the coefficient of x^0.

15. The general form of an equation of the nth degree is

$$x^n + ax^{n-1} + bx^{n-2} + \cdots + lx + q = 0,$$

in which n may represent any number, odd or even. The coefficient of x^n, the first term, is 1, not expressed, but understood; while $a, b \cdots, l$ are the coefficients of the following terms, and q is the product of the n factors or roots of the equation.

16. A **Root of an Equation** is any number, letter, character, or expression of quantity that will satisfy all the expressed conditions of the equation. Thus: in the equation $x^3 - 6x^2 + 11x - 6 = 0$, the roots are 1, 2, and 3, because if we divide the equation by any one of the expressions $x - 1$, $x - 2$, $x - 3$, the last term will become 0.

17. A **Natural Equation** is an equation in the general form all of whose roots can be accurately expressed.

18. A **Forced Equation** is an equation in the general form all of whose roots cannot be accurately expressed by present known methods.

19. When we discover a method making a rational fraction (that is, a fraction in its lowest terms), a root of $f(x) = 0$, all equations may then be said to be *Natural.*

20. The discovery of its Natural is practically the solution of a Forced Equation.

21. A **Real Quantity** is an intelligible expression of quantity.

22. An **"Imaginary" Quantity,** so called, because not properly understood at the time its name was coined, is the indicated square root of a negative quantity, and as such, is properly defined to mean the indicated square root of the difference of the squares (with its sign changed) of the bases of two right triangles having a common perpendicular which is the radius of a circle.

23. Imaginary Quantities are properly divided into three classes: Imaginary Origins, Real Imaginaries, and Pure Imaginaries.

24. When the sum of the squares of a pair of such quantities is a zero quantity, it is an *Imaginary Origin;* when the sum of the squares is a real plus quantity, the imaginary is Real; and when the sum of squares is a minus quantity, the imaginary is Pure. $\pm 1 \pm \sqrt{-1}$ *is the unit of an Imaginary Origin.*

25. The **Numerical Sum of the Roots of an Equation** is their sum when all the roots are regarded plus quantities.

26. The **Algebraic Sum** is the excess of plus or minus roots in the formation of an equation; and the algebraic sum, *plus* or *minus* the numerical sum, is always an *even number.*

27. A **Proposition** is the simple statement of something to be done.

28. The most important of mathematical propositions are Axioms, Theorems, Corollaries, Postulates, and Problems.

29. Axioms are self-evident truths, requiring no process of reasoning to satisfy the mind that they are true. They may be said to be inherent principles of a sound mind: for he who denies or cannot conceive that "the whole is equal to the sum of all its parts," is not of sound mind.

30. A **Postulate** is the simple statement that a thing can be done; and like the Axiom requires no proof to satisfy the mind that the statement is true.

ILL. — "An apple can be divided into four equal parts," is a postulate.

31. Theorems are propositions requiring proof to establish either their truth or falsity.

ILL. — "If the sum of the squares of the roots of an equation of the Second Degree be a minus quantity, the equation contains a pair of pure imaginary roots," is a theorem. It becomes an Absolute Theorem, when we understand the formation of equations and the nature of imaginaries.

32. A **Corollary** is a theorem the truth of which becomes established by the demonstration of a prior theorem.

33. A **Problem** is a proposed proposition of something to be done.

34. An **Angle** is the opening between two lines that meet in a common point.

35. A **Triangle** is a figure that has three sides and three angles.

36. A **Right Angle** is the opening between two lines that meet in a common point forming a square corner.

37. A **Right Triangle** is a figure having three sides and one right angle.

38. An **Isosceles Triangle** is a triangle having two equal sides and equal angles opposite the equal sides.

39. A **Square** is a figure bounded by four equal sides and having four square corners.

40. Magnitude (size) is the result of extension, and includes lines, surfaces, solids.

NOTE. — The definition that quantity is anything that can be measured, also is meant to include the determination of quantity by weight; and, strictly speaking, imaginary quantities may be said to be included, because they can be measured.

41. Theorem I. — *Twice the sum of the squares of two lines or numbers is equal to the square of their sum plus the square of their difference; three times the sum of the squares of three lines or numbers is equal to the square of their sum plus the sum of the squares of their differences; four times the sum of the squares of four lines or numbers is equal to the square of their sum plus the sum of the squares of their differences; five times the sum of the squares of five lines or numbers is equal to the square of their sum plus the sum of the squares of their differences, and so on, without limit.*

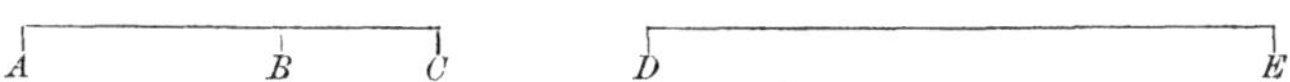

Dem. — Let AB and AC represent any two lines. Then BC will be their difference. Let their sum be represented by the line DE.

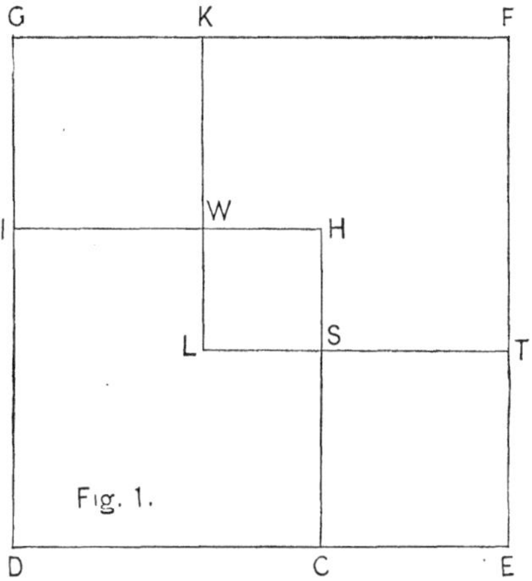

Fig. 1.

Then we are to prove that the square described upon DE + the □ of BC = twice the □ of AC + twice the □ of AB, or that $2\,\overline{AC}^2 + 2\,\overline{AB}^2 = \overline{DE}^2 + \overline{BC}^2$.

Upon the line DE construct the □ $DEFG$. Upon DE, the side of the □ $DEFG$, lay off $DC = AC$, and construct the □ $DCHI$; and upon FG, the side of the □ $DEFG$, lay off $FK = AC$, and construct the $\square$ $FKLT$. Then we have by construction the additional $\square$ $CETS$ and $KGIW$, which are each equal to the square described upon AB; for the side DE is, by hypothesis, equal to $AC + AB$; and DC, by construction, is equal to AC. $\therefore$ If we take from the side DE the side $DC = AC$, there will remain $CE = AB$. We now have twice the square AB and twice the square AC + the square $SHWL$, which, by construction, is equal to the square described upon BC, their difference. $\therefore$ If we add to $\square$ $DEFG$, the $\square$ $SHWL$, we have $2\,\overline{AB}^2 + 2\,\overline{AC}^2 = \overline{DE}^2 + \overline{BC}^2$. Q.E.D.

42. To prove the theorem for n lines or numbers, let a, b, c, $\cdots$, l, m represent n lines or numbers; and $(a^2 + b^2 + c^2 + \cdots + l^2 + m^2)$ represent the sum of the squares of the n lines or numbers.

Then we are to prove that $n\,(a^2 + b^2 + c^2 + \cdots + l^2 + m^2) = (a + b + c + \cdots + l + m)^2$ + the sum of the squares of the differences of the n lines.

(i.) The square of difference of two lines or numbers is equal to the sum of the squares of the lines or numbers diminished by twice the rectangle of the lines, or twice the product of the numbers. [See any algebra or geometry.]

(ii.) Since we have in n times the sum of the squares of the n lines or numbers, not only the square of their sum, but the sum of the squares of the differences of the n lines, each line must appear as many times as there are other lines to compare with it, or in all, $(n - 1)$ times.

(iii.) $\therefore$ The sum of the squares of the differences of the n lines or numbers is equal to

$$(n-1)(a^2 + b^2 + c^2 + \cdots + l^2 + m^2) - (2\,ab + 2\,ac + \cdots + 2\,al + 2\,am + \cdots + 2\,bc + \cdots 2\,bm + 2\,bl + \cdots + 2\,lm).$$

(iv.) $(a + b + c + \cdots + l + m)^2 = (a^2 + b^2 + c^2 + \cdots + l^2 + m^2) + (2\,ab + 2\,ac + \cdots 2\,al + 2\,am + 2\,bc + \cdots 2\,bm + 2\,bl + \cdots 2\,lm).$

(v.) Adding (iii. and iv.), we have

(vi.) $n(a^2 + b^2 + c^2 + \cdots + l^2 + m^2) =$ the square of the sum of the n lines or numbers + the sum of the squares of the differences of the n lines or numbers. Q.E.D.

(vii.) To prove the theorem for $(n + 1)$ lines or numbers. let us introduce another line or number, say t.

43. Then we have, according to the theorem,

(viii.) $(n + 1)(a^2 + b^2 + c^2 + \cdots + e^2 + \cdots + l^2 + m^2 + t^2)$ $= (a + b + c + \cdots + e + \cdots + l + m + t)^2 +$ the sum of the squares of the differences of the $(n + 1)$ lines or numbers.

(ix.) $(a + b + c + \cdots + e + \cdots + l + m + t)^2 = a^2 + b^2 + c^2 + \cdots + e^2 + \cdots + l^2 + m^2 + t^2 + 2ab + 2ac + \cdots + 2ae + \cdots + 2al + 2am + 2at + \cdots + 2nt.$

(x.) The sum of the squares of the differences of the $(n + 1)$ lines or numbers is equal to

$$n(a^2 + b^2 + c^2 + \cdots + e^2 + \cdots + l^2 + m^2 + t^2) - (2ab + 2ac + \cdots + 2ae + \cdots + 2al + 2am + 2at + \cdots + 2mt).$$

Adding (ix. and x.), we have

$$(n + 1)(a^2 + b^2 + c^2 + \cdots + e^2 + \cdots + l^2 + m^2 + t^2) = \cdots,$$

which proves the theorem for $(n + 1)$ lines or numbers.

Thus we have shown that the theorem holds good for two lines, for n lines or numbers, and for $(n + 1)$ lines or numbers. Therefore, if the theorem holds good for *two* lines, for n lines or numbers, and for $(n + 1)$ lines or numbers, it will hold good for $(n + 2)$ lines or numbers, and if the theorem holds good for two, n, $n + 1$, and $(n + 2)$ lines or numbers, it will hold good for $(n + 3)$ lines or numbers. Therefore the theorem holds good for any number of lines or numbers.

44. To illustrate the application of the theorem numerically, take the numbers 6 and 8.

Here we have two numbers. The sum of their squares will be $6^2 + 8^2 = 100$. Then, according to Th. I,

$$100 \times 2 = (6 + 8)^2 + (8 - 6)^2.$$

$100 \times 2 = 200$. $(6 + 8)^2 = 14^2 = 196$, and $(8 - 6)^2 = 2^2 = 4$, $\therefore$ $200 = 196 + 4$.

Let $14 =$ sum of ⓢ of three numbers, $14 \times 3 = 42 =$ □ of sum of numbers + sum of ⓢ of the differences of the numbers. (Th. I.) The side of the greatest □ in 42 whose side is integral is 6, = the sum of the three numbers. $\therefore$ $42 - (6)^2 = 6 =$ sum of the ⓢ of the differences of the numbers. There being three numbers, there are three differences, the sum of whose ⓢ $= 6$. $\therefore$ $6 \times 3 = 18 =$ □ of sum of differences + sum of ⓢ of the differences of differences. The side of the greatest □ in 18, whose side is integral, is $4 -$, which is the sum of the differences of the three numbers whose sum of ⓢ $= 42$. $4 \div 2 = 2 =$ the difference between the first and third number taken in the order of their magnitude. $\therefore$ 1, 2, and 3 are the numbers, and $1^2 + 2^2 + 3^2 = 14$; and $14 \times 3 = 42 = (1 + 2 + 3)^2 + (3 - 1)^2 + (2 - 1)^2 + (3 - 2)^2$, which illustrates the application of Th. I to three numbers.

In the same way the student can apply the theorem to any number of integers.

THEOREMS ALGEBRAICALLY DEMONSTRATED.

45. Theorem A. — *The square described upon the sum of two lines diminished by twice their rectangle is equal to the sum of their squares.*

Dem. — Let a and b be any two lines, and ab their rectangle. Then we are to prove that $(a + b)^2 - 2\,ab = a^2 + b^2$.

1. $(a + b)^2 = a^2 + b^2 + 2\,ab$ [See any algebra.]
2. $2 \times ab \quad = \quad 2\,ab$

$\therefore$ $(a + b)^2 - 2\,ab = a^2 + b^2$ [Taking 2 from 1.] Q.E.D.

46. Theorem B. — *The square described upon the difference of two lines plus twice the rectangle of the lines is equal to the sum of their squares.*

DEM. — Let a and b be any two lines, and ab their rectangle. Then we are to prove that $(a - b)^2 + 2\,ab = a^2 + b^2$.

$$\begin{array}{ll} 1. & (a-b)^2 = a^2 + b^2 - 2\,ab \\ 2. & 2 \times ab \quad = \qquad\qquad 2\,ab \end{array}$$

Adding (1) and (2), we have $a^2 + b^2 = (a - b)^2 + 2\,ab$. Q.E.D.

Theorem C. — *The square described upon the sum of two lines diminished by four times the rectangle of the lines is equal to the square of their difference.*

DEM.

$$\begin{array}{ll} 1. & (a+b)^2 = a^2 + b^2 + 2\,ab \\ 2. & 4 \times ab \quad = \qquad\qquad 4\,ab \end{array}$$

Taking (2) from (1), we have $a^2 + b^2 - 2\,ab = (a - b)^2$. Q.E.D.

47. Theorem D. — *The square described upon the sum of any number of lines diminished by twice the sum of their rectangles, taken two and two, is equal to the sum of their squares.*

DEM. — Let $(a + b + c + d + \cdots + l + m)$ represent the sum of n lines, in which $a, b, c, \cdots$ represents any magnitude, great or small, and n any number of such magnitudes.

Then we are to prove that $(a + b + c + d + \cdots + l + m)^2 - (2\,ab + 2\,ac + \cdots + 2\,lm) = a^2 + b^2 + c^2 + d^2 + \cdots + l^2 + m^2$.

It has been shown that $(a + b)^2 - 2\,ab = a^2 + b^2$. (Th. A.)

The square of the sum of n lines is equal to the sum of the squares of each of the lines + twice each line into the sum of the lines that follow it.

$$\begin{aligned} \therefore\ (a + b + c + d + \cdots + l + m)^2 \\ = a^2 + b^2 + c^2 + d^2 + \cdots + l^2 + m^2 + 2\,a\,(b + c + d + \cdots + l + m) \\ + 2\,b\,(c + d + \cdots + l + m) + 2\,c\,(d + \cdots + l + m) + 2\,lm. \end{aligned}$$

If we take from the right-hand member their equivalent magnitudes, there will remain $a^2 + b^2 + c^2 + d^2 + \cdots + l^2 + m^2 =$ to the sum of the squares of the n magnitudes. Q.E.D.

If it holds good for n magnitudes or lines, let us introduce another magnitude, say o. Then, let $n + 1 = h$ magnitudes, and

$(a+b+c+d+\cdots+l+m+o)$ will represent the sum of $n+1$ or h magnitudes. Then will the square of the sum of h magnitudes be equal to

$$a^2+b^2+c^2+d^2+\cdots+l^2+m^2+o^2+2a(b+c+\cdots+l+m+o)$$
$$+2b(c+d+\cdots+l+m+o)+\cdots+2mo.$$

And if the right-hand member be reduced by its equivalent magnitude, there will remain $a^2+b^2+c^2+d^2+\cdots+l^2+m^2+o^2=$ the sum of the squares of h magnitudes or lines. Q.E.D. ∴ If the theorem holds good for n magnitudes or lines, and for $n+1$ magnitudes or lines, it will hold good for any number of lines or magnitudes. Q.E.D.

48. Theorem E. — *The square described upon the difference of any number of lines so combined as to form one difference, minus twice the sum of the rectangles of such lines, is equal to the sum of the squares of the lines.*

DEM. — (i.) Let $(a+b+c+-d+-\cdots+-e+-\cdots+-l+-m)$ represent the difference of n lines, in which a, b, c, $-d$, $\cdots$ represent any magnitudes or lines great or small, and n any number of such magnitudes or lines so taken.

(ii.) Then we are to prove that the square described upon

$$(a+b+c+-d+-\cdots+-e+-\cdots+-l+-m)^2$$
$$-(2ab+2ac+-2ad+-2ae+\cdots+2lm)$$
$$=a^2+b^2+c^2+d^2+\cdots+e^2+\cdots+l^2+m^2.$$

(iii.) We have shown that the sum of the squares of n lines is equal to the square of their sum minus twice the sum of their rectangles taken two and two. (Th. D.) We have also shown that the sum of the squares of two lines is equal to the square of their difference *plus* twice their rectangle. (Th. B.)

(iv.) The square of the difference of n lines so combined as to make one difference, is equal to the sum of the squares of the n lines diminished by twice the sum of the rectangles of such lines taken two and two.

$$\therefore\ (a+b+c+-d+-\cdots-e+-\cdots+-l+-m)^2$$
(v.) $$=a^2+b^2+c^2+d^2+\cdots+e^2+\cdots+l^2+m^2$$
$$+(2ab+2ac+-2ad+-\cdots+2lm).$$

(vi.) Twice the sum of their rectangles two and two

$$=(2ab+2ac+-2ad+-\cdots+-2ae+-\cdots+2lm).$$

Subtracting (v. and vi.) we have $(a^2 + b^2 + c^2 + d^2 + \cdots + e^2 + \cdots + l^2 + m^2)$ = the sum of their squares. Q. E. D.

[The demonstration can be carried further by introducing another *line* (letter) as in Dem. of Th. D.]

49. Theorem F. — *The square described upon the sum of any number of lines diminished by the sum of the squares of the lines is equal to twice the sum of the rectangles of the lines taken two and two.*

Dem. — Let $(a + b + c + d + \cdots + l + m)$ represent the sum of n lines, in which a, b, c, d $\cdots$ represents any magnitude, integer, or line, and n the number, or any number of such lines, magnitudes, or integers. Then we are to prove that

$$(a + b + c + d + \cdots + l + m)^2 - (a^2 + b^2 + c^2 + d^2 + \cdots + l^2 + m^2)$$
$$= 2\,(ab + ac + ad + \cdots + lm).$$
$$(a + b + c + d + \cdots + l + m)^2$$
$$= a^2 + b^2 + c^2 + d^2 + \cdots + l^2 + m^2 + 2\,ab + 2\,ac + 2\,ad + \cdots + 2\,lm.$$

(Th. D.) If the sum of the squares of the n lines be taken from $a^2 + b^2 + c^2 + d^2 + \cdots + l^2 + m^2 + 2\,ab + \cdots + 2\,lm$, there will remain $2\,ab + 2\,ac + 2\,ad + \cdots + 2\,lm$ = twice $(ab + ac + ad + \cdots + lm)$.

Q. E. D.

Cor. 1. — The square described upon the sum of any number of lines, diminished by four times the sum of the rectangles of the lines taken two and two, is equal to the sum of the squares of the lines, minus twice the sum of their rectangles taken two and two.

50. Theorem G. — *If the sum of the squares of any three given lines be reduced by a certain magnitude, and the sum of their rectangles, taken two and two, be reduced by a like magnitude, the sum of the differences of such lines will remain unchanged, and the square of the sum of such lines will be reduced by three times such magnitude.*

Dem. — Let a, b, and c represent the lines, and l the sum of their squares, and m the sum of their rectangles taken two and two.

We then have

$$(x.)\ \begin{cases} a^2 + b^2 + c^2 = l, \text{ and} \\ ab + ac + bc = m. \end{cases}$$

1. $3 \times l = 3l$ = square of sum + sum of squares of differences of lines. (Th. I.)

2. $2 \times l - 2 \times m = 2l - 2m$ = sum ▢ of differences. (140.)

3. $\therefore 3l - (2l - 2m) = l + 2m = (a + b + c)^2$.

Let l and m be each reduced by t. We now have

$$(y.)\ \begin{cases} a^2 + b^2 + c^2 = l - t, \text{ and} \\ ab + ac + bc = m - t. \end{cases}$$

4. $(l - t) \times 3 = 3l - 3t = (a + b + c)^2$ + sum ▢ of diffs. (Th. I.)

5. $2 \times (l - t) - 2(m - t) = 2l - 2m$.

6. $\therefore (2) = (5)$. Q.E.D.

7. $3l - (3l - 3t) = 3t$. [Taking 4 from 1.] Q.E.D.

COR. 1.—Increasing the sum of squares, and sum of rectangles taken two and two by like magnitudes, increases the square of their sum by three times such magnitude, while the square of their sum of differences will remain unchanged.

51. Theorem H.—*If the sum of the squares of any three given lines be increased by a certain magnitude, and the sum of their rectangles taken two and two remain unchanged, the square of the sum of such lines will be increased by such magnitude, and the square of their sum of differences will be increased by twice such magnitude.*

DEM.—Let a, b, and c represent the lines, and l the sum of their squares, and m the sum of their rectangles taken two and two. Let l become $l + t$. Then

$$(x.)\ \begin{cases} a^2 + b^2 + c^2 = l + t, \text{ and} \\ ab + ac + bc = m. \end{cases}$$

1. Th. I, $3l + 3t = (a + b + c)^2$ + sum ▢ of diffs.

2. $2(l + t) - 2m = 2l - 2m + 2t$ = sum ▢ of diffs.

3. $(a + b + c)^2 = l + 2m$. (140.)

4. $(3l + 3t) - (2l - 2m + 2t) = l + 2m + t$. [Taking 2 from 1.]

5. $\therefore (l + 2m + t) - (l + 2m) = t$. Q.E.D.

6. $\therefore (2l - 2m + 2t) - (2l - 2m) = 2t$. Q.E.D.

COR. 1.—If the sum of the squares of three lines be reduced by a certain magnitude, and the sum of their rectangles two and two remain unchanged, the square of the sum of lines will be decreased by such magnitude, and the square of the sum of their differences will be reduced by twice such magnitude.

52. Theorem I. — *If the sum of the squares of any three given lines remain unchanged, and the sum of their rectangles taken two and two be reduced by a certain magnitude, the sum of squares of differences will be increased by twice such magnitude, and the square of the sum of such lines will be reduced by twice such magnitude.*

DEM.—Let a, b, and c represent the lines, and l the sum of their squares, and m the sum of their rectangles taken two, and let m become $m - t$. Then we have

$$(\text{x.}) \begin{cases} a^2 + b^2 + c^2 = l, \text{ and} \\ ab + ac + bc = m - t. \end{cases}$$

1. $l + 2m = (a + b + c)^2$. (Th. H, 3.)

2. $2l - 2m =$ sum $\boxed{\text{s}}$ of diffs. (Th. G, 2.)

3. $3l = (a + b + c)^2 +$ sum $\boxed{\text{s}}$ of diffs. (Th. I.)

4. $2l - 2(m - t) = 2l - 2m + 2t =$ sum $\boxed{\text{s}}$ of diffs.

5. $\therefore 3l - (2l - 2m + 2t) = l + 2m - 2t = (a + b + c)^2$.

6. $\therefore (l + 2m) - (l + 2m - 2t) = 2t$. Q.E.D.

7. $\therefore (2l - 2m + 2t) - (2l - 2m) = 2t$. Q.E.D.

COR. 1.—If the sum of the squares of any three lines remain unchanged, and the sum of their rectangles two and two be increased by a certain magnitude, the square of the sum of lines will be increased by twice such magnitude, and the sum of the squares of the differences of such lines will be reduced by twice such magnitude.

53. Theorem K. — *If the sum of the squares of any four lines be reduced by a certain magnitude, and the sum of their rectangles taken two and two be reduced by a like magnitude, the square of the sum of such lines will be reduced by three times such magnitude, and the square of the sum of differences of such lines will be reduced by once such magnitude.*

DEM. — Let a, b, c, and d represent the lines, and l the sum of their squares, and m the sum of their rectangles two and two. We then have

$$(\text{x.}) \begin{cases} a^2 + b^2 + c^2 + d^2 = l, \\ \qquad p_2 \qquad = m. \end{cases}$$

1. Th. I, $4 \times l = 4\,l =$ □ of sum + sum of [s] of diffs.
2. $3 \times l - 2 \times m = 3\,l - 2\,m =$ sum [s] of diffs. (140.)
3. $\therefore\ 4\,l - (3\,l - 2\,m) = l + 2\,m = (a + b + c + d)^2$.

Let l become $l - t$, and m become $m - t$. Then

$$(\text{y.}) \begin{cases} a^2 + b^2 + c^2 + d^2 = l - t, \text{ and} \\ \qquad p_2 \qquad = m - t. \end{cases}$$

4. Th. I, $4 \times (l - t) = 4\,l - 4\,t =$ □ of sum + sum [s] of diffs.
5. $3\,(l - t) - 2\,(m - t) = 3\,l - 2\,m - t =$ sum [s] of diffs.
6. $\therefore\ 4\,l - (4\,l - 4\,t) = 4\,t =$ diffs. of squares of sums, and sums of diffs. of squares.
7. $(4\,l - 4\,t) - 3\,l - 2\,m - t = l + 2\,m - 3\,t$.
8. $\therefore\ l + 2\,m - 3\,t$ taken from $l + 2\,m = 3\,t$. Q.E.D.
9. $\therefore\ 3\,l - 2\,m - 3\,l - 2\,m - t = t$. Q.E.D.

COR. 1. — If the sum of squares and sum of p_2 be increased by a certain magnitude, the square of the sum of such lines will be increased by three times such magnitude and the square of sum of differences will be increased by once such magnitude.

54. Theorem L. — *If the sum of the squares of four lines be increased by a certain magnitude, and the sum of their rectangles remain unchanged, the square of the sum of such lines will be increased by* once *such magnitude, and the square of sum of differences will be increased by three times such magnitude.*

DEM. — Let a, b, c, and d represent the lines, and l the sum of their squares, and m the sum of their rectangles two and two. Then will

$$(x.) \begin{cases} a^2 + b^2 + c^2 + d^2 = l, \text{ and} \\ \quad p_2 \quad = m. \end{cases}$$

1. From Th. K, $4l = \square$ of sum + sum $\boxed{s}$ of diffs.

2. From Th. K, $3l - 2m =$ sum of $\boxed{s}$ of diffs.

Let l be increased by t, then

$$(y.) \begin{cases} a^2 + b^2 + c^2 + d^2 = l + t, \text{ and} \\ \quad p_2 \quad = m. \end{cases}$$

3. $4(l + t) = 4l + 4t = \square$ of sum + sum $\boxed{s}$ of diffs.

4. $3(l + t) - 2m = 3l - 2m + 3t =$ sum $\boxed{s}$ of diffs.

5. $\therefore 4l + 4t - (3l + 2m - 3t) = l + 2m + t.$

6. $\therefore l + 2m + t > l + 2m$, by t. Q.E.D.

7. $\therefore 3l - 2m + 3t - 3l - 2m = 3t.$ Q.E.D.

COR. 1. — If the sum of the squares of four lines be reduced by a certain magnitude while the sum of their rectangles two and two remain unchanged, the square of the sum of lines will be reduced by such magnitude, and the square of sum of differences of lines will be reduced by three times such magnitude.

COR. 2. — If the sum of rectangles of four lines be decreased by a certain magnitude, and the sum of their squares remain unchanged, the square of sum of lines will be reduced by twice such magnitude, and the square of sum of differences will be increased by twice such magnitude.

COR. 3. — If the sum of squares of four lines be increased by a certain magnitude, and the sum of their rectangles two and two be decreased by a like magnitude, the square of the sum of such lines will be decreased by *once* such magnitude, and the sum of the squares of their differences will be increased by *five* times such magnitude.

55. Theorem M. — *If the sum of the squares, and the sum of the rectangles taken two and two, of* **five** *lines be reduced by* *like magnitudes, the square of the sum of such lines will be reduced by three times such magnitude, and the sum of squares of differences will be reduced by twice such magnitude.*

DEM. — Let a, b, c, d, and e represent such lines, and l the sum of their squares, and m the sum of their rectangles two and two. Then

$$(\text{x.}) \begin{cases} a^2 + b^2 + c^2 + d^2 + e^2 = l, \text{ and} \\ \qquad\qquad p_2 \qquad\qquad = m. \end{cases}$$

1. $5 \times l = 5l = \square$ of sum + sum $\boxed{s}$ of diffs. (Th. I.)

2. $4 \times l - 2 \times m =$ sum $\boxed{s}$ of diffs. $= 4l - 2m$.

3. $5l - 4l - 2m = l + 2m = \square$ of sum $= (a + b + c + d + e)^2$.

Let l now become $l - t$, and m, $m - t$. Then we have

$$(\text{y.}) \begin{cases} a^2 + b^2 + c^2 + d^2 + e^2 = l - t, \text{ and} \\ \qquad\qquad p_2 \qquad\qquad = m - t. \end{cases}$$

4. $5 \times (l - t) = 5l - 5t = \square$ of sum + sum $\boxed{s}$ of diffs.

5. $4(l - t) - 2(m - t) = 4l - 2m - 2t =$ sum $\boxed{s}$ of diffs.

6. $\therefore (5l - 5t) - 4l - 2m - 2t = l + 2m - 3t$.

7. $4l - 2m - 2t < 4l - 2m$ by $2t$. Q.E.D.

8. $l + 2m - l + 2m - 3t = 3t$. Q.E.D.

COR. 1. — If the sum of the squares of five lines remain unchanged, and the sum of their rectangles two and two be reduced by a certain magnitude, the square of the sum of such lines will be reduced by twice such magnitude, and the sum of squares of differences of such lines will be increased by twice such magnitude.

COR. 2. — If the sum of the squares of five lines be reduced by a certain magnitude, and the sum of their rectangles remain unchanged, the square of the sum of such lines will be reduced by *once* such magnitude, and the sum of squares of differences of lines will be reduced by *four* times such magnitude.

COR. 3. — If the sum of the squares of five lines remain unchanged, and the sum of their rectangles two and two be increased by a certain magnitude, the square of sum of lines will be *increased* by twice such magnitude, and the square of sum of differences of lines will be *reduced* by *twice* such magnitude.

FORMATION OF EQUATIONS. BINOMIAL THEOREM.

56. Equations containing two or more roots represented by one unknown quantity, and in the general form,

$$(x^n + ax^{n-1} + bx^{n-2} + \cdots + ex^2 + mx + v = 0),$$

are all built in the same way, being the continued product of the unknown quantity combined with the several values (roots) assigned to it.

If a and b represent two values of x, then $x - a = 0$, and $x - b = 0$. If we multiply $x - a$ by $x - b$, we obtain

$$x^2 - (a + b)x + ab = 0.$$

Introduce another letter, say c, then $x - c = 0$, and

$$(x - a)(x - b)(x - c)$$
$$= x^3 - (a + b + c)x^2 + (ab + ac + bc)x - abc = 0.$$

Introducing another letter, say d, then $x - d = 0$, and

$$(x - a)(x - b)(x - c)(x - d) = x^4 - (a + b + c + d)x^3$$
$$+ (ab + ac + ad + bc + bd + cd)x^2$$
$$- (abc + abd + acd + bcd)x + abcd = 0.$$

Introducing another letter (*value*, root), say e, then $x - e = 0$, and

$$(x - a)(x - b)(x - c)(x - d)(x - e)$$
$$= x^5 - (a + b + c + d + e)x^4$$
$$+ (ab + ac + ad + ae + bc + bd + be + cd + ce + de)x^3$$
$$- (abc + abd + abe + acd + ace + ade + bcd + bce + bde + cde)x^2$$
$$+ (abcd + abce + abde + acde + bcde)x - abcde = 0.$$

Examining the foregoing equations, we find the following relations to exist:

(1) The number of terms of each equation is *one* more than the highest power of the unknown quantity.

(2) The exponent of x decreases by *one* with each successive term, and that the last term is the product of all the letters or roots, and may be considered the coefficient of x^0.

(3) That the coefficient of the *first term* is 1, not expressed, but understood.

(4) That the coefficient of the *second term* is the *sum* of the several letters $(a, b, c, \cdots)$ with their *sign changed.*

(5) That the coefficient of the *third term* is the *sum* of the products of the letters taken *two* and *two.*

(6) That the coefficient of the *fourth term* is the *sum* of the products of the letters taken in pairs of *three*, or taken *three* and *three*, with their *sign changed.*

(7) That the coefficient of the *fifth term* is the *sum* of the products of the letters taken *four* and *four.*

(8) That the *last term* is the continued product of all the letters that enter into the formation of the equation.

(9) We also notice that when the letters are $+$ quantities that the coefficient of the *odd* powers of x will be $+$, and the coefficient of the *even* powers of x will be $-$. It therefore follows that if all the values assigned to x be *minus* quantities, all the terms of the equation will be $+$. Therefore, when all the roots of an equation are *plus* quantities, the terms of the equation will be alternately $+$ and $-$, and when they are all *minus* quantities, the terms will be all $+$; for if $a, b, c, \cdots$ become $-a, -b, -c, \cdots$,

$$x+a=0, \quad x+b=0, \quad x+c=0, \quad \cdots.$$

57. The *general law* governing the formation of the coefficients of complete equations may be stated as follows:

The coefficient of the second term is the sum of all the

roots with their signs changed; the coefficient of third term is the sum of the products of the roots taken two and two; the coefficient of fourth term is the sum of the products of the roots taken three and three with their signs changed, etc.; and that the last term is the product of all the roots with their signs changed.

58. Should all the letters (roots) be equal, then the coefficient of the second term would be represented by $-5a$, third term coefficient by $10 \times (-a)^2 = 10a^2$, and so on, so that an equation of the fifth degree whose roots are equal may be written

$$x^5 - 5ax^4 + 10a^2x^3 - 10a^3x^2 + 5a^4x - a^5 = 0.$$

Examining this last equation, we notice that the exponent of x decreases by 1 with each successive term, and that the *exponent of a increases* by 1 with each successive term; and that the numerals -5, $+10$ are the number of the several quantities that enter into the formation of the equation. This fact led Newton to the discovery of the Binomial Theorem, which, briefly stated, is as follows:

Take $(x+a)^5 = x^5 + 5ax^4 + 10a^2x^3 + 10a^3x^2 + 5a^4x + a^5 = 0.$

59. (1) The leading letter (x) enters all the terms except the last, and the following letter (a) all the terms except the first.

(2) The exponent of the leading letter (x) decreases by 1, while those of the following letter, beginning with the second term, increases by 1; and the sum of the exponents in any term is equal to the exponent of the given power. Thus, the exponents of $(x+a)^5$ will be x^5, ax^4, a^2x^3, a^3x^2, a^4x, a^5.

(3) If the coefficient of any term be multiplied by the exponent of the leading letter of the same term, and the

product divided by the number of such term from the left, the result will be the coefficient of the term next following.

Thus the coefficient of the first term (x^5) is 1, of the second term $\frac{1 \times 5}{1} = 5$, of the third $\frac{4 \times 5}{2} = 10$, and so on.

60. Expand $(x+a)^n$.

$$(x+a)^n = x^n + nax^{n-1} + \frac{n(n-1)}{1 \times 2} a^2x^{n-2} + \frac{n(x-1)(n-2)}{1 \times 2 \times 3} a^3x^{n-3}$$

$$+ \cdots + \frac{n(n-1)}{1 \times 2} a^{n-2}x^2 + nax^{n-1} + a^n.$$

The above is the general formula for the expansion of a binomial.

If the second term is *plus*, the terms are all *plus*. If the second term is *minus*, the *even* powers of the leading letter will be *minus*, and odd powers *plus*.

61. We have discovered that when the roots of any equation are all equal, that the sum of the squares of the roots multiplied by the degree of the equation is equal to the square of the sum of the roots; and that the sum of the squares of the roots of any equation higher than the second degree is independent of the absolute term of the equation.

62. Equations containing all equal roots in the *Natural* are easily solved, no matter what the degree of the equation or magnitude of absolute term.

Take the equation

$$(a) \quad x^5 - 2.5\,x^4 + 2.5\,x^3 - 1.25\,x^2 + .3125\,x - 3 = 0.$$

Here we have

1. $(-2.5)^2 - 2(2.5) = 1.25 =$ sum of ⊡ of roots. (Th. D.)
2. $1.25 \times 5 = 6.25$, which $= (-2.5)^2$. (Th. I.)
3. $\therefore$ Roots are all equal, being $\frac{1}{5}$ of $2.5 = .5$.
4. $(.5)^5 = .03125 =$ absolute term of the *Natural*.

5. $\therefore\ 3 - .03125 = 2.96875$; and the *real* roots of (a) will be $.5 + (2.96875)^{\frac{1}{5}}$.

The other roots of this equation will be equal conjugate imaginaries, because $(.3125)^2 - 2(-1.25 \times -3) =$ a minus quantity. [See Th. V and Absolute Theorems.]

63. All determinate equations of two unknown quantities can be written in the form of a *quadratic*. Thus, if $x+y=11$, and $xy=10$, we may write $x^2 - 11x + 10 = 0$. (57.)

All determinate equations containing three unknown quantities may be written in the form of a *cubic*.

Thus, if $a+b+c=6$, $ab+ac+bc=11$, and $abc=7$, we may write the cubic

$$x^3 - 6x^2 + 11x - 7 = 0. \quad (57.)$$

The same way we write for determinate equations of *four*, *five*, and *six* unknown quantities, equations of the *fourth*, *fifth*, and *sixth* degrees, and so on.

64. It has been long established by prior mathematicians that an equation of the mth degree has precisely m roots and no more.

65. It is seen that the coefficients of an equation in the general form are the combinations of its roots. The coefficient of the second term being the sum of the roots, and the coefficients of the following terms being the sum of the combination products in sets of two, three, four, and so on.

66. The rule of combinations shows how many products enter into each coefficient.

This rule may be stated as follows:

The number of combinations of A things taken b at a time may be written in the form of a fraction, — writing for its numerator the continued product of b successive numbers from A downward; and for its denominator the continued product of b successive numbers from 1 upward.

To Illustrate: Let it be required to find the number of combinations in 5 things taken in sets of two, three, four, and five.

In sets of two we have $\frac{5 \times 4}{1 \times 2} = 10$; and

in sets of three we have $\frac{5 \times 4 \times 3}{1 \times 2 \times 3} = 10$; and

in sets of four we have $\frac{5 \times 4 \times 3 \times 2}{1 \times 2 \times 3 \times 4} = 5$; and

in sets of five we have $\frac{5 \times 4 \times 3 \times 2 \times 1}{1 \times 2 \times 3 \times 4 \times 5} = 1$,

which is the continued product of the five things or numbers.

EXAMPLES. PROPOSITIONS.

67. Build an equation whose roots are 1, 2, 3; and one whose roots are 1, 2, and -3; and then build an equation whose roots are the products of these roots taken two and two. What kind of equations do we call them?

68. Build an equation whose roots are 1, 6, $3+\sqrt{2}$, $3-\sqrt{2}$. What kind of an equation will you have?

69. Form an equation of the second, one of the third, one of the fourth, and one of the fifth degree, having 0 for the sum of the squares of its roots.

70. Form an equation of the second, one of the third, one of the fourth, and one of the fifth degree, all of whose roots can be expressed in the form of irrational fractions or imaginary quantities.

71. Separate into quadratic equations the following biquadratics:

$$x^4 + 2x^3 + 2x^2 + 4x + 8 = 0,$$
$$x^4 + 2x^3 + 2x^2 + 4x + 4 = 0,$$
$$x^4 + x^3 + x^2 + x + 1 = 0,$$
$$x^4 + 2x^3 + 2x^2 + 4x + 7 = 0,$$
$$x^4 - 2x^3 - x^2 + 2x + 8 = 0.$$

72. Factor the following equations, that is, separate them into the several binomial factors which build the equations:

$$x^3 - 6x^2 + 11x - 6 = 0,$$
$$x^3 - 6x^2 + 12x - 8 = 0,$$
$$x^4 - 8x^3 + 24x^2 - 64x + 16 = 0,$$
$$x^5 - 15x^4 + 85x^3 - 225x^2 + 274x - 120 = 0,$$
$$x^5 - 2x^4 - 16 = 0,$$
$$x^5 + 2x^4 - 3x^3 - 3x^2 + 2x + 1 = 0,$$
$$x^5 - px^4 - px^3 - px^2 - px - (p+1) = 0,$$
$$5x^5 - 51x^4 + 160x^3 - 160x^2 + 51x - 5 = 0.$$

73. Find its *Natural* to each of the following equations:

$$x^3 - 7x + 7 = 0,$$
$$x^3 - 6x - 9 = 0,$$
$$x^4 - 8x^3 + 21x^2 - 22x + 7 = 0,$$
$$x^4 - 6x^3 + 3x^2 + 26x - 23 = 0,$$
$$x^7 + x^6 - 14x^5 - 14x^4 + 49x^3 + 49x^2 - 36x - 43 = 0.$$

74. Can all the roots of an odd degree equation be accurately expressed if its roots are not integral?

75. What class of odd degree equations have we shown, whose roots can all be accurately expressed when such roots are not integral?

TWO UNKNOWN QUANTITIES. FUNCTIONS OF SQUARES.

76. Application of theorems in the solution of equations containing two unknown quantities.

77. To find x and y.

$$\text{Given}\begin{cases}(1)\ x-y=3,\\(2)\ x^2+y^2=117.\end{cases}$$

SOLUTION. (*a*) $(117\times 2-3^2)^{\frac{1}{2}}=x+y=15.$ (Th. I.)

(*b*) $\therefore\ x=\dfrac{15+3}{2}=9$; and $y=\dfrac{15-3}{2}=6.$

$$\text{Given}\begin{cases}(1)\ x^2-y^2=28,\\(2)\ (x^2+y^2)^{\frac{1}{2}}=10.\end{cases}$$

SOLUTION.

(*a*) $(10)^2\times 2=200=2\,x^2+2\,y^2=(x+y)^2+(x-y)^2.$ (Th. I.)

(*b*) $28\times 2=56=2\,x^2-2\,y^2.$ (From 1.)

(*c*) $\therefore\ (256)^{\frac{1}{2}}=2\,x=16.$ Whence, $x=8$ (Adding (*a*) and (*b*), and taking square root.)

(*d*) $\therefore\ x^2-y^2=64-y^2=28.$ Whence, $y=\sqrt{64-28}=6.$ (Substituting the value of x^2 in (1).)

78. $$\text{Given}\begin{cases}(1)\ x^2y+xy^2=30,\\(2)\ x^4y^2+x^2y^4=468.\end{cases}$$

SOLUTION.

(*a*) $468\times 2-(30)^2=36=(x^2y-xy^2)^2.$ (Th. I.)

(*b*) $\therefore\ x^2y-xy^2=6=\sqrt{36}.$

(*c*) $\therefore\ x^2y=\dfrac{30+6}{2}=18$; and $xy^2=\dfrac{30-6}{2}=12.$

(*d*) $\therefore\ x=\sqrt{\dfrac{18}{y}}$, and $x=\dfrac{12}{y^2}\cdot$ (From c.)

(*e*) $\therefore\ \sqrt{\dfrac{18}{y}}=\dfrac{12}{y^2}\cdot$ Squaring both sides and multiplying by $\dfrac{y^4}{18}$,

(*f*) $y^3=8.$ Whence, $y=\sqrt[3]{8}=2.$

Substituting the value of y in (*d*) or (*e*), we have $x=3.$

79. Given $\begin{cases} (1)\ x^2+y^2=25, \\ (2)\ 2\,xy=24. \end{cases}$

SOLUTION. (*a*) $(25+24)^{\frac{1}{2}} = x + y = 7.$

(*b*) $(25-24)^{\frac{1}{2}} = x - y = 1.$

(*c*) $\therefore\ x = \frac{7+1}{2} = 4;\ y = \frac{7-1}{2} = 3.$

80. Given $\begin{cases} (1)\ \frac{1}{x}+\frac{1}{y}=\frac{1}{2}, \\ (2)\ x^2y+xy^2=162. \end{cases}$

SOLUTION. (*a*) $x + y = \frac{xy}{2}.$ (Multiplying (1) by xy.)

(*b*) $x^2y + xy^2 = \frac{x^2y^2}{2}.$ (Multiplying (*a*) by xy.)

(*c*) $\therefore\ \frac{x^2y^2}{2} = 162.$ $(2 = b.)$

(*d*) $\therefore\ xy = 18.$ (Multiplying (*c*) by 2 and taking the square root of both sides.)

(*e*) $\therefore\ x + y = 9.$ (Substituting xy in (*a*).)

(*f*) $9^2 - 4 \times 18 = 9 = (x-y)^2.$ (Th. C.)

(*g*) $\therefore\ x - y = 3 = \sqrt{9}.$

(*h*) $\therefore\ x = \frac{9+3}{2} = 6,$ and $y = \frac{9-3}{2} = 3.$

81. Given $\begin{cases} (1)\ \frac{x+y}{x-y}+\frac{x-y}{x+y}=\frac{10}{3}, \\ (2)\ x^2+y^2=45. \end{cases}$

SOLUTION. (*a*) $45 \times 2 = 90 = (x+y)^2 + (x-y)^2.$

If the values of x and y are integral, and their diff. is less than either x or y, the side of the greatest square (integral) in 90 will be their sum. This we see to be

$$9 = x + y, \text{ and } 90 - (9)^2 = 9 = (x-y)^2.$$

Whence $x - y = 3.$ $\therefore\ x = \frac{9+3}{2} = 6,$ and $y = \frac{9-3}{2} = 3.$

Substituting these values in (1), the equation is satisfied. $\therefore$ 6 and 3 are respectively the values of x and y.

82. Given $\begin{cases} (1)\ \dfrac{x+y}{x-y}+\dfrac{x-y}{x+y}=\dfrac{11}{3}, \\ (2)\ x^2+y^2=45. \end{cases}$

SOLUTION.

(*a*) $2x^2+2y^2=\frac{11}{3}(x^2-y^2)=(x+y)^2+(x-y)^2$. (Th. I.)

(*b*) $2x^2+2y^2=90=(x+y)^2+(x-y)^2$. (Th. I.)

(*a*) is obtained from (1) by multiplying the equation through by $(x-y)(x+y)=x^2-y^2$, and (*b*) is found by multiplying both sides of (2) by 2.

(*c*) $\therefore\ \frac{11}{3}(x^2-y^2)=90$. Whence

(*d*) $x^2-y^2=90\times\frac{3}{11}=\frac{270}{11}$. (Dividing both sides of (*c*) by $\frac{11}{3}$.)

Adding (2) and (*d*), we have

(*e*) $2x^2=45+\frac{270}{11}=69\frac{6}{11}$. Whence

(*f*) $x^2=34\frac{17}{22}$, and $x=\sqrt{34\frac{17}{22}}$; and $y=(45-34\frac{17}{22})^{\frac{1}{2}}=(10\frac{5}{22})^{\frac{1}{2}}$.

83. Given $\begin{cases} (1)\ x^2+y^2=208, \\ (2)\ \ x+y=20. \end{cases}$

SOLUTION. $(208\times 2-\overline{20}^2)^{\frac{1}{2}}=4=x-y$. (Th. I.)

$$\therefore\ x=\frac{20+4}{2}=12,\text{ and } y=\frac{20-4}{2}=8.$$

84. Given $\begin{cases} (1)\ x^3-y^3=56, \\ (2)\ x^2y-xy^2=16. \end{cases}$

SOLUTION. (*a*) $x^3+x^2y-xy^2-y^3=72$. (Adding (1) and (2).)

(*b*) $x^2+2xy+y^2=\dfrac{72}{x-y}$. (Dividing (*a*) by $x-y$.)

(*c*) $xy=\dfrac{16}{x-y}$. (Dividing (2) by $x-y$).

(*d*) $\therefore\ \dfrac{72}{x-y}-4\left(\dfrac{16}{x-y}\right)=\dfrac{8}{x-y}=(x-y)^2$. (Th. C.)

(*e*) $\therefore\ x-y=\sqrt[3]{8}=2$.

(*f*) $\therefore\ x+y=\sqrt{\frac{72}{2}}=6$. (Substituting $(x-y)$ in (*b*) and taking the square root of both sides.)

(*g*) $\therefore\ x=\dfrac{6+2}{2}=4$; $y=\dfrac{6-2}{2}=2$.

85. Given $\begin{cases} (1)\ x^4 + y^4 = 706, \\ (2)\ x^2 - y^2 = 16. \end{cases}$

SOLUTION.

(*a*) $706 \times 2 = 1412 = (x^2 + y^2)^2 + (x^2 - y^2)^2$. (Th. I.)

(*b*) $1412 - (16)^2 = 1156 = (x^2 + y^2)^2$. Whence $x^2 + y^2 = 34$.

(*c*) $(x^2 + y^2) + (x^2 - y^2) = 34 + 16 = 2x^2 = 50$. Whence $x = \pm 5$.

(*d*) $x^2 + y^2 - (x^2 - y^2) = 34 - 16 = 18 = 2y^2$. Whence $y = \pm 3$.

86. Given $\begin{cases} (1)\ x^4 + y^4 = 705, \\ (2)\ x^2 - y^2 = 17. \end{cases}$

SOLUTION. (*a*) $(705 \times 2 - (17)^2)^{\frac{1}{2}} = x^2 + y^2 = \sqrt{1121}$.

(*b*) $\therefore\ 2x^2 = 17 + \sqrt{1121}$. Whence $x = \sqrt{8.5 + \sqrt{280.25}}$.

(*c*) $\therefore\ y = \sqrt{8.5 - \sqrt{280.25}}$.

(Substituting the value of x in 2.)

x and y may be either + or −; but one cannot be + and the other −.

87. Given $\begin{cases} (1)\ x^2 - xy = 54, \\ (2)\ xy - y^2 = 18. \end{cases}$

SOLUTION. (*a*) $x - y = 6$. (Taking (2) from (1) and extracting the square root.)

(*b*) $x^2 - y^2 = 72$. (Adding (1) and (2).)

(*c*) $\therefore\ x + y = 12$. (Dividing (*b*) by (*a*).)

(*d*) $\therefore\ x = \frac{12 + 6}{2} = 9$, and $y = \frac{12 - 6}{2} = 3$.

x and y may be both + or both −, but cannot have opposite signs.

88. Given $\begin{cases} (1)\ x^2 + y^2 = 8.5, \\ (2)\ x - y = 1. \end{cases}$

SOLUTION. (*a*) $[8.5 \times 2 - (1)^2]^{\frac{1}{2}} = x + y = 4$. (Th. I.)

(*b*) $\therefore\ x = \frac{4 + 1}{2} = 3$; $y = \frac{4 - 1}{2} = 1.5$.

89. Given $\begin{cases} (1)\ x^3 + y^3 = 35, \\ (2)\ x + y = 5. \end{cases}$

SOLUTION.

(*a*) $x - y = \sqrt{7 - xy}$. (Dividing (1) by (2), and subtracting xy from both sides, and extracting the square root of both members.)

(*b*) $x + y = \sqrt{7 + 3\,xy}$. (Dividing (1) by (2), adding $3\,xy$ to both sides, and taking square root.)

(*c*) $\therefore\ \sqrt{7 + 3\,xy} = 5$. ($b = 2$.) Whence

(*d*) $7 + 3\,xy = 25$. (Squaring both sides of (*c*).)

(*e*) $\therefore\ xy = 6$. (Transposing and reducing (*d*).)

(*f*) $\therefore\ x - y = 1$. (Substituting xy in (*a*), and taking square root of the right-hand member.)

(*g*) $\therefore\ x = \frac{5 + 1}{2} = 3$; $y = \frac{5 - 1}{2} = 2$. (x and y may exchange values, but both are plus.)

90. Given $\begin{cases} (1)\ x^3 - y^3 = 218, \\ (2)\ x + y = 12. \end{cases}$

SOLUTION. Let $x - y = d$.

Then by (137) we write the cubic

$d^3 + 432\,d = 872$. Whence $d = 2 = x - y$; $x = \frac{12 + 2}{2} = 7 \cdot\ y = 5$.

(See solution of cubics.)

91. Given $\begin{cases} (1)\ x^2 + y^2 = \frac{5\,xy}{2}, \\ (2)\ x - y = \frac{1}{4}xy. \end{cases}$

SOLUTION.

(*a*) $\frac{5\,xy}{2} \times 2 = 5\,xy = (x + y)^2 + (x - y)^2$. (Th. I.)

(*b*) $\therefore\ 5\,xy - (\frac{1}{4}\,xy)^2 = (x + y)^2 = 5\,xy - \frac{x^2y^2}{16}$.

(*c*) $\therefore\ x + y = \sqrt{5\,xy - \frac{x^2y^2}{16}}$.

(*d*) $x + y = \sqrt{\frac{9\,xy}{2}}$. (Adding $2\,xy$ to both sides of (1), and taking the square root of both members.)

(e) $\therefore$ ($c = d$) $5\,xy - \frac{x^2y^2}{16} = \frac{9\,xy}{2} = xy = 8$. (Multiplying both sides by 16, and dividing the result by xy.)

(f) $\therefore\ x - y = 2$. (Substituting xy in (2).)

(g) $\therefore\ x + y = 6$. (Substituting xy in (c) or (d).)

$$\therefore\ x = \frac{6+2}{2} = 4\text{; and } y = \frac{6-2}{2} = 2.$$

92. Given $\begin{cases} (1)\ x + y = s. \\ (2)\ x^2 + y^2 = t. \end{cases}$

SOLUTION. (a) $t \times 2 = 2\,t = (x+y)^2 + (x-y)^2$. (Th. I.)

(b) $2\,t - (s)^2 = (x-y)^2$. Whence $x - y = \sqrt{2\,t - s^2}$.

(c) $\therefore\ x = \frac{s + \sqrt{2\,t - s^2}}{2}$; and $y = \frac{s - \sqrt{2\,t - s^2}}{2}$.

93. Given $\begin{cases} (1)\ x + \sqrt{xy} + y = 19, \\ (2)\ x^2 + xy + y^2 = 133 \end{cases}$

SOLUTION.

(a) $133 \times 3 = 399 = (x + \sqrt{xy} + y)^2 +$ sum [s] of diffs. (Th. I.)

(b) $399 - (19)^2 = 38 =$ sum [s] of three diffs.

(c) $(38 \times 3)^{\frac{1}{2}} = 10 =$ sum of diffs. (The side of the greatest square whose side is integral is taken from 38×3.)

(d) $\therefore\ 2\,x - 2\,y = 10 = x - y = 5$. (From ($d$) we readily find $x = 4$, or 9, and $y = 9$, or 4.)

SECOND SOLUTION.

(e) $x + y = 19 - \sqrt{xy}$. (Transposing terms in (1).)

(f) $x^2 + y^2 = 133 - xy$. (Transposing terms in (2).)

(g) $(133 - xy) \times 2 = 266 - 2\,xy = (19 - \sqrt{xy})^2 + (x-y)^2$. (Th. I.)

(h) $\therefore\ 38\sqrt{xy} = 228$. (Transposing and reducing (g).)

(i) $\therefore\ \sqrt{xy} = 6$, whence $xy = 36$.

(j) Substituting the values of $\sqrt{xy}$ and xy in (1) and (2), we have $x + y = 13$, and $x^2 + y^2 = 97$.

$$\therefore\ (97 \times 2 - (13)^2)^{\frac{1}{2}} = 5 = x - y. \quad \text{(Th. I.)}$$

$$\therefore\ x = \frac{13 \pm 5}{2} = 9\text{, or } 4\text{, and } y = \frac{13 \mp 5}{2} = 4\text{, or } 9.$$

94. *Problem.* — The sum of the squares of the extremes of four numbers in arithmetical progression is 200, and the sum of the squares of the means is 136. What are the numbers?

95. *When any four numbers have a common difference, the sum of the extremes will equal the sum of the means; also, the square root of the difference of the sum of the squares of the extremes and means, divided by 2, will be their common difference.*

SOLUTION of 94. $\frac{(200 - 136)^{\frac{1}{2}}}{2} = 4 =$ common difference. (95)

$\therefore$ We may write for the numbers

$$a = \text{1st},$$
$$a + 4 = \text{2d},$$
$$a + 8 = \text{3d},$$
$$a + 12 = \text{4th}.$$

$\therefore\ a^2 + (a + 12)^2 = 200 = a^2 + 12\,a = 28.$

$$a^2 + (\ ) + \overline{\tfrac{12}{2}}|^2 = 28 + \overline{\tfrac{12}{2}}|^2 = 64,$$
$$a + 6 = 8.$$

Whence, $a = 8 - 6 = 2.$

$\therefore$ 2, 6, 10, and 14 are the numbers.

96. *Problem.* — Find six numbers in arithmetical progression such that the sum of the squares of the first and sixth shall be 148; and the sum of the squares of the second and fifth shall be 115; and the sum of the squares of the third and fourth shall be 97.

SOLUTION. (a) $\frac{(115 - 97)^{\frac{1}{2}}}{2} = \frac{\sqrt{18}}{2} = \sqrt{4.5} =$ common difference. (95)

Having found the common difference, find the numbers as in solution of 94.

97. The sum of the sixth and seventh of seven terms in geometrical progression is 96; and the sum of the two preceding terms is 24. What are the numbers?

97 *a.* *The sum of any two consecutive terms in geometrical progression, divided by the sum of the two immediately preceding terms, is equal to the square of their ratio.*

SOLUTION of 97. Letting a, b, c, d, e, and f represent the terms, we then have $f + g = 96$, and $d + e = 24$.

$$\therefore \frac{f+g}{d+e} = \frac{96}{24} = 4 = r^2 \text{ (the square of their ratio).}$$

$\therefore r = 2$. $\therefore$ 1, 2, 4, 8, 16, 32, and 64 are the numbers.

97 *b.* *Problems.* (1) What would the numbers be in the last example, if $f + g = 48$, and $d + e = 24$?

(2) $\begin{cases} x^2 + y^2 = -14, \\ xy = 7. \end{cases}$

(3) $\begin{cases} x^2 + y^2 = 100, \\ xy = 51. \end{cases}$

(4) $\begin{cases} x + \sqrt{xy} + y = 17, \\ x^2 + xy + y^2 = 22. \end{cases}$

(5) $\begin{cases} xy^6 + xy^8 = 648, \\ x^2y^3 + x^2y^4 = 648. \end{cases}$

(6) A, B, and C meet at a hotel. Says A to B and C, if you will give me one-half of your money, I will have \$100; B says to A and C, give me one-half of your money, and I then will have \$100; C says to A and B, give me one-fourth of your money and I will have \$100.

How much money did each have?

Can you give an arithmetical solution for 6?

ABSOLUTE THEOREMS.

98. If the sum of the squares of the roots of an equation of the second degree be equal to 0, the equation contains a pair of imaginary roots; and the square of the real part of the imaginary is numerically equal to that part of the root affected by the radical, with its sign changed.

99. If the sum of the squares of the roots of an equation of the second degree be a minus quantity, the equation contains a pair of pure imaginary roots.

100. If the *sum of the squares* of the roots of *any equation* be a *minus quantity,* the equation contains imaginary roots.

101. If the sum of the squares of the products of the roots taken two and two, three and three, four and four, and so on, be, in either case, a minus quantity, the equation contains imaginary roots.

102. If the sum of the squares of the roots of an equation be equal to 0, the equation contains imaginary roots; and the sum of the squares of the real roots of such an equation is numerically equal to the sum of the squares of the imaginary roots.

103. Even degree equations whose last term is negative must have two real roots of opposite signs.

104. When the second term of any equation is wanting, and the sign of its third term plus, the equation always contains pure imaginary roots.

105. If the absolute term of an equation be 0, the equation is, at least, one degree lower than the highest power of the unknown quantity.

106. If the sum of the squares of the roots be equal to the sum of the squares of the products of the roots indicated by the first power of the unknown quantity, the equation contains real roots when the sum of the squares is plus, and imaginary roots when the sum of the squares is minus.

107. The square of a real root is a plus quantity; also, the sum of the squares of a pair of Real Imaginaries is a plus quantity; and the sum of the squares of a pair of Pure Imaginaries is a minus quantity.

108. If the absolute term of any Natural Equation be separated into as many factors as the equation contains degrees, and if the sum of the squares of such factors be equal to the square of the coefficient of the second term, minus twice the coefficient of the third term, then will such factors be the true numerical roots of such equation, *if the sum of such factors be equal to the true sum of roots.*

109. If an equation is built according to the general law, the true signs and characters of its roots can be determined by the relations that exist between the signs of the coefficients of the second and third term and absolute term.

110. An equation of odd degree, if it be true, has an odd number of real roots; and, therefore, must have, at least, one real root affected by a sign contrary to its absolute term.

111. An equation whose terms are all plus, and roots real, can have no real plus roots; and if its roots are real, and its terms alternately plus and minus, it can have no real minus roots.

112. If an equation of the *third degree* contains all real roots, and in the form of $x^3 - px + q = 0$ be so changed that q becomes $> q$, the roots of such an equation will be alternately increased and decreased, such that the increase in sum of roots plus the decrease of roots shall equal the sum of increase in roots. Thus, $x^3 - 7x + 6 = 0$ has for its three roots $1, 2, -3$. Should the equation read $x^3 - 7x + 7 = 0$, then the roots will be > 1, < 2, > -3; numerical sum of roots > 6. The increase in 1 plus the increase in 3 will equal the decrease in 2 plus the increase in 6. This law will hold good as long as the roots are real.

113. If the absolute term of any equation be increased within certain limits, the roots of such equation will be alternately increased and decreased, and this law will hold good while all the roots are real. If the equations be of even degree, and its terms alternately plus and minus, or all plus, the sum of increases shall equal the sum of decreases.

114. If all the terms of an equation of the *third degree* be expressed, and the sum of the squares of its roots, taken two and two, a perfect square, the square root of sum of squares of roots, two and two, will be equal to $ac+bc-ab$. All such equations have one root equal to the sum of the other two roots.

Proposition. Prove that if $a+b=c$,

that $$\sqrt{(\overline{ab}^2+\overline{ac}^2+\overline{bc}^2)}=ac+bc-ab.$$

115. An equation of even degree having its odd terms missing, and all its terms plus except the last, can contain but two equal real roots of opposite signs, — the other roots of the equation being imaginary roots in pairs. Thus, $x^6+4x^4+2x^2-136=0$, and $x^4+4x^2-326=0$, are equations of this class.

116. If any number of lines or integers be arranged in the order of their magnitude, so that the difference between the first and second shall equal the difference between the third and fourth, and the difference between the fifth and sixth, and so on, without limit, then will the sum of the first and fourth equal the sum of the second and third; and the sum of the first and sixth will equal the sum of the second and fifth, and so on, without limit.

117. An equation of the sixth degree, whose terms are alternately plus and minus, and whose odd terms are missing, contains real and imaginary roots in pairs; and if such an equation be formed from the cubic in the form of $x^3-px+q=0$, the roots of such sixth degree equation will be double the roots of the cubic; and if the roots of the cubic are all real, the roots of the sixth will be all real;

and if the cubic contains real and imaginary roots, the sixth will contain real and imaginary roots.

118. Letting a, b, and c represent the roots of an equation of the third degree, when $a + b = c$, then will

$$c(a^2+b^2)+b(c^2+a^2)+a(b^2+c^2)=c^2(a+b)+b^2(c+a)+a^2(b+c).$$

119. If the second and third term of any equation higher than the second degree be wanting, the equation contains imaginary roots.

120. An equation of odd degree, whose terms are alternately plus and minus, may contain imaginary roots; and if it be of even degree, the roots may be all real, or all imaginary.

121. If it be found that the roots of any Natural equation of even degree are consecutive, or have a common difference, the roots of such equation will always sustain the same relation to each other, even should the absolute term be increased or diminished. Thus,

$$x^4 - 10\,x^3 + 35\,x^2 - 50\,x + 24 = 0,$$

has for its three roots 1, 2, 3, 4; should the absolute term be greater or less than 24, the roots will always sustain the same relation as in the Natural.

122. If all the terms of an equation of the third degree be expressed, and alternately plus and minus, or all plus, and the sum of the squares of its roots, and sum of squares of its roots taken two and two, equal to 0, the equation contains but one real root, which is the cube root of absolute term if it be a perfect square.

123. The middle term of three consecutive numbers and numbers having a common difference is equal to one-third their sum.

124. The sum of the squares of the differences of the roots of any equation is equal to the sum of the squares of the roots multiplied by the degree of the equation less 1, minus twice the sum of the products of the roots taken two and two.

125. Letting a, b, c, d, and e represent the roots of an equation in the order of their magnitude, then will the sum of the differences of the roots of an equation of the third degree be represented by $(2c-2a)$, and of an equation of the fifth degree by $(4e+2d)-(4a+2b)$.

126. The sum of the differences of any odd number of integers is always an even number.

127. If the sum of the squares of the roots of an odd degree equation be equal to the sum of the squares of its roots indicated by the first power of the unknown quantity, the equation is generally called "recurring" or "reciprocal"; and if the sum of squares of roots is plus, the roots are real.

128. If the quotient of two numbers be a perfect square, their product will be a perfect square.

129. The sum of the squares of roots, sum of squares of products of roots, taken two and two, three and three, and so on, are always plus when the equation contains all real roots.

130. If the sum of the squares of the roots multiplied by the degree of the equation is numerically less than the square of their algebraic sum, or numerical sum of roots, the equation contains imaginary roots.

131. The difference of any two numbers divided by the difference of their cube roots, minus the square of the difference of the roots, is equal to three times the product of the roots; and the product of the roots, plus the quotient arising from dividing the difference of the numbers by the difference of their roots, is equal to the square of the sum of the roots.

132. Any equation of the *fourth degree* having the sum of the squares of its roots, and the sum of the squares of its roots taken three and three, in both cases, *a zero quantity*, the roots of such equation will be *equal conjugate imaginaries*, unless it be a "reciprocal" equation.

$$x^4 - 8x^3 + 32x^2 - 64x + 64 = 0$$

is an equation of this class, and can readily be separated into two quadratics.

133. The general equation in the form of

$$(A)\ x^n - px^{n-1} - px^{n-2} - px^{n-3} - \cdots - px - (p+1) = 0$$

always has $(p+1)$ for its real root; and when such an equation is reduced by $(p+1)$, it becomes

$$(B)\ x^{n-1} + x^{n-2} + x^{n-3} + \cdots + 1 = 0.$$

If (A) be *odd*, it will contain but one real root, $(p+1)$; if it be *even*, it will contain two real roots, $p+1$ and -1. The imaginary roots of all such equations of the third degree are always the same, being $\frac{-1 \pm \sqrt{-3}}{2}$, and the imaginary roots of such equations of the fifth degree being

$$\tfrac{1}{4}(-1 \pm \sqrt{5} \pm \sqrt{-10 \pm 2\sqrt{5}}).$$

134. If an equation of the *third degree* have all its terms plus, and the sum of the squares of roots a minus quantity, the imaginary roots of such an equation will be plus; and if its terms be alternately plus and minus, its imaginary roots will be minus.

$$x^3 - 2x^2 + 3x - 7 = 0 \text{ and } x^3 + 2x^2 + 3x + 7 = 0$$

are equations of this class. The roots of such equations are numerically the same but of opposite signs.

NOTE.—When reference is made to an imaginary, as *plus* or *minus*, we mean such conjugate imaginaries that have real parts, and the *initial* of the imaginary means its *real part.*

135. A cubic equation in the form of $x^3 - px + q = 0$ may be changed to an equation of the *sixth degree* by changing it to the following form, $y^6 - 2py^4 + p^2y^2 - q^2 = 0$, in which $-2p$ is the sum of the squares of the roots of the cubic with its sign changed; p^2 is the sum of the squares of the products of the roots, taken two and two, of the cubic; $-q^2$ is the square of the absolute term of cubic with sign changed.

136. If one-half of the sum of the squares of the roots of an equation of the *fourth degree* be a perfect square, and if one-third of the sum of the squares of the roots of an equation of the *sixth degree* be a perfect square, and so on, for even-degree equations, the roots of such equations are the sides of right triangles, or isosceles triangles, standing on the same base which is the diameter of a circle, and equal to the square root of such perfect square.

137. Four times the difference of the cubes of any two numbers is equal to the cube of their difference, plus three times the square of their sum into their difference.

138. If twice the sum of the squares of three numbers be equal to twice the sum of their products taken two and two, the numbers are equal; and if three times the sum of the squares of four numbers be equal to twice the sum of their products taken two and two, the numbers are equal; and if four times the sum of the squares of five numbers be equal to twice the sum of their products taken two and two, the numbers are equal, and so on, without limit.

139. The sum of the cubes of the roots of an equation of the third degree may be expressed algebraically as follows:

Let $x^3 + mx^2 + nx + q = 0$ be an equation of the third degree, and, in the general form, in which m, the coefficient of x^2, represents the sum of the roots, and n the sum of the products of roots two and two, and q the product of all the roots, then $a^3 + b^3 + c^3 = m^3 + 3q - 3mn$.

140. The sum of the squares of the differences of the roots of any equation is equal to the sum of the squares of the roots multiplied by the degree of the equation less one, minus twice the products of the roots taken two and two.

141. The sum of the cubes of the roots of an equation of the fourth degree in the form of $x^4 + mx^3 + nx^2 + ox + q = 0$ may be expressed algebraically as follows:

$$a^3 + b^3 + c^3 + d^3 = m^3 + 3o - 3mn.$$

THREE OR MORE UNKNOWN QUANTITIES.

142. Application of theorems in the solution of equations containing *three* or *more unknown quantities*, introductory to methods for the solution of *Higher Numerical Equations*.

143. Given $\begin{cases} a^2 + b^2 + c^2 = 133, \\ ab + ac + bc = 94, \end{cases}$ to find values for a, b, c.

SOLUTION.

(a) $(133 \times 2) - (2 \times 94) = 78 =$ sum [s] of differences. (140.)

(b) $133 \times 3 - 78 = 321 = (a + b + c)^2$. (Th. I.)

(c) $\therefore a + b + c = 17.9164 + = \sqrt{321}$.

(d) $78 \times 3 = 234 =$ □ of sum of diffs. + sum [s] of the diffs. of diffs.

(e) The side of the greatest □ in 234, whose side is integral, is 15, which is rejected (26). 14 is then taken, and we have

(f) $2c - 2a = 14$, (125). Whence $c - a = 7$.

(g) $c = 17.9164 - (a + b)$. (From (c).)

(h) $c = 7 + a$. (From (f).)

(i) $\therefore 2c = 24.9164 - b$. (Adding ($g$) and ($h$).)

(j) $c = 12.4582 - \frac{b}{2}$. (Dividing ($i$) by 2.)

(k) $a = 5.4582 - \frac{b}{2}$. (Taking (h) from (g) and dividing by 2.)

(l) Squaring both sides of (j) and (k), and adding b^2 to both sides, and substituting for $(a^2 + b^2 + c^2)$, 133, and transposing and collecting terms, we have

(m) $b^2 - 11.9442\,b = -34.66579$, from which we find $b = 6.9721+$. Substituting in (j) and (k) the value of (b), we obtain $a = 1.9721$, $c = 8.9721$.

144. The foregoing (143) illustrates the method in full. We will now show how the work may be *greatly abbreviated.*

145. If we *increase* the *sum* of *squares,* and the *sum* of *products,* each by 1, the sum of differences will remain unchanged (Th. G, Cor. 1). If the sum of the squares and the sum of the products are each increased by 1 in (143), the sum of $a + b + c = 18$.

$\therefore 18 - 17.9164 = .0836 =$ the sum of *three equal reductions* in the original numbers, which, if their sum equals 18, and their sum of squares, 134, and sum of products *two* and *two,* 95, will be 2, 7, 9.

$\therefore$ The values of a, b, and c will be $\frac{1}{3}$ of .0836 less than 2, 7, and 9.

$$\therefore a = 2 - \tfrac{1}{3} \text{ of } .0836 = 1.9721+,$$
$$b = 7 - \tfrac{1}{3} \text{ of } .0836 = 6.9721+,$$
$$c = 9 - \tfrac{1}{3} \text{ of } .0836 = 8.9721+.$$

NOTE. — The greater portion of the operation in an example of this kind can be performed mentally.

146. We will now place another condition upon the problem, — that of the product of the numbers. Taking the equations

$$(1) \quad a + b + c = 18,$$
$$(2) \quad ab + ac + bc = 95,$$
$$(3) \quad abc = 125,$$

we have found that 2, 7, and 9 will satisfy the first and second conditions of the problem, but will not satisfy its *third condition: that of its product. The sum of numbers and sum of products taken two and two have remained unchanged*, while their *natural* product has been *reduced by* 1.

(a) $\therefore$ The values of a, b, and c will be <2, >7, and <9 (113); so that $<2\times>7\times<9=125$, and $<2+>7+<9=18$; and $<2\times>7+<2\times<9+>7\times<9=95$.

(b) These products will be so affected that 14 will be >14, 18, <18, and 63, >63. $\therefore$ $<2\times>7=>14$, $<2\times<9=<18$, and $>7\times<9=>63$.

(c) As the change of only 1 in the product can produce but a slight change in the values (original) of a, b, and c, $125\div>63=1.9=a$ to one decimal place. If we divide the remainder by $63+\frac{1}{2}\times.9^2$, we will obtain the next decimal part of $a=.07$.

$$\therefore\ a=1.97 \textit{ to two places of decimals.}$$

(d) $125\div>14=8.92=c$ *to two places of decimals.* By adding the approximate values of a and c together, and taking their sum from 18, we obtain 7.10, which is b *to two places of decimals.*

(e) Having found a, b, and c to two places of decimals, we find the sum of the differences of a, b, and c, thus far found, to be 13.90.

Should we change the equation to a cubic, and approximate the roots by the Horner method, we cannot find for sum of roots a value closer than 17.9999+, *which will necessitate the approximation of each root to at least six places of decimals.*

(f) $\therefore$ $17.9999-(1.97+7.10+8.92)=.0099$. If we divide .009 by 3, and .0009 by 3^2, and add the results, we will obtain .0031, *which is the third and fourth decimal place in one-half their sum of differences.*

(*g*) $\therefore \dfrac{13.90}{2} + .0031 = 6.9531 = c - a.$

From $c - a = 6.9531$ we find a, b, and c, as in (143), to be

$$a = 1.9717,$$
$$b = 7.1034,$$
$$c = 8.9248,$$

each to four places of decimals.

147. In the solution of (146) we have solved the *cubic* built by $(x-2)(x-7)(x-9) =$

(*A*) $$x^3 - 18x^2 + 95x - 126 = 0,$$

with its absolute term reduced by 1, *so that it becomes*

(*B*) $$x^3 - 18x^2 + 95x - 125 = 0.$$

NOTE.—*It will be shown in the solution of cubics that* (*A*) *can readily be reduced to a quadratic; and that the solution of either* (*A*) *or* (*B*) *is the simple solution of a quadratic equation; but as all equations of the third degree, having all its terms expressed, cannot be solved by quadratics without removing second term, the method* (146) *may be used to advantage in cases where the roots are all real quantities.*

148. Given $\begin{cases} a + b + c = 6, \\ ab + ac + bc = 12, \\ abc = 39, \text{ to find } a, b, \text{ and } c. \end{cases}$

SOLUTION.

(*a*) $6^2 - 2 \times 12 = 12 = a^2 + b^2 + c^2$. (Th. D.)

(*b*) $12 \times 2 - 2 \times 12 = 0 =$ sum ⓢ of differences. (124.)

(*c*) $\therefore a = b = c$ (138) $\doteq 6 \div 3 = 2$.

Their sum equals 6, the sum of their products taken two and two $= 12$; but their product $= 8$. But 39 is given as the product of abc. Are the values of a, b, and c all *real values?* $(12)^2 - 2(6 \times 39) = -324 = \overline{ab}^2 + \overline{ac}^2 + \overline{bc}^2$. $\therefore$ Only one of the values are *real.* (101.) Then $a = 2 + \sqrt[3]{(39-8)}$. *Find b and c.* It solves the cubic

$$x^3 - 6x^2 + 12x - 39 = 0.$$

149. Given $\begin{cases} a^2+b^2+c^2=48, \\ ab+ac+bc=48, \\ abc=67, \text{ to find } a, b, c. \end{cases}$

SOLUTION.

(*a*) $48 \times 2 - 2(48) = 0 =$ sum [s] of diffs.

(*b*) $\therefore$ The values of a, b, and c are equal, and $48 \div 3 = 16 = a^2$, or b^2, or c^2. $\therefore (16)^{\frac{1}{2}} = 4 = a$, b, or c. Their product, 64, is less by 3 than the *assumed* product. $\therefore a = 4 + \sqrt[3]{3}$. The other two values ($b$ and c) are found from a quadratic.

$12 \div 3 = 4 =$ either one of the roots in the *natural*, and $\sqrt[3]{3}$ indicates the equation $y^3 = 3$, whence $y = \sqrt[3]{3}$.

$(y^3 - 3 = 0) \div (y - \sqrt[3]{3}) = 0 = y^2 + \sqrt[3]{3}\,y + \sqrt[3]{9}$, which solved, gives for a or b

$$4 \pm \frac{\sqrt[3]{3} \pm \sqrt{-3\sqrt[3]{9}}}{2}.$$

150. Given $\begin{cases} a^2+b^2+c^2+d^2=134, \\ p_2=175, \\ (c+d)-(a+b)=6, \\ abcd=720. \end{cases}$

SOLUTION.

(*a*) $134 \times 3 - 2(175) = 52 =$ sum [s] of diffs. (124.)

(*b*) $(134 \times 4 - 52)^{\frac{1}{2}} = 22 = a + b + c + d$. (Th. I.)

(*c*) $\therefore \frac{22+6}{2} = 14 = c + d$; and $\frac{22-6}{2} = 8 = a + b$.

(*d*) $(c+d)^2 + (a+b)^2 = a^2 + b^2 + c^2 + d^2 + 2\,ab + 2\,cd = 260$.

(*e*) $\therefore 2\,ab + 2\,cd = 126$. (Taking from both sides of (*d*) 134.)

(*f*) $\therefore ab + cd = 63$. (Dividing (*e*) by 2.)

(*g*) $ab = 63 - cd$. (Transposing cd in (*f*).)

(*h*) $ab = \frac{720}{cd}$. (From problem.)

(*i*) $\therefore 63 - cd = \frac{720}{cd}$. (Ax. 1.)

(*j*) Solving (*i*), we obtain $cd = 48$, whence $ab = 15$.

(*k*) From $a + b = 8$,
$ab = 14$, $a = 3$, $b = 5$; and from
$c + d = 14$,
$cd = 48$, $c = 6$, $d = 8$.

151. *Problem.* — *What would be the value of a, b, c, or d, if* $abcd = 719$? *If* $abcd = 13$?

152. Given $\begin{cases} a^2 + b^2 + c^2 + d^2 + e^2 = 151, \\ p_2 = 237, \\ abc - de = -26, \\ (a+b+c) - (d+e) = -5, \\ abcde = 1680, \text{ to find } a, b, c, d, e. \end{cases}$

SOLUTION.

(*a*) $151 \times 4 - 2(237) = 130 =$ sum [S] of diffs. (140.)

(*b*) $(151 \times 5 - 130)^{\frac{1}{2}} = (625)^{\frac{1}{2}} = 25 = a + b + c + d + e.$

(*c*) $\therefore \frac{25 + -5}{2} = 10 = a + b + c$; $\frac{25 - (-5)}{2} = d + e = 15.$

(*d*) $abc = de - 26$. (From problem.)

(*e*) $abc = \frac{1680}{de}.$

(*f*) $\therefore de - 26 = \frac{1680}{de}$, whence

(*g*) $de = 56$. (Solving (*f*).)

(*h*) We now have $d + e = 15$, and $de = 56$, from which we find $d = 7$, $e = 8$.

(*i*) $151 - (7^2 + 8^2) = 38 = a^2 + b^2 + c^2.$

(*j*) $38 \times 3 - (10)^2 = 14 =$ sum [S] of diffs.

(*k*) $(14 \times 3)^{\frac{1}{2}} = 6 = 2c - 2a$. (By taking side of greatest square in (14×3).)

(*l*) $c - a = 3$, by which we readily find $a = 2$, $b = 3$, $c = 5$.

Problem. — Find the values of a, b, c, d, and e, if their product in the foregoing (152) was 1200.

153. Given $\begin{cases} a + b + c = 18, \\ p_2 = 95, \\ abc = 126, \text{ to find } a, b, \text{ and } c. \end{cases}$

SOLUTION.

(*a*) $\overline{ab}^2 + \overline{ac}^2 + \overline{bc}^2 = 4489 = \overline{95}^2 - 2(18 \times 126)$. (Th. D.)

(*b*) $(4489)^{\frac{1}{2}} = 67 = ac + bc - ab$. (114.)

(c) $(ab + ac + bc) - (ac + bc - ab) = 2\,ab = 28 = (95 - 67)$.

(d) $\therefore\ ab = 14$, whence $c = \frac{126}{14} = 9$.

(e) $18 - 9 = 9 = a + b$; and from $a + b = 9$, and $ab = 14$, we find $a = 2,\ b = 7$.

154. Given $\begin{cases} a + b + c = 6, \\ p_2 = 11, \\ abc = 6, \text{ to find } a,\ b,\ c. \end{cases}$

SOLUTION.

(a) $a^3 + b^3 + c^3 = 36 = 6^3 + (3 \times 6) - (3 \times 6 \times 11)$. (139.)

(b) $\therefore$ 1, 2, 3, are respectively the values of a, b, c.

155. *The sum of the cubes of the first n natural numbers, as 1, 2, 3, 4, 5, $\cdots$, n, is always equal to the square of their sum.*

It, therefore, follows

That if the sum of the cubes of the roots of any equation is equal to the square of their sum, the roots of such equation are the first n natural numbers.

PROBLEMS FOR SOLUTION

(1) Given $\begin{cases} x^2 - y^2 = 0, \\ xy = 5. \end{cases}$ (2) Given $\begin{cases} x^2 + y = 11, \\ xy = 6. \end{cases}$

(3) Given $\begin{cases} x^2 + y^2 + z^2 = 38, \\ xy + xz + yz = 30, \\ xyz = 30. \end{cases}$

(4) Given $\begin{cases} x^2 + y^2 + z^2 = 62, \\ z - x = 5, \\ xyz = 42. \end{cases}$

(5) Given $\begin{cases} x + y = z, \\ x^2 + y^2 + z^2 = \frac{217}{72}, \\ xyz = \frac{17}{24}. \end{cases}$

(6) Given $\begin{cases} x^2 + y^2 + z^2 = \frac{21}{64}, \\ xy + xz + yz = \frac{7}{32}, \\ xyz = \frac{1}{64}. \end{cases}$

(7) Given $\begin{cases} (x-y)^2+(x-z)^2+(y-z)^2=56, \\ x^2+y^2+z^2=115, \\ xz+yz-xy=57. \end{cases}$

(8) Given $\begin{cases} x^2+y^2+z^2=0, \\ xy+xz+zy=8, \\ xyz=8. \end{cases}$

(9) Given $\begin{cases} x^2+y^2+z^2+w^2=54, \\ (x+w)=(z+y), \\ xw+yz=22, \\ (x-y)^2+(x-z)^2+(x-w)^2+(y-z)^2 \\ \qquad +(y-w)^2+(z-w)^2=20. \end{cases}$

(10) Given $\begin{cases} x^2+y^2+z^2+w^2+u^2=0, \\ xy+zw=12, \\ xyzwu=128, \\ p_2=32. \end{cases}$

(11) Given $\begin{cases} x^2+y^2+z^2+w^2+t^2+u^2=219, \\ p_2=435, \\ (x+u)=(y+t)=(z+w), \\ xyzwtu=13{,}000. \end{cases}$

(12) Given $\begin{cases} x^2+y^2+z^2+w^2+u^2=90, \\ p_2=155, \\ zu+yw=27, \\ xz+xw=20. \end{cases}$

(13) Given $\begin{cases} x^2+y^2+z^2+w^2=0, \\ p_3=0, \\ xyzw=1, \\ x+y+z+w=2. \end{cases}$

(14) Given $\begin{cases} x+y+z+w=-3, \\ p_2=-121, \\ xyzw=-540. \end{cases}$

(15) The sum of the squares of the three sides of a triangle is 434; the difference between the greater and less side is 2. What is the length of a line drawn from any of the vertices of the triangle to a point within the triangle that will be equally distant from the three vertices (corners) of the triangle?

(16) (*a*) The product of three numbers in geometrical progression is 729. What are the numbers if their sum equals 39? (*b*) The product of four numbers in geometrical progression is 64. What are the numbers if their sum equals 15?

(17) An army 25 miles long starts upon a journey of 50 miles; and at the same time a courier starts from the rear to deliver a message to the front. He delivers his message, and returns to the rear at the time the army completes its journey. How far did the courier travel?

(*You can solve* (17) *in ten minutes. Try it.*)

SYNTHETIC MULTIPLICATION.

156. *Let it be required to multiply* $x + a = 0$ *by* $x + b = 0$.

There being two values assigned to x, the highest power of x will be ^{2}. (13) Therefore x^2 will be the first term, and its coefficient is 1, *not expressed, but understood* (**56** — (3)). The next power of x will be x', or simply x, the index ' being understood. Its coefficient will be the sum of the values assigned to x, *with their signs changed* (**56** — (4)). Therefore, $(x + a)(x + b) =$

(A) $x^2 + (a + b)x + ab = 0$ (their product being equal to 0, because $x + a = 0$ and $x + b = 0$).

Let us now introduce another value, say $-c$, in (A); then, $x + c = 0$. We write for the terms of the new equation:

$$\left.\begin{array}{r} x^3 \textit{ for the first term} \\ (a+b+c)\,x^2 \textit{ for the second term} \\ (c\,(a+b)+ab)\,x \textit{ for the third term} \\ (ab \times c + 0)\,x^0 \textit{ for the fourth term} \end{array}\right\} (B).$$

Adding the terms of (B) and putting the result equal to 0, we have

$$(C) \qquad x^3 + (a+b+c)\,x^2 + (ab+ac+bc)\,x + abc = 0.$$

Let us now assign another value to x, say $-d$, and multiply (C) by $x + d = 0$, and we have

$$\left.\begin{array}{r} x^4 \textit{ for the first term} \\ (a+b+c+d)\,x^3 \textit{ for the second term} \\ ((a+b+c)\,d + ab + ac + bc)\,x^2 \textit{ for the third term} \\ ((ab+ac+bc)\,d + abc)\,x \textit{ for the fourth term} \\ (abc \times d)\,x^0 \textit{ for the fifth term,} \\ \textit{or absolute term.} \end{array}\right\} (D).$$

Performing the indicated operations, and adding the terms of (D), we have

$$(E) \quad x^4 + (a+b+c+d)\,x^3 + (ab+ac+ad+bc+bd+cd)\,x^2 \\ + (abc+abd+acd+bcd)\,x + abcd = 0.$$

Examining (B) we find that it is derived from (A) by multiplying it by $(x + c)$. We notice,

(1) That x^3, the *degree* of equation (C), represents the number of roots (values) assigned to x.

(2) That the coefficient of x^2, in (C), is made up of the coefficient of x, in (A), $+ c$.

(3) That the coefficient of x, in (C), is made up by $c \times (a + b) + ab$, in (A).

(4) That the coefficient of x^0, in (C), is made up of $(c \times ab + 0)$, in (A).

(5) That the same law of formation of the terms in (D) are the same, that of multiplying (C) by $(x + d)$.

From the foregoing $(B - D)$ we may deduce the following

Rule.

To introduce another root in a given equation,

(1) *Raise the degree of the given equation by* 1.

(2) *Add the proposed root with its sign changed to the coefficient of the second term of the given equation, for the coefficient of the second term of the new equation, — writing for the exponent of* x, *the degree of the new equation, less* 1.

(3) *Multiply the coefficient of the second term of the given equation by the proposed root, and add the product to the coefficient of the third term of the given equation, for the coefficient of the third term of the new equation, — writing for the exponent of* x, *the degree of the new equation, less* 2.

(4) *Multiply the coefficient of the third term of the given equation by the proposed root, adding the result to the coefficient of the fourth term of the given equation, for the coefficient of the fourth term of the new equation, — writing for the exponent of* x, *the degree of the new equation, less* 3. *Proceed in like manner till all the terms of the given equation are dealt with by the proposed root; and placing the new equation equal to* 0, *the work is accomplished.*

157. From the foregoing rule let us write a *general formula* for the introduction of a new root in a given equation. To do this, we let

$$(F) \quad x^n + mx^{n-1} + nx^{n-2} + ox^{n-3} + px^{n-4} + \cdots + sx + q = 0$$

be a general equation of the nth degree in which it is proposed to introduce another root, say $-\frac{m}{n}$; then $x + \frac{m}{n} = 0$. Multiplying the given equation (F) by $x + \frac{m}{n}$, we have, by the rule,

$$(G)\ x^{n+1}+\left(m+\frac{m}{n}\right)x^n+\left(\frac{m^2}{n}+n\right)x^{n-1}+(m+o)\,x^{n-2}$$
$$+\left(\frac{mo}{n}+p\right)x^{n-3}+\left(\frac{mp}{n}+(\ )\right)x^{n-4}+\cdots+\left(\frac{ms}{n}+q\right)x$$
$$+\frac{mq}{n}=0.$$

Let $-\dfrac{m}{n}=-a$, then $(x+a)=0$, and multiplying (F) by $(x+a)$, we have

$$(C)\ x^{n+1}+(m+a)x^n+(am+n)x^{n-1}+(an+o)x^{n-2}+(ao+p)x^{n-3}$$
$$+(ap+o)x^{n-4}+\cdots+(as+q)x+aq=0,$$

and the rule is established in its most general form.

158. To illustrate numerically, take the equation,

$$(A') \qquad x^2+4\,x+4=0;$$

and introducing another root, say -3, then $x+3=0$. Then, $(x+3)(A')=$

$$(C') \qquad x^3+7\,x^2+16\,x+12=0.$$

Introducing in (C') another root, say -2, then $x+2=0$, and we have

$$(E') \qquad x^4+9\,x^3+30\,x^2+48\,x+24=0.$$

Introducing in (E') another root, say $+6$, then $x-6=0$, and we have

$$(I) \qquad x^5+6\,x^4-24\,x^3-132\,x^2-264\,x-144=0.$$

Introducing in (I) another root, say $+6$, then $x-6=0$, and we have,

$$(T)\ \ x^6\pm 0\,x^5-60\,x^4+12\,x^3+528\,x^2+1440\,x+864=0.$$

Introducing in (T) another root, say -5, then $x+5=0$, and writing the process in full, we have,

$$\begin{array}{lccccccccc} & x^6 & \pm 0x^5 & -60x^4 & +\ 12x^3 & +528x^2 & +1440x & +\ 864 & = & 0 \\ \text{Then,} & +5 & \pm\ 0 & -300 & +\ 60 & +2640 & +7200 & +4320 & & \\ \hline & x^7+5x^6 & -60x^5 & -288x^4 & +588x^3 & +4080x^2 & +8064x & +4320 & = & 0 \end{array}$$

SYNTHETIC DIVISION. HORNER'S METHOD.

159. Synthetic Division, which was first used by W. G. Horner, of Bath, England, about the year 1829, is the reverse of **Synthetic Multiplication,** which we have just explained.

160. In Horner's method for approximating the roots of numerical equations the method of synthetic division is employed, and, briefly stated, is as follows:

Suppose that a root of the equation

(1) $x^n + ax^{n-1} + bx^{n-2} + cx^{n-3} + \cdots + ex^2 + tx + q = 0$

is found to lie between l and $l+1$. Transform the given equation into another whose roots shall be less by l, and we have one in the form

(2) $y^n + a'y^{n-1} + b'y^{n-2} + c'y^{n-3} + \cdots + e'y^2 + t'y + q' = 0,$

one of whose roots is less than 1. If that is found to lie between the decimal fraction l' and $l' + .1$, transform equation (2) into another whose roots shall be less by l', and we have an equation of the form

(3) $e^n + a''e^{n-1} + b''e^{n-2} + c''e^{n-3} + \cdots + e''e^2 + t''e + q'' = 0,$

one of whose roots is less than .1. If that root is found to be a little greater than l'', proceed in the same way with (3) as (2), and we obtain

$$x = l + l' + l'' + \cdots$$

to any degree of accuracy.

As e in (3) represents a small fraction, its higher powers will be so small that they may be neglected, and its value is nearly $\frac{-q''}{t''}$; therefore, l', l'', $\cdots$, may be found in this way with more and more accuracy the smaller e becomes.

This is briefly the Horner method, and *the only method of any satisfaction prior to the methods offered here.*

161. How the Horner method can be applied to greater advantage than it has ever been in any prior work the reader is referred to our method of changing equations, *by which imaginary roots may be approximated as real roots.*

QUADRATIC EQUATIONS.

162. A **Quadratic Equation** is the simplest form of a *General Equation* whose roots are two in number, and represented by one unknown quantity; as, $x^2 + 4x + 4 = 0$, $x^2 - 5x + 6 = 0$, and $x^2 + mx + q = 0$.

163. **Quadratics** are also called *Second Degree* equations, and the roots of such equations are either *Real Quantities*, *Real Imaginaries*, or *Pure Imaginaries.*

164. The roots of quadratics represent the sides of *right triangles* when *Real Quantities;* the sides of *isosceles triangles* when *Real Imaginaries;* and when *Pure Imaginaries*, may be represented by *lines.*

165. *The roots of any numerical quadratic equation, whether real quantities or imaginary quantities, can be measured.*

166. To illustrate (§ 164), let ABC (Fig. 2) be any right triangle. Let $AB=a$, and $AC=b$, and $BC=c$. Then $a^2 + b^2 = c^2$. (See any geometry.)

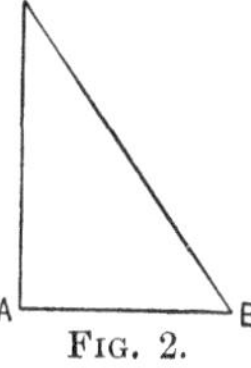

Fig. 2.

Letting a and b represent the roots of a quadratic, then $x - a = 0$ and $x - b = 0$. Their product will be the quadratic

$$x^2 - (a + b)x + ab = 0. \quad \textbf{(56.)}$$

(3) Then, $(a + b)^2 - 2 \times ab = a^2 + b^2$. (Th. A.) But it has been shown that $a^2 + b^2 = c^2$. Now, let $ab = p$, and we have the equations

$$(1) \quad a^2 + b^2 = c^2,$$

$$(2) \quad ab = p,$$

to find a and b in terms of p and c.

SOLUTION. (3) $a^2 + b^2 + 2ab = c^2 + 2p$. Whence,

(4) $a + b = \sqrt{c^2 + 2p}$.

(5) $a - b = \sqrt{c^2 - 2p}$.

(6) $\therefore\ a = \dfrac{\sqrt{c^2 + 2p} + \sqrt{c^2 - 2p}}{2} = AB$.

(7) $\therefore\ b = \dfrac{\sqrt{c^2 + 2p} - \sqrt{c^2 - 2p}}{2} = BC$.

Squaring (6) and (7), we have $a^2 + b^2 = c^2$. (By adding the [S] of (6) and (7).)

167. It is now seen that in all algebraic expressions in the form of $x^2 + y^2 = n$, *in which n represents any positive integer or fraction*, that the square root of the right-hand member, n, is the hypotenuse of a right triangle; and, as the hypotenuse of any right triangle may be taken as the diameter of a circumscribed circle, we may also say that *in all algebraic expressions in the form of $x^2 + y^2 = n$, that the square root of the right-hand member, n, is the diameter of a circle*, of which *the semicircle is the compass for all true rectangles of the lines represented by x and y;* and, being the compass for all true rectangles, xy, *it is also the compass for all true or positive values of the lines represented by x and y, drawn from the termini of its diameter, and meeting in the semicircumference.*

168. To further illustrate the foregoing statements, let us draw a circle whose diameter is the hypotenuse of the rt. △ ABC (Fig. 2). Let ADC–E (Fig. 3) represent such ⊙. Draw the lines or chords AB and CB, meeting at the point B, in the semicircumference AEC. Designate all lines by x to the *left*, and y to the *right*. Then will $AB = x$, and $CB = y$.

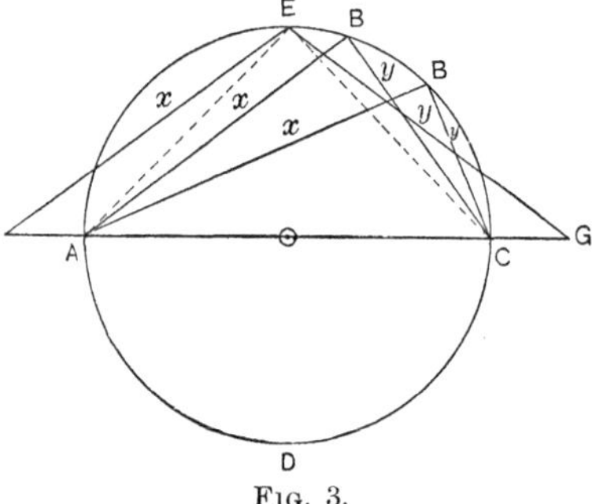

FIG. 3.

Whence, $x^2 + y^2 = \overline{AC}^2 = c^2$.

Letting $xy = p$, then will the values of x and y be the same in this last equation as already found in (**166**).

169. Let us now increase their rectangle by any positive quantity, say t; then $xy = p + t$. $(p + t)$, *to be true, must be less* than *one-half the square of c;* that is, $(p + t)$ must be $< \frac{c^2}{2}$: because, *the true greatest rectangle of any two lines that can be drawn from the termini of its diameter, and meeting in the semicircumference, is equal to one-half the square of the diameter of the circle.* (See any geometry.) If p represents the rectangle of the lines x and y, when $xy = p + t$, and $p + t < \frac{c^2}{2}$, and $p + t > p$, the lines now represented by x and y, let us assume to be AB' and CB'. Therefore, *increasing the rectangle of the lines, the sum of their squares always remaining permanent*, x gradually grows *less*, and y gradually grows *greater*, in consequence of which the point of meeting of the lines moves in the semicircumference towards the point E; and when their rectangle equals $\frac{\overline{AC}^2}{2}$, the lines become numerically equal, being then represented by the dotted lines AE and CE (Fig. 3).

It is now seen that x may assume all *possible values* from AC to 0, and y all *possible values* from 0 to AC. Therefore, by *increasing* or *decreasing* the *rectangle* of the lines represented by x and y, *within the limit of* $\frac{\overline{AC}^2}{2}$, *the lines assume new positions and magnitudes in the semicircle.* And as the sum of the squares of any two lines drawn from the termini of the diameter of any circle, and meeting in its semicircumference, is equal to the square of the diameter, such lines, with the diameter of the circle, form *rt. triangles;* and the *rectangle* of any two of such lines, so formed, *is the absolute term of a quadratic;* and the *sum of such lines is the numerical sum of the roots of such equation*, and, as such, *are real quantities.*

170. Letting $x^2 + y^2$ always remain permanent, and increasing their greatest true rectangle by any positive value, say t, then $xy = \frac{c^2}{2} + t$, and we have the equations

(*a*) $$x^2 + y^2 = c^2, \text{ and}$$

(*b*) $$xy = \frac{c^2}{2} + t,$$

to find new values for x and y.

Adding to (*a*) twice (*b*), and taking the square root of both members, we have

(*c*) $$x + y = \sqrt{2\,c^2 + 2\,t} = \textit{sum of lines.}$$

And taking $2 \times$ (*b*) from (*a*), and extracting the square root of both members, we have

(*d*) $$x - y = \sqrt{-2\,t} = \textit{their difference.}$$

(*e*) $$\therefore\ x = \frac{\sqrt{2\,c^2 + 2\,t} + \sqrt{-2\,t}}{2}, \text{ and}$$

(*f*) $$y = \frac{\sqrt{2\,c^2 + 2\,t} - \sqrt{-2\,t}}{2}.$$

Here we meet with this "vexed" imaginary, for a full meaning of which the reader is referred to the *General Theorem of Imaginary Quantities*, given in another part of this work. It will be sufficient, however, at this time, to point out the location of the lines now represented by $\frac{\sqrt{2\,c^2+2\,t} \pm \sqrt{-2\,t}}{2}$. It has been shown that when $xy = \frac{c^2}{2}$, x and y are, respectively, represented by the dotted lines AE and CE (Fig. 3). When their rectangle exceeds $\frac{c^2}{2}$ by t, we have $x + y = \sqrt{2\,c^2 + 2\,t}$, which is greater than $x + y = \sqrt{2\,c^2}$: for, by our hypothesis, t is a *positive real quantity*. It has been shown: that when $xy = \frac{c^2}{2}$, that x and y are, respectively, equal to $\frac{\sqrt{2\,c^2}}{2}$, and lie wholly within the semicircle AEC (Fig. 3), being represented by the dotted lines AE and CE. When $xy = \frac{c^2}{2} + t$, x and y are, respectively, equal to $\frac{\sqrt{2c^2+2t}+\sqrt{-2t}}{2}$ and $\frac{\sqrt{2c^2+2t}-\sqrt{-2t}}{2}$.

To locate the real part of x in this last expression is now our object. The $\frac{\sqrt{2c^2+2t}}{2}$ being $> \frac{\sqrt{2c^2}}{2}$, it must lie partly *without* the semicircle. Beginning at the point (E) in the semicircumference, where the lines AE and CE meet, forming the true greatest rectangle of the lines, we lay off the real part of x, $\left(\frac{\sqrt{2c^2+2t}}{2}\right)$, to meet AC extended in F, and the real part of y, $\left(\frac{\sqrt{2c^2+2t}}{2}\right)$, to meet AC extended in G (Fig. 3). We now have the *isosceles triangle* FEG, whose sides EF and EG represent the real part of the *Real Imaginary*, $\frac{\sqrt{2c^2+2t} \pm \sqrt{-2t}}{2}$. It will be shown in the discussion of the *General Theorem of Imaginary Quantities* that the imaginary parts, $\pm \frac{\sqrt{-2t}}{2}$ are represented by the lines FA and CG, that lie in the same direction of the line AC, the diameter of the circle.

171. To illustrate, numerically, take the equation,

$$x^2 - 14x + 48 = 0.$$

Here, $\quad a^2 + b^2 = 100 = (-14)^2 - 2 \times 48.$ (Th. A.)

And, $\quad ab = 48.$

Whence, by a solution of $a^2+b^2=100$, and $ab=48$, we find

$$a = 8 \text{ and } b = 6.$$

To locate the lines representing the values of a and b, draw a circle whose diameter is the $\sqrt{100} = 10$, which represents, also, the hypotenuse of the right triangle. Then draw the chords a and b, and we have, respectively, the other two sides of the right triangle.

172. In the same way determine, by actual measurement, the roots of the following quadratics:

(*l*) $x^2 - 4x + 5 = 0,$

(*m*) $x^2 - 6x + 11 = 0,$

(*n*) $x^2 - 7x + 12 = 0,$

(*o*) $x^2 - 6x + 9 = 0,$

(*p*) $x^2 - 10x + 37.5 = 0.$

Multiply n and p together, and show what *absolute theorem* will apply in its solution.

173. Theorem II. *The sum of the squares of the roots of any general equation is equal to the square of the coefficient of the second term, minus twice the coefficient of the third term; and the sum of the squares of the roots multiplied by the degree of the equation is equal to the square of the sum of the roots plus the sum of the squares of the differences of the roots.*

174. To prove the theorem, take the general equation

$$x^n + mx^{n-1} + nx^{n-2} + ox^{n-3} + \cdots + px + q = 0.$$

Letting $a + b + c + d + \cdots + l + m + \cdots$ to n, represent the roots of the equation; then, according to the theorem, we have

(1) $m^2 - 2n = a^2 + b^2 + c^2 + d^2 + \cdots + l^2 + m^2 + \cdots$ to n factors or roots = the sum of the squares of the n roots of the equation. (Th. D.)

(2) $n(a^2 + b^2 + c^2 + \cdots) = \square$ of sum of n factors or roots + the sum of the Ⓢ of the differences of the n factors or *roots* that enter into the formation of the equation. (Th. I.)

175. To illustrate the universal application of the theorem in the solution of numerical equations, let it be required to find the roots of the following equations:

(1) $x^2 - 4x + 5 = 0.$

(2) $x^2 + 4x + 5 = 0.$

(3) $x^2 + 4x + 8 = 0.$

(4) $x^2 - 4x + 8 = 0.$

(5) $x^2 + dx + q = 0.$

(6) $x^2 - dx + q = 0.$

(7) $x^3 + 6x^2 + 12x + 8 = 0.$

(8) $x^3 - 6x^2 + 12x - 9 = 0.$

(9) $x^3 - 16x^2 + 76x - 96 = 0.$

(10) $x^3 - 7x + 6 = 0.$

(11) $x^4 - 14x^3 + 71x^2 - 154x + 120 = 0.$

(12) $x^4 + 2x^3 + 2x^2 + 4x + 4 = 0.$

(13) $x^4 - 14x^3 + 78x^2 - 196x + 176 = 0.$

(14) $x^5 - 4x^4 - 49x^3 + 64x^2 + 780x + 1008 = 0.$

(15) $x^5 - 31x^3 + 2x^2 + 192x + 160 = 0.$

Solutions. Letting $a, b, c, \cdots$, or any other unknown quantities, represent the roots, then, from the general law (**56**) of the formation of the coefficients of the foregoing equations, we have

From equation (1),

(1) $(a + b) = -4$, and $ab = 5$.

(2) $\therefore (-4) - 2(5) = a^2 + b^2 = 6.$ (Th. II.)

(3) $a^2 + b^2 + 2ab = 16 = (6 + 10).$

(4) $a + b = 4.$

(5) $a^2 + b^2 - 2ab = -4 = (6 - 2x^5).$

(6) $a - b = \sqrt{-4} = 2\sqrt{-1}.$

(7) $\therefore a = \dfrac{4 + \sqrt{-4}}{2} = 2 + \sqrt{-1}.$

$b = \dfrac{4 - \sqrt{-4}}{2} = 2 - \sqrt{-1}.$

$\therefore$ The roots of the equation are Real Imaginaries (**24**).

From equation (2),

(1) $a + b = 4$, and $ab = 5$.

The roots of which are numerically the same as (1), but the sign of the real part of the imaginary is —.

From equation (3),

(1) $a + b = 4$, $ab = 8$. (2) $a^2 + b^2 = (4)^2 - 2 \times 8 = 0$.

(3) $\therefore$ the roots are conjugate *imaginary origins*, and (**98**), $-2 + \sqrt{-4}$, and $-2 - \sqrt{-4}$ are the roots, or $2 \pm 2\sqrt{-1}$.

From equation (4),

$$(1)\ a + b = -4, \text{ and } ab = 8.$$

The roots are the same as the roots of (3), but the real part of the imaginary is $+$. $\therefore 2 \pm 2\sqrt{-1}$ are the roots.

From equation (5),

(1) $a + b = -d$, and $ab = q$.

(2) $a^2 + b^2 = d^2 - 2q$.

(3) $a - b = \sqrt{d^2 - 4q}$.

(4) $\therefore a = -\dfrac{d + \sqrt{d^2 - 4q}}{2}$.

(5) $\therefore b = -\dfrac{d - \sqrt{d^2 - 4q}}{2}$.

If $d^2 - 4q$ is *minus*, the equation contains imaginary roots; if *plus*, the roots of the equation will be *real* quantities.

From equation (6),

$$(1)\ a + b = -d, \text{ and } ab = q.$$

The roots of (6) will be the same as the roots of (5), except as to sign.

From equation (7),

(1) $(a + b + c) = 6$, $p_2 = 12$, p_3 or $abc = 8$.

(2) $(6)^2 - 2 \times 12 = 12 = a^2 + b^2 + c^2$. (Th. II.)

(3) $2 \times 12 = 2p_2$. $\therefore$ (**138**), -2, -2, -2 are the roots.

From equation (8),

(1) $a^2 + b^2 + c^2 = 12$. (Th. II.)

(2) $\therefore$ The numbers are equal, as $2 \times 12 = 2p_2$.

The roots being the same as the roots of (7), except as to sign. But $2 \times 2 \times 2 = 8$, while the absolute term of (8) is 9 $\therefore$ One of the roots at least will be $2 + \sqrt[3]{9 - 8} = 3$. The sum of the other two roots will be $6 - 3 = 3$. Their product will be $9 \div 3 = 3$. *As four times their product is greater than the square of their sum, the numbers, or roots, are imaginary.* $\therefore a - b = \sqrt{(3)^2 - 4 \times 3} = \sqrt{-3}$. Whence a and b are, respectively, equal to

$$\frac{3 + \sqrt{-3}}{2} \text{ and } \frac{3 - \sqrt{-3}}{2}.$$

From equation (9),

(1) $a + b + c = -16$, $p_2 = 76$, and $abc = -96$.

(2) $a^2 + b^2 + c^2 = (-16)^2 - 2 \times 76 = 104$. (Th. II.)

(3) $104 \times 3 = 312 = \square$ of sum + sum $\boxed{s}$ of diffs.

(4) $312 - (-16)^2 = 56 =$ sum $\boxed{s}$ of diffs.

(5) $56 \times 3 = 168 = \square$ of sum of diffs. + sum $\boxed{s}$ of diffs. of diffs. (Th. I.) The side of the greatest square in 168, whose side is integral, is 12, $= 2c - 2a$, $c - a = 6$. Having found $c - a = 6$, we readily find the values of a, b, and c to be 2, 6, and 8, which will satisfy all the conditions of the problem.

From equation (10),

(1) $a + b + c = \pm 0$, and $abc = 6$, and $p_2 = -7$.

(2) $a^2 + b^2 + c^2 = 14 = (\pm 0)^2 - 2(-7.)$ (Th. II.)

(3) $(3 \times 14)^{\frac{1}{2}} = 6 = a + b + c$.

(4) $\therefore \dfrac{6 + 0}{2} = 3 =$ sum + roots; true sign $-$. $\therefore$ 1, 2, $-$ 3.

From equation (11),

(1) $a^2 + b^2 + c^2 + d^2 = (-14)^2 - 2 \times 71 = 54$. (Th. II.)

(2) $54 \times 4 = 216 = \square$ of sum + sum $\boxed{s}$ of diffs. (Th. II.)

(3) $216 - (-14)^2 = 20 =$ sum $\boxed{s}$ of diffs. of roots.

(4) $20 \times 6 = 120 = \square$ of sum of diffs. + sum $\boxed{s}$ of diffs. of diffs.

(5) $(120)^{\frac{1}{2}} = 10 =$ sum of diffs.

(6) Separating 20 into 6 squares by trial, or by factoring the absolute term, 120, into 4 factors, we readily find 2, 3, 4, 5 as the roots of (11).

(See full solutions of biquadratics.)

From equation (12),

(1) $e^2 + b^2 + c^2 + d^2 = 0 = (+2)^2 - 2(2)$. (Th. II.)

(2) $(4)^2 - (2 \times 4) 2 = 0 =$ sum $\boxed{s}$ of p_3.

(3) $\therefore$ The roots are all imaginary; and the equation can be separated into two quadratics, which are

$$x^2 + (1 + \sqrt{3})x + 2 = 0, \text{ and } x^2 + (1 - \sqrt{3})x + 2 = 0.$$

(See full solution of biquadratics.)

From equation (13),

(1) $a^2 + b^2 + c^2 + d^2 = (-14)^2 - 2(78) = 40.$ (Th. II.)

(2) $40 \times 4 = 160 = \square$ of sum + sum $\boxed{s}$ of diffs.

(3) As $160 < (-14)^2$, the equation contains imaginary roots (130). We now factor the absolute term in order to determine whether the equation contains *all* imaginary roots, or is made up of *real* and imaginary roots. $176 =$ the factors $2 \times 2 \times 4 \times 11$. We try 2, and find that it satisfies the condition of the problem. ∴ The equation contains two real + roots and two imaginary roots; for *even degree equations contain an even number of real roots or none.* But we have discovered that it contains *one real* root, therefore it must contain two *real* roots.

We now represent the roots by

$$a,\ b,\ \text{and}\ c \pm \sqrt{-l}.$$

$$\therefore\ a^2 + b^2 + 2c^2 + -2l = 40.\quad \text{(Th. II.)}$$

$$a^2 \qquad = 4\ (\text{letting}\ a = 2).$$

Whence $\qquad b^2 + 2c^2 + -2l = 36.$

We now try 4 one of the factors, and we find it is a root. Taking its square from 36, we have

$$2c^2 - 2l = 20,$$

whence $\qquad c^2 - l = 10.$

$$(c + \sqrt{-1})(c - \sqrt{-l}) = c^2 + l = 22 = 176 \div (2 \times 4).$$

$$2c^2 = 32.$$

$$c^2 = 16.$$

$$c = 4 = \sqrt{16}.$$

$$\therefore\ (c^2 + l) - (c^2 - l) = 22 - 10 = 12 = 2l.$$

Whence $\qquad l = 6$, and $\sqrt{-l} = \sqrt{-6}.$

∴ 2, 4, and $4 \pm \sqrt{-6}$ are the roots of (13).

(See solution of biquadratics.)

From equation (14),

(1) $a^2 + b^2 + c^2 + d^2 + e^2 = (-4)^2 - 2(-49) = 114.$ (Th. II.)

(2) $114 \times 5 = 570 = \square$ of sum + sum $\boxed{s}$ of diffs. (Th. II.)

(3) $(570)^{\frac{1}{2}} = 22 =$ sum of roots. (The side of the greatest square in 570, whose side is integral, is taken for the sum of roots. It must be an even number (**26**).)

(4) $\therefore$ (26), $\frac{22 + - 4}{2} = 9 =$ sum of + roots in formation of equations; true sign −; and

(5) (26), $\frac{22 - (-4)}{2} = 13 =$ sum of − roots in formation of equations; true sign +.

From algebraic sum and sign of *absolute* term the equation contains *three minus* roots and *two plus* roots. Putting $a + b + c = 9$ and $d + e = 13$, and adding $(a + b + c)^2$, $+(d + e)^2$, and from algebraic sum of p_2 we find for p_2 185. From this we readily find for the roots of (14), − 2, − 3, − 4, 6, and 7.

(See full solutions of fifth degree equations.)

From equation (15),

(1) $a^2 + b^2 + c^2 + d^2 + e^2 = 62 = (\pm 0)^2 - 2(-31)$. (Th. II.)

(2) $62 \times 5 = 310 = \square$ of sum + sum [s] of diffs. (Th. II.)

(3) $(310)^{\frac{1}{2}} = 16 = a + b + c + d + e$. (17 being rejected (**26**).)

(4) $\therefore \frac{16 + 0}{2} = 8 =$ sum + roots in formation of equation; true sign −.

(5) $\frac{16 - 0}{2} = 8 =$ sum *minus* roots in formation of equation; true sign +.

Now form the *cubic* and *quadratic*; for we have discovered that the equation contains three + roots and two *minus* roots in its formation.

Let $x^3 + 8x^2 + ax + y = 0$,

and $x^2 - 8x + e = 0$ represent the equations.

Their product

$= x^5 + (a + e + - 64)x^3 + (8e + y + - 8a)x^3 + (ae + - 8y)x + ey = 0$,

the coefficients of which are respectively equal to the coefficients of (15).

(1) $\therefore a + e + - 64 = -31$, whence $a + e = 33 = (-31 + 64)$.

(2) $8e + y + - 8a = + 2$, whence $8e + y = 2 + 8a$.

(3) $ae + - 8y = + 192$, whence $ae = 192 + 8y$, and $e = \frac{192 + 8y}{a}$.

(4) $ey = + 160$, whence $e = \frac{160}{y}$.

(5) $a = 33 - e$. (From (1).)

(6) $a = \frac{8e + y - 2}{8}$. (From (2) by transposition and division.)

(7) Whence (5) = (6), $\frac{8e + y - 2}{8} = 33 - e = 16e + y = 266$.

(8) $e = \frac{266 - y}{16}$. (From (7).)

(9) $\therefore$ (4) = (8) $\frac{266 - y}{16} = \frac{160}{y}$. Solving (9) we have

(10) $y = 10$, whence $e = \frac{160}{10} = 16$.

We may now complete the *cubic* and *quadratic*, which solved gives for the roots of (15)

$$-1, \ -2, \ -5, \ 4, \text{ and } 4.$$

176. Thus far we have shown that Th. II holds good in the solutions of equations containing *two, three, four,* or *five* roots. Therefore the theorem will hold good, and is true, for equations of all degrees. (Ths. I and D.)

177. Theorem III. *The sum of the squares of the products of the roots, taken two and two, of an equation of the third degree, is equal to the square of the coefficient of the third term, minus twice the coefficient of the second term into the absolute term.*

To apply the theorem, let

$$x^3 + mx^2 + nx + q = 0,$$

be an equation (in the general form) of the *third degree.*

Then we have, according to the theorem,

$$\overline{ab}^2 + \overline{ac}^2 + \overline{bc}^2 = n^2 - 2\,(m \times n).$$

To apply the theorem to the following cubes:

(i) $x^3 - 13\,x^2 + 54\,x - 70 = 0$.

$$\overline{ab}^2 + \overline{ac}^2 + \overline{bc}^2 = (+54)^2 - 2\,(-13 \times -70) = 1096.$$

(ii) $x^3 + 9\,x^2 - 4 = 0$.

$$\overline{ab}^2 + \overline{ac}^2 + \overline{bc}^2 = (\pm 0)^2 - 2\,(+9 \times -4) = 72.$$

(iii) $x^3 - 7x + 7 = 0$.

$$\overline{ab}^2 + \overline{ac}^2 + \overline{bc}^2 = (-7)^2 - 2(\pm 0 \times + 7) = 49.$$

(iv) $x^3 + 9x^2 + 18x + 18 = 0$.

$$\overline{ab}^2 + \overline{ac}^2 + \overline{bc}^2 = (+18)^2 - 2(+9 \times + 18) = 0.$$

(v) $x^3 \pm 1 = 0$.

$$\overline{ab}^2 + \overline{ac}^2 + \overline{bc}^2 = (\pm 0)^2 - 2(\pm 0 \times \pm 1) = 0.$$

(vi) $x^3 + 2x^2 - 3x - 5 = 0$.

$$\overline{ab}^2 + \overline{ac}^2 + \overline{bc}^2 = (-3)^2 - 2(+2 \times - 5) = 29.$$

(vii) $x^3 - 7x^2 - 11x - 8 = 0$.

$$\overline{ab}^2 + \overline{ac}^2 + \overline{bc}^2 = (-11)^2 - 2(-7 \times - 8) = 9.$$

178. Theorem IV. *The sum of the squares of the products of the roots, taken two and two, of an equation of the fourth degree, is equal to the square of the coefficient of the third term, minus twice the difference between the product of the second and fourth term coefficients, and absolute term; and the sum of the squares of the products of the roots, taken three and three, is equal to the square of the coefficient of the fourth term, minus twice the coefficient of the third term into absolute term.*

To apply the theorem take the general equation,

$$x^4 + mx^3 + nx^2 + ox + q = 0.$$

(1) $\overline{ab}^2 + \overline{ac}^2 + \overline{bc}^2 + \overline{ad}^2 + \overline{bd}^2 + \overline{cd}^2 = n^2 - 2(mo - q)$. (Th. IV.)

(2) $\overline{abc}^2 + \overline{abd}^2 + \overline{acd}^2 + \overline{bcd}^2 = o^2 - 2(nq)$.

To apply the theorem to the following *biquadratics:*

(i) $x^4 - 21x^3 + 158x^2 - 504x + 576 = 0$.

(1) $\overline{ab}^2 + \overline{ac}^2 + \overline{ad}^2 + \overline{bc}^2 + \overline{bd}^2 + \overline{cd}^2 = 4948$
$= (+158)^2 - 2[(-21 \times - 504) - 576]$,

(2) $\overline{abc}^2 + \overline{abd}^2 + \overline{acd}^2 + \overline{bcd}^2 = 72000$
$= (-504)^2 - 2(+158 \times + 576)$.

(ii) $x^4 + 2x^3 + 2x^2 + 4x + 4 = 0$.

(1) $\overline{ab}^2 + \overline{ac}^2 + \cdots + \overline{cd}^2 = -4 = (2)^2 - 2[(2 \times 4) - 4]$,

(2) $\overline{abc}^2 + \overline{abd}^2 + \cdots + \overline{bcd}^2 = 0 = (4)^2 - 2(2 \times 4)$.

(iii) $x^4 - x^3 - 3x^2 + 4x + 5 = 0$.

(1) $\overline{ab}^2 + \overline{ac}^2 + \cdots + \overline{cd}^2 = 27 = (-3)^2 - 2[(-\times +4) - +5]$,

(2) $\overline{abc}^2 + \overline{abd}^2 + \cdots + \overline{bcd}^2 = 46 = (+4)^2 - 2(-3 \times +5)$.

(iv) $x^4 \pm 1 = 0$.

(1) $\overline{ab}^2 + \overline{ac}^2 + \cdots + \overline{cd}^2 = \pm 2$

$= (\pm o)^2 - 2[(\pm 0 \times \pm 0) - \pm 1]$,

(2) $\overline{abc}^2 + \cdots + \overline{bcd}^2 = \pm 0$.

179. Theorem V. *The sum of the squares of the products of the roots, taken two and two, of an equation of the fifth degree, is equal to the square of the coefficient of the third term, minus twice the difference between the product of the coefficients of the second and fourth term, and the coefficient of the fifth term; and the sum of the squares of the products of the roots, taken three and three, is equal to the square of the coefficient of the fourth term, plus twice the coefficient of the second term into absolute term, minus twice the coefficient of the third term into coefficient of fifth term; and the sum of the squares of the products of the roots, taken four and four, is equal to the square of the coefficient of fifth term, minus twice the coefficient of fourth term into absolute term.*

To illustrate the application of the theorem take the general equation of the fifth degree,

$$x^5 + mx^4 + nx^3 + ox^2 + px + q = 0.$$

(1) $\overline{ab}^2 + \overline{ac}^2 + \cdots + \overline{de}^2 = n^2 - 2(mo - p)$.

(2) $\overline{abc}^2 + \overline{abd}^2 + \cdots + \overline{cde}^2 = (o^2 + 2mq) - 2(n \times p)$.

(3) $\overline{abcd}^2 + \overline{abde}^2 + \cdots + \overline{bcde}^2 = p^2 - 2oq$.

To apply the theorem take the following quintics:

(i) $x^5 + x^4 - 26x^3 - 12x^2 + 134x + 119 = 0$.

(1) $\overline{ab}^2 + \overline{ac}^2 + \cdots + \overline{de}^2 = (-26)^2 - 2[(+1 \times -12) - 134]$
$= 968$,

(2) $\overline{abc}^2 + \overline{abd}^2 + \cdots + \overline{cde}^2 = (-12)^2 + (2 \times +1 \times +119)$
$-2(-26 \times +134) = 7350$.

(3) $\overline{abcd}^2 + \overline{abce}^2 + \cdots + \overline{bcde}^2 = (+134)^2 - 2(-12 \times +119)$
$= 20812$.

(ii) $x^5 + 2x^4 + 2x^3 + 2x^2 + 4x + 4 = 0$.

(1) $\overline{ab}^2 + \overline{ac}^2 + \cdots + \overline{de}^2 = (2)^2 - 2[(2 \times 2) - 4] = 4$.

(2) $\overline{abc}^2 + \overline{abd}^2 + \cdots + \overline{cde}^2 = (2)^2 + 2(2 \times 4) - 2(2 \times 4) = 4$.

(3) $\overline{abcd}^2 + \cdots + \overline{bcde}^2 = (4)^2 - 2(2 \times 4) = 0$.

180. The functions of the squares of the products of the roots, taken in pairs of *two*, *three*, *four*, and so on, become of especial importance in the solution of Higher Numerical Equations. It is not necessary, however, that they be called into use to effect the solution of many problems; but, should any difficulty arise in which the character (*real or imaginary*) and signs of the roots, and their location, are not easily determined by application of Theorem II and Absolute Theorems, by the proper use of the foregoing theorems, the character and location of the roots of any equation of the class to which they apply can be determined without the aid of the Sturm Theorem or "Descartes' rule of signs"; and while the pupil is thus determining the character and location of the roots, he is also performing the operation of a solution of the problem, and the time spent in determining the character and location of the roots is not lost, but gained.

NOTE. — In applying the foregoing theorems, care should be taken to preserve the well-established uses of the signs, + and −, as used in algebraic operations.

LOCATION AND CHARACTER OF ROOTS.

181. Application of theorems in determining the location and character of the roots of an equation.

182. Let it be required to determine the *location* and *character* of the *roots* of the following *cubics:*

(1) $x^3 - 4x^2 + 7x - 8 = 0.$ (5) $x^3 + 7x - 92 = 0.$

(2) $x^3 - 2x^2 + 3x - 18 = 0.$ (6) $x^3 \pm 1 = 0.$

(3) $x^3 + 3x^2 - 5x + 12 = 0.$ (7) $x^3 - 67x + 127 = 0.$

(4) $x^3 + 7x^2 - 90 = 0.$

From equation (1),

$$(-4)^2 - 2(+7) = 2 = a^2 + b^2 + c^2. \quad \text{(Th. II.)}$$

$3 \times 2 = 6 = \square$ of sum of roots + sum ⓢ of diffs. (Th. II.)

As $6 < (-4)^2$, the equation contains imaginary roots (**130**). ∴ It being of the third degree, it can contain but *one real* + root (**110**). Substituting the side of the greatest integral square in 6, which is 2, we find the real root $> +2$ and $< +3$. By Theorem III we have

$$(+7)^2 - 2(-4 \times -8) = -15 = \overline{ab}^2 + \overline{ac}^2 + \overline{bc}^2.$$

∴ The imaginaries are pure. (**24.**)

From equation (2),

$$(-2)^2 - 2(+3) = -2 = a^2 + b^2 + c^2. \quad \text{(Th. II.)}$$

∴ Only one real + root, and a pair of pure imaginary roots. And by (**134**), the real parts of the imaginary roots will be −.

NOTE. — It will be shown in the solution of cubics that equation (2) is readily changed to the quadratic $x^2 - \frac{24}{7}x + \frac{9}{7} = 0$, the solution of which will be the real root of (2).

From equation (3),

$$(+3)^2 - 2(-5) = 19 = a^2 + b^2 + c^2. \quad \text{(Th. II.)}$$

$$(-5)^2 - 2(+3 \times +12) = -47 = \overline{ab}^2 + \overline{ac}^2 + \overline{bc}^2. \quad \text{(Th. III.)}$$

∴ The equation contains but one real − root, and a pair of pure imaginary roots (**110—24**).

Theorem II does not immediately detect the character of the roots, but Theorem III does. Substituting in the equation the side of the greatest integral square in 19, which is 4, and making its sign contrary to absolute term, we find that the real root lies between −4 and −5.

From equation (4),

$$(+7)^2 - 2(\pm 0) = 49 = a^2 + b^2 + c^2. \quad \text{(Th. II.)}$$

$$(\pm 0) - 2(+7 \times -90) = 1260. \quad \text{(Th. III.)}$$

Here both theorems give + quantities for sum of squares of roots, and sum of squares of products of roots taken two and two; but we know that the third term being wanting, the equation contains imaginary roots, which must be *real imaginaries*. $49 \times 3 = 147 = \square$ of sum of roots + sum Ⓢ of diffs. of roots (Th. II). The side of the greatest square in 147 whose side is integral is 12; but 12 is rejected (26). As the equation contains a pair of real imaginaries, the sum of whose squares is a + quantity, we take 11 as the numerical sum of roots. ∴ $\frac{11+7}{2} = 9 =$ sum of + roots in formation of equation, true sign −; and $\frac{11-7}{2} = 2 =$ sum of *minus* roots in formation of equation; true sign +. Try 2, and find it too small. ∴ 13 is taken, and we have

$$\frac{13+7}{2} = 10 = \text{sum } + \text{ roots; true sign } \textit{minus}.$$

$$\frac{13-7}{2} = 3 = \text{sum } - \text{ roots; true sign } \textit{plus}.$$

3 is tried, and satisfies the condition of the problem. ∴ Write $-5+\sqrt{-l}$ and $-5-\sqrt{-l}$ for the imaginary roots. Their product $25 + l = \frac{90}{3} = 30$. ∴ $-l = -5$ and $-5 \pm \sqrt{-5}$ are the other two roots. Thus we have performed an actual solution of the problem. It can be readily

seen, that as soon as the reader becomes acquainted with this method, the entire process can be performed *mentally* and *rapidly*.

From equation (5). The second term is wanting, and the sign of the third term +. ∴ Only one real root (**104**) and a pair of pure imaginaries. The sign of absolute term is −. ∴ Real root will be +. Separating 92 into its prime factors, we have $2 \times 2 \times 23$. If the real root is integral, it must be $2 \times 2 = 4$, which we find satisfies the problem.

∴ $\frac{4}{2} = 2$ = real part of imaginary. Its sign is *minus*.

$$\therefore\ (-2 + \sqrt{-l})(-2 + \sqrt{-l}) = \tfrac{92}{4} = 23.$$

Whence $\quad -l = -19$, and $\sqrt{-l} = \sqrt{-19}$.

∴ The roots of (5) are 4, and $-2 \pm \sqrt{-19}$.

From equation (6). The second and third term are wanting. ∴ Only one real root, which is $\sqrt[3]{\pm 1}$, and a pair of imaginary roots.

From equation (7),

$$(\pm 0)^2 - 2(-67) = 134 = a^2 + b^2 + c^2. \quad \text{(Th. II.)}$$

$134 \times 3 = 402 = \square$ of sum of roots + sum ⊡ of diffs. of roots (Th. II.). The side of the greatest integral square in 402 is 20, which will give for one of the roots, −10. This is found to be too great. The next lower number, 19, is rejected. (26.) 18 is then taken, and we have

$$\frac{18 + 0}{2} = 9 = \text{sum of + roots; true sign −; and}$$

$$\frac{18 - 0}{2} = 9 = \text{sum of − roots; true sign +.}$$

From the algebraic sum and sign of absolute term, the equation contains two + roots and one − root. We now substitute −9 in the equation. To do so, we divide the equation by $x + 9$, and find that −9 is a little too small. We now discover the *Natural* to be $x^3 - 67 \times - 126 = 0$, the roots of which are 2, 7, and -9. (To discover the Natural we divide (5) by -9, synthetic division, and solve the quadratic.) Thus:

$$\begin{array}{r} x^3 \pm 0 - 67 + 127 \\ -9 + 81 - 126 \\ \hline x^2 - 9 + 14 + \quad 1 \end{array}$$

(Solve $x^2 - 9x + 14 = 0$, and we obtain 2 and 7.)

If the absolute term of (5) was $+126$, the roots would be 2, 7, and -9; but the absolute term of the Natural has been increased by 1. ∴ The roots of (5) will be

$$>2, \ <7, \text{ and } > -9. \quad (\mathbf{112.})$$

This means that one of the roots lies between 2 and 3, one between 6 and 7, and one between -9 and -10.

183. To determine the location and character of the roots of the following *biquadratics*:

(1) $x^4 + 5x^3 + 30x^2 - 85x - 6 = 0.$

(2) $x^4 - 8x^3 + 23x^2 - 10x - 42 = 0.$

(3) $x^4 + 4x^3 - .5x^2 - 16x - 14 = 0.$

(4) $x^4 - 8x^3 + 33x^2 - 68x + 71 = 0.$

(5) $x^4 - 16x^3 + 128x^2 - 480x + 900 = 0.$

(6) $x^4 - 100x^3 + 3748x^2 - 62400x + 398375 = 0.$

(7) $x^4 - 2x^3 + 2x^2 - 16x + 64 = 0.$

(8) $x^4 + x^3 + x^2 + x + 1 = 0.$

(9) $x^4 - 3x^3 - 3x^2 - 3x - 4 = 0.$

From equation (1),

$(+5)^2 - 2(+30) = -35 = a^2 + b^2 + c^2 + d^2.$ (Th. II.)

∴ The equation contains imaginary roots. (**100.**) The sign of absolute term is *minus*. ∴ Two real roots of opposite signs (103), and two pure imaginary roots. (**26.**) The absolute term separates into the prime factors 2 and 3; 2 will satisfy the conditions of the problem, and is therefore a root. (16.) If we divide equation (1) by $x-2$, we obtain the cubic

$$x^3+7x^2+44x+3=0,$$

the real root of which is *minus*, and cannot be greater than

$$\frac{3}{<4}=>-.07 \text{ and } <-.08.$$

The imaginary roots can be readily found from a quadratic.

From equation (2),

$(-8)^2-2(23)=18=a^2+b^2+c^2+d^2$. (Th. II.)

$4\times 18=72=\square$ of sum + sum $\boxed{s}$ of diffs. of roots. (Th. II.)

The side of the greatest square in 72 whose side is integral is 8. If 8 is the true numerical sum of roots, then

$\dfrac{8+-8}{2}=0=$ sum of + roots in formation of equation; true sign −.

$\dfrac{8-(-8)}{2}=8=$ sum − roots in formation of equation; true sign +.

Then would the equation contain no *minus* root, which we see is not true from the signs of its terms; for the equation contains *two real* roots, *one* + and *one* −. We have seen that the side of the greatest square in 72, which is 8, is too small. Therefore, say 9; but 9 is rejected. (**26.**) 10 is then taken as the true *numerical* sum of roots; and $\dfrac{10+-8}{2}$ $=1=$ sum + roots; true sign −; and $\dfrac{10-(-8)}{2}=9=$ sum − roots; true sign +. -1 satisfies the conditions of the problem. ∴ $10=$ true *numerical* sum of roots. The absolute term separates into 1, 2, 3, and 7 as prime factors. $+3$ is also found to be a root. ∴ -1 and $+3$ are the real roots. The sum of their squares $=(1)^2+(3)^2=10$, which we take from the whole sum of squares, and we obtain

$18-10=8=$ sum of ⓢ of the imaginary roots, say $a \pm \sqrt{-l}$; or, $2a^2 + -2l = 8$. Their product will be $\frac{42}{1 \times 3} = 14 =$ $a^2 + l = 14$. Multiplying this last by 2 and subtracting it from the *sum* of squares, we have $-2l = -20$. Whence $-l = -5$ and $\sqrt{-l} = \sqrt{-5}$. And, adding and extracting square root of both members, we have $a = 3$. $\therefore$ The roots of (2) are -1, $+3$, and $+3 \pm \sqrt{-5}$.

From equation (3),

$(+4)^2 - 2(-.5) = 17 = a^2 + b^2 + c^2 + d^2$. (Th. II.)

$(-16)^2 - 2(-.5 \times -14) = 242 = \overline{abc}^2 + \overline{abd}^2 + \cdots$. (Th. IV.)

$17 \times 4 = 68 = \square$ of sum of roots + sum ⓢ of diffs. (Th. II.)

$(68)^{\frac{1}{2}} = 8 =$ sum of roots. (The side of the greatest square in 68 being taken for numerical sum of roots. If it should be too great, or too small, it will be detected as we proceed.)

$\therefore \frac{8+4}{2} = 6 =$ sum + roots in formation of equation; true sign $-$; and

$\frac{8-4}{2} = 2 =$ sum $-$ roots in formation of equation; true sign $+$.

From algebraic sum and signs of the terms there are three *minus* roots and one *plus* root. 2 is tried, and it satisfies the equation. $+2$ is therefore a root. We also try -2, and find it to be a root. By dividing equation (13) by $(x+2)(x-2)$, we obtain,

$$x^2 + 4x + 3.5 = 0.$$

Solving the quadratic, which we can do mentally, we find the other two roots to be also *real*, being

$$-2 \pm \sqrt{.5}.$$

NOTE. — While we have been determining the location and character of the roots we have solved the equation.

From equation (4),

$$(-8)^2 - 2(+33) = -2 = a^2 + b^2 + c^2 + d^2. \quad \text{(Th. II.)}$$

$$(-68)^2 - 2(+33 \times +71) = -62 = \overline{abc}^2 + \cdots + \overline{bcd}^2. \quad \text{(Th. IV.)}$$

Both theorems give for sum of squares of roots, and sum of squares of products of roots, taken three and three, *minus quantities*. ∴ It is safe to conclude that the equation contains all pure imaginary roots, which we may now represent as follows for unequal roots:

$$a \pm \sqrt{-l},$$

$$b \pm \sqrt{-m}.$$

Should the roots be equal conjugate imaginaries, then

$$2 \pm \sqrt{-l},$$

$$2 \pm \sqrt{-l}$$

may represent the roots. Trial is made with the equal roots, and we obtain as the roots of (4)

$$2 \pm \sqrt{-4.5 \pm \sqrt{1.25}}.$$

(See general solutions of biquadratics.)

From equation (5),

$$(-16)^2 - 2(128) = 0 = a^2 + b^2 + c^2 + d^2. \quad \text{(Th. II.)}$$

$$(-480)^2 - 2(128 \times 900) = 0 = \overline{abc}^2 + \cdots + \overline{bcd}^2. \quad \text{(Th. IV.)}$$

∴ The equation contains all imaginary roots. (**132.**)

REMARK. — To separate (5) into two quadratics.

Let $(i)\ x^2 - ax + 30 = 0,$

and $(e)\ x^2 - bx + 30 = 0$

be the equations whose products equal equation (5). $30 = \sqrt{900}$. Find $-a$, and $-b$, and substitute in (i) and (e) and solve by quadratics. The roots of the quadratics will be the roots of the biquadratic.

From equation (6),

$(-100)^2 - 2(3748) = 2504 = a^2 + b^2 + c^2 + d^2$. (Th. II.)

$(2504) \times 4 = 10016 = \square$ of sum + sum ⓢ of diffs. of roots. $10016 - (100)^2 = 16 =$ sum ⓢ of diffs. From the signs and magnitude of the coefficients, and absolute term, and sum of ⓢ of differences of roots, we have no hesitancy in saying that the equation contains four *real imaginaries.* The problem is easily solved by submitting it to a *general solution,* in which case no attention is given to the signs or character of the roots, *as their true signs and character are developed in the solution.*

From equation (7). By inspection we discover, mentally, that the equation contains all imaginary roots; and by separating the equation into quadratics, the roots are obtained and their signs and character determined.

Equations (8) and (9) are readily solved by (**133**).

184. To determine the location and character of the roots of the following quintics:

(1) $x^5 + x^4 - 26x^3 - 12x^2 + 134x + 119 = 0.$

(2) $x^5 + 2x^4 - 3x^3 - 3x^2 + 2x + 1 = 0.$

(3) $x^5 \pm 1 = 0.$

(4) $x^5 + x^4 + 2x^3 + 2x^2 + 3x + 3 = 0.$

(5) $x^5 - 30x^4 + 340x^3 - 1800x^2 + 4384x - 3830 = 0.$

(6) $x^5 - 73x^4 + 89x^3 + 103x^2 + 771x + 29 = 0.$

(7) $x^5 + 14x^4 + 73.7x^3 + 457x^2 + 1307x + 1218 = 0.$

(8) $x^5 - 37 = 0.$

(9) $x^5 - 16x^4 + 126x^3 - 539x^2 + 1295x - 1218 = 0.$

From equation (1),

$(+1)^2 - 2(-26) = 53 = a^2 + b^2 + c^2 + d^2 + e^2$. (Th. II.)

$53 \times 5 = 265 = \square$ of sum + sum ⓢ of diffs. (Th. II.)

The side of the greatest square in 265, whose side is integral, is 16, which is rejected. (**26.**) 15 is then taken for numerical sum of roots, and we have

$$\frac{15+(+1)}{2}=8=\text{sum}+\text{roots in formation of equation;}$$

true sign $-$.

$$\frac{15-(+1)}{2}=7=\text{sum}-\text{roots in formation of equation;}$$

true sign $+$.

$\therefore\ 265-(15)^2=40=$ sum $\boxed{S}$ of diffs.; ten in number, $10\times 40=400$, which is a perfect square. $\therefore\ \sqrt{400}=20=(4\,e+2\,d)-(4\,a+2\,c)$. (**125.**) From the sum of the diffs. and sum of the roots we readily separate 15 into the numbers 1, 2, 3, 4, 5. Fitting these numbers to the sum of $+$, and $-$ roots, we have in either case three *minus* roots and two *plus* roots. We now try $+5$, or any of the other numbers (1, 2, 3, 4), to obtain the combination of the roots. In either case we find for *minus* roots -1, -2, -5, and *plus* roots 3 and 4. With these roots we build the *cubic* and *quadratic*, respectively,

$$x^3+8\,x^2+17\,x+10=0, \text{ and}$$

$$x^2-7\,x+12=0.$$

Their product $=0=x^5+x^4-27\,x^3-13\,x^2+134\,x+120$, which is the *Natural Equation* from which (1) is derived, by changing the coefficients of $-x^3$, $-x^2$, and x^0, or absolute term. The sum of the $\boxed{S}$ of the roots of the *Natural* will be $55=1^2+2^2+3^2+4^2+5^2$.

The products of the roots of the *Natural*, taken *four* and *four*, are $abcd=24$, $abce=30$, $abde=40$, and $acde=60$, and $bcde=120$. The absolute term has been decreased by 1. $\therefore$ The roots will be

$$<-1,\ >-2,\ <-5,\ <3,\ >4;$$

and the products, four and four, will be

$$>24, \ <30, \ >40, \ <60, \text{ and } >120.$$

$$\therefore\ 119 \div > 24 = -\ 4 = e,$$

$$119 \div < 60 = -\ 2 = b,$$

$$119 \div > 120 = -\ .9 = a.$$

Having now obtained the first figures of the three *minus* roots, we proceed to find another figure of the root, as follows:

$119 \div 24 = 4$, and a remainder of 23. To obtain the next figure of the root we divide 23 by $24 + \frac{4}{2}$, or 26. $23 \div 26 = .8$. $\therefore\ -4.8 = e$ to two places; and, having found $a = -.9$, if we divide 119 by $120 + \frac{.9}{2}$, we obtain $a = .98+$, to two places of decimals; and $119 \div (60 - 2) = 2.05 = b$ to two places of decimals. The other two roots will be found to be *real* and *equal*. [See solution elsewhere.]

From equations (2), (3), (4) it is easily discovered that such equations are easily solved. [See solutions.]

From equation (5),

$$(-30)^2 - 2(340) = 220 = a^2 + b^2 + c^2 + d^2 + e^2. \quad \text{(Th. II.)}$$

$$220 \times 5 = 1100 = \square \text{ of sum} + \text{sum} \boxed{\text{s}} \text{ of diffs.} \quad \text{(Th. II.)}$$

$$1100 - (30)^2 = 200 = \text{sum} \boxed{\text{s}} \text{ of diffs.}$$

$200 \times 10 = 2000 = \square$ of sum of diffs. + sum $\boxed{\text{s}}$ of the *differences* of *differences*. 2000 is made up of two perfect squares, viz. 1600 and 400. $\sqrt{1600} = 40 =$ sum of differences; and $\sqrt{400} = 20 =$ sum *first order* of differences. And $40 \div 20 = 2 =$ common difference of roots.

$$\therefore\ a + a + 2 + a + 4 + a + 6 + a + 8 = 30.$$

Whence $a = 2$, and the roots are 2, 4, 6, 8, 10. Trial proves these roots to satisfy all the conditions of the problem, *but that of the absolute term,* which has been decreased by 10.

$\therefore$ The roots of (5) are

$$< 2, \ > 4, \ < 6, \ > 8, \text{ and } < 10,$$

which means that the roots lie between 1 and 2, 4 and 5, 5 and 6, 8 and 9, and 9 and 10. We have now accomplished all that the "Sturm Theorem" is capable of doing for us, but with far less labor and in much less time. We will now carry the *location* of the roots a step farther than that capable of being accomplished by the "Sturm Theorem." Letting a, b, c, d, and e represent the roots, then, from the Natural we have for the products of roots taken *four* and *four:*

$$\begin{aligned} abcd &= 384, \\ abce &= 480, \\ abde &= 640, \\ acde &= 960, \\ bcde &= 1920. \end{aligned}$$

$$\frac{3830}{abcd} = e = 3830 \div > \ 384 = 9.97,$$

$$\frac{3830}{abce} = d = 3830 \div < \ 480 = 8.10,$$

$$\frac{3830}{abde} = c = 3830 \div > \ 640 = 5.84,$$

$$\frac{3830}{acde} = b = 3830 \div < \ 960 = 4.11,$$

$$\frac{3830}{bcde} = a = 3830 \div > 1920 = 1.97.$$

Beginning with a, for $bcde$ we add 2×10 to 1920 for divisor; for b, decrease 960 by 3×10; for c, *increase* 640 by 1×10; for d, decrease 480 by 1×10; and e is found by taking $(a + b + c + d)$ from 29.99; for if we approximate the roots by any known method, we cannot find for sum of roots a closer approximation than 29.99999+, which will necessitate the approximation of each root to at least six places of decimals.

From equation (6),

$$x^5 - 73x^4 + 89x^3 + 103x^2 + 771x + 29 = 0.$$

We give the method in full, as this equation was submitted for solution by A. H. Godby of Carder, Missouri, who regards the problem as a difficult one. It will be seen that the equation is easily solved by our method, *while its solution by the Horner method and Sturm Theorem* is long and tedious.

(1) $(-73)^2 - 2(89) = 5151 = a^2 + b^2 + c^2 + d^2 + e^2.$ (Th. II.)

(2) $(+771)^2 - 2(103 \times 29) = 588{,}467$

$$= \overline{abcd}^2 + \cdots + \overline{bcde}^2. \quad \text{(Th. V.)}$$

(3) $(103)^2 + 2(-73 \times 29) - 2(89 \times 771) = -130{,}953$

$$= \overline{abc}^2 + \overline{abd}^2 + \overline{abe}^2 + \cdots + \overline{cde}^2. \quad \text{(Th. V.)}$$

∴ (Th. V), the equation contains imaginary roots. (**101.**)

But every *odd* degree equation contains at least *one real root affected by a sign contrary to its absolute term.* (**110.**) ∴ The equation contains a *minus* root; and by inspection of the equation we can see that such *real* root is < -1.

We now proceed to discover its Natural, if possible.

Dividing the equation by $x + 1$, we obtain

$$(A) \qquad x^4 - 74x^3 + 163x^2 - 60x + 831 = 0.$$

If the absolute term of equation (6) was 831, -1 would be a root. So a, the first root, is < -1 (**113**). From (A) (Th. IV), $(-74)^2 - 2(+163)$ is largely a + quantity, while $(-60)^2 - 2(163 \times 831)$ is largely a $-$ quantity.

Therefore (A) will contain a real root contrary to sign of absolute term; and being of *even degree,* if it contains *one* real root, it must contain *two* real roots. ∴ (A) contains two real and two imaginary roots. ∴ Equation (6) contains *three real roots and two imaginary roots.* (**110.**)

831 is exactly divisible by 3, so we divide equation (A) by $x - 3$, and obtain

$$(B) \qquad x^3 - 71\,x^2 - 50\,x - 210 = 0.$$

If the absolute term of (A) was 630, (3×210), $+3$ would be a root.

We now multiply B, $x + 1$, and $x - 3$ together, and obtain

$$(C) \qquad x^5 - 73\,x^4 + 89\,x^3 + 103\,x^2 + 570\,x + 630 = 0.$$

∴ (C) is the *Natural* equation from which (6) is derived by *increasing the coefficient of x in the Natural by 201, and decreasing the absolute term of the Natural by 601.*

From (B) it is seen that the real root will be $+$, and > 71, but < 72; and this would be the case should the absolute term of (B) be as small as -1. Therefore, the roots of (6) will be < -1, $> +3$, but $< +4$, and $> +71$, but $< +72$, and two imaginary roots. We will now locate or determine the roots more definitely. Letting a, b, and c represent the real roots in the order of their magnitude, $29 \div 771 = .037 = a$ *to three places of decimals,* with a remainder, after division, of .473, which we divide by 601, the decrease in absolute term, $.473 \div 601 = .00078$, the next two figures of the root. ∴ $a = -.03778$ to five places of decimals.

The next root is > 3 but < 4, so we divide the equation by $+3$, using the method of synthetic division, and obtain $+2$ for a quotient. Continuing the division of the remainder by $+3$, we obtain as a divisor of $+2$, -3687.

∴ $2 \div 3687 = .00054 =$ the decimal part of b to five places of decimals. Whence, $b = 3.00054+$.

Again, dividing equation (6) by $(x+.03778)(x-3.00054)$, we obtain the cubic

$$(D) \quad x^3 - 70.03724\,x^2 - 118.3901731824\,x - 255.70108 = 0,$$

which may be written for solution,

$$(E) \qquad x^3 - 70.04\,x^2 - 118.4\,x - 255.70 = 0.$$

(E), solved, gives $c = 71.7398+$.

To obtain the imaginary roots,

$$(.03778)^2 + (3.00054)^2 + (71.7398)^2 = a^2 + b^2 + c^2.$$

Taking the sum of the squares of the roots thus far found from the sum of ⓢ *of all the roots, we obtain the sum of the* ⓢ *of the imaginary roots.*

Letting $d \pm \sqrt{-l}$ represent the imaginary roots, their product $= d^2 + l = \dfrac{29}{(.03778)(3.00054)(71.7398)} = 3.5672126+,$

$$5151 - (a^2 + b^2 + c^2) = -4.60328714 = 2\,d^2 + -\,2\,l.$$

$\therefore\ d^2 + -\,l = -2.30164357.$ (Dividing $(2\,d^2 + -\,2\,l)$ by 2.)

Whence, $2\,d^2 = 1.2655691.$ (Adding $(d^2 + -\,l)$ and $a^2 + l$.)

$$\therefore\ d = \sqrt{\frac{1.265569}{2}} = .7954+.$$

And $\pm\sqrt{-\,l} = \pm\sqrt{-2.929428}.$ (Subtracting $(a^2 + -\,l)$ and $(a^2 + l)$, dividing by 2, and taking square root of both members.)

$\therefore$ The roots of equation (6) are

$$71.7398,\ 3.00054,\ -.03778,\ \text{and}\ -.7954 \pm \sqrt{-2.929428}.$$

From eq. (7) $a^2 + b^2 + c^2 + d^2 + e^2 = 48.6.$ (Th. II.)

$$\overline{ab}^2 + \overline{ac}^2 + \cdots + \overline{de}^2 = -4722.31. \quad \text{(Th. V.)}$$

$\therefore$ The equation contains imaginary roots. (**101.**) It also contains a real *minus* root. (**110.**) Theorem V also gives a plus quantity for sum of squares of roots, taken three and three, and four and four. [Equation 7 was submitted for solution by A. H. Godby, of Carder, Missouri.]

To determine its Natural (if possible), and locate the roots.

(1) $48.6 \times 5 = 243 = \square$ of sum of roots + sum of ⓢ of diffs.

(2) $243 \div 2 = 121.5$.

(3) $243 \div 3 = 81$.

(4) The side of the greatest integral square in 121.5 is 11.

(5) The side of the greatest square in 81 is 9.

(6) $\dfrac{9+11}{2} = 10$. (One root lies between -9 and -11.)

We now divide the equation by $x + 10$, and obtain the *biquadratic*,

$$(A) \qquad x^4 + 4x^3 + 33.7x^2 + 120x + 107 = 0.$$

∴ If the absolute term of (7) was 1070, -10 would be a root; and as the absolute term of (7) is > 1070, one of the real roots is > -10, but < -11. (**113.**)

Increase the coefficient of x^2 in (A) by .3, and we have

$$(B) \qquad x^4 + 4x^3 + 34x^2 + 120x + 107 = 0.$$

Introducing -10, by synthetic multiplication, we have

$$(C) \qquad x^5 + 14x^4 + 74x^3 + 460x^2 + 1307x + 1070 = 0.$$

(C) is the *Natural* from which (7) is derived, by changing the coefficients of x^3, x^2, and absolute term in (C).

Does the equation (7) *contain more than one real root?*

We will now investigate whether it contains another real root; and, if it does, *it will contain three real roots.* (**110.**)

Dividing equation (7) by -10, by synthetic division, we obtain -148 for a quotient; and dividing the remainder by -10, we obtain $+8277$ for a divisor of -148. $\frac{148}{8277} = .01$, which is the first two figures of the decimal part of the root whose real part is -10. $\therefore$ 10.01. Then for correction divisor add .01 of 8277 to 8277, and we obtain 8360, *nearly*. $\therefore \frac{148}{8360} = .0177 =$ four decimals of the root. $\therefore -10.0177$ is one of the roots of (7). $48.6 - (-10.0177)^2 = -51.7553 + =$ sum of ⓢ of the other four roots of (7). The sum of ⓢ of the roots of the *biquadratic* being largely a *minus* quantity, *the other four roots of* (7) *will be imaginary.*

NOTE. — *When it becomes known that an equation of the fifth contains but one real root, the simplest and most satisfactory method is found by changing the equation to one of the tenth degree, and approximating the product of each pair of imaginaries.* When the product of each pair becomes known, they may be placed equal to $a^2 + l$, and $b^2 + m$.

To illustrate. Take the equation

$$(A) \qquad x^5 + mx^4 + nx^3 + ox^2 + px + q = 0.$$

Let (A) contain but one real root. Then we may represent the roots, algebraically, as follows:

$$a,\ b \pm \sqrt{-l},\ c \pm \sqrt{-m}.$$

The sum of the squares of the roots are found by Theorem II to be

$$a^2 + 2\,b^2 + -2\,l + 2\,c^2 + -2\,m = m^2 - 2\,n.$$

When $b^2 + l$ and $c^2 + m$ are found it is seen that all the roots of the fifth are easily obtained.

[See solutions of quintics and general formula for changing an equation of the fifth into an equation of the tenth, given in another part of this volume.]

From equation (8): One real + root, and four equal conjugate imaginaries. The real root is $\sqrt[5]{37}$.

From eq. (9):

$$(-16)^2 - 2(126) = 4 = a^2 + b^2 + c^2 + d^2 + e^2. \qquad \text{(Th. II.)}$$

As 4×5 is $< (-16)^2$, the equation contains imaginary roots. (**130.**) The sum of ⓢ of roots is a perfect □, and we try $(4)^{\frac{1}{2}}$ or 2 for the real root. It is found to satisfy all the conditions of the equation, and is therefore a root. (**16.**)

∴ The sum of the squares of the remaining roots will be a *zero quantity;* and dividing equation (9) by $(x-2)$, by synthetic division, we obtain the *biquadratic.*

$$(A) \qquad x^4 - 14x^3 + 98x^2 - 343x + 609 = 0.$$

The four roots of which are found to be

$$3.5 + \sqrt{-12.25 + \sqrt{-8.75}},$$

$$3.5 - \sqrt{-12.25 + \sqrt{-8.75}},$$

$$3.5 + \sqrt{-12.25 - \sqrt{-8.75}},$$

$$3.5 - \sqrt{-12.25 - \sqrt{-8.75}}.$$

[See general solutions of biquadratics given in another part of this work.]

185. To determine the location and character of the following miscellaneous equations:

(l) $x^4 - 7x^3 + 17x^2 - 16.625x + 5 = 0.$

(m) $x^4 - 756x^3 + 142885x^2 - 378x + 2700 = 0.$

(n) $x^4 + 114x^3 + 11x^2 - 184566x + 1601 = 0.$

(o) $x^4 - x^3 - 43x^2 + 86.5x + 119 = 0.$

(p) $x^6 + 21x^5 + 170x^4 + 665x^3 + 1176x^2 + 343x - 117 = 0.$

(q) $x^7 + 2x^6 - 13x^5 - 46x^4 - 41x^3 + 100x^2 + 296x + 184 = 0.$

(r) $x^9 + 2x^8 - 2x^7 - 4x^6 + 99x^5 + 478x^4 + 658x^3$
$+ 196x^2 - 2499x + 4878 - 0.$

From (l).

$(-7)^2 - 2(17) = 15 = a^2 + b^2 + c^2 + d^2.$ (Th. II.)

$(17)^2 - 2[(-7 \times -16.625) - 5] = 66.25 = \overline{ab}^2 + \cdots + \overline{cd}^2.$ (Th. IV.)

By inspection we see that the sum of squares of products of roots taken *three* and *three* will also be a plus quantity. We would therefore infer that the equation contains all real + roots. The same we will find is true of the other biquadratics (m), (n), and (o).

To solve these apparently difficult equations we submit them to a general solution, which we will now briefly illustrate.

186. Let $x^4 + mx^3 + nx^2 + ox + q = 0$ be an equation of the *fourth degree*, of which we are required to represent the roots in terms of the coefficients.

(1) Let $$n - \frac{m^2}{4} = \frac{2o}{m} = z + y.$$

(2) Put $$zy = q.$$

(3) Find e and y from (1) and (2).

(3) Write for quadratics

$$x^2 + \frac{m}{2}x + z = 0,$$

$$x^2 + \frac{m}{2}x + y = 0.$$

(5) Substitute the values of z and y in their respective quadratics, which solved gives the roots in terms of the coefficients.

187. *By this method the biquadratics* **185** *can be solved, and their roots determined to a far greater degree of accuracy, and in less time than it takes to solve any one of the equations by the old methods. It is the only satisfactory solution for this class of biquadratics ever discovered, and does not depend upon Cardan's rule, nor does it require the removal of the second term. It will be further illustrated under the head of general solutions.*

188. To solve (l) by quadratics.

$$x^4 - 7x^3 + 17x^2 - 16.625x + 5 = 0.$$

$$(1)\quad z + y = 17 - \frac{49}{4} = 4.75 = \frac{2x - 16.625}{-7}.$$

$$(2)\qquad zy = 5.$$

$$((4.85)^2 - 4(5))^{\frac{1}{2}} = z - y = \sqrt{2.5625}.$$

$$\therefore\ z = 2.375 + \sqrt{.640625},$$

$$y = 2.375 - \sqrt{.640625}.$$

We now write the quadratics

$$(e)\ x^2 - 3.5x + 2.375 + \sqrt{.640625} = 0.$$

$$(i)\ x^2 - 3.5x + 2.375 - \sqrt{.640625} = 0.$$

Their product equals equation (l).

It will be discovered in the solution of the quadratic (e) that the equation contains two real roots and a pair of real imaginaries. *Almost an entire solution of the equation is required by the Sturm Theorem in determining the character of the roots.* In the general solution no attention is given to the character of roots, for their true character and signs are developed by the solution.

From (p): It will be shown in the solution of equations of the Sixth Degree that they depend upon the solution of a cubic.

From (q),

$$(2)^2 - 2(-13) = 30 = a^2 + b^2 + c^2 + d^2 + e^2 + f^2.\quad \text{(Th. II.)}$$

184 = the product of the prime factors 2, 2, 2, and 23.

The equation is of odd degree, therefore one real root at least. (**110.**) We now try -2, and find that it satisfies the condition of the equation, and is therefore a root. (**16.**)

We now separate the equation, if possible, into a *cubic* and *biquadratic*, letting $2 \times 2 \times 2 = 8 =$ absolute term of the cubic. If -2 is one of the roots of the cubic, then will $2 \times 2 = 4$ be the product of the other two roots. We easily form the cubic

$$(A) \qquad x^3 + 4x^2 + 8x + 8 = 0,$$

which has -2 for a root. Dividing (l) by (A) we obtain the biquadratic

$$(B) \qquad x^4 - 2x^3 - 13x^2 + 14x + 23 = 0.$$

The roots of (B) are easily found, as in the solution of (l). The roots of (B) are all real, two + and two −.

∴ (q) contains five real roots and a pair of imaginaries.

From equation (r), $(+2)^2 - 2(-2) = 8 =$ sum of squares of roots (Th. II.). The equation is of odd degree; therefore, one real + root at least. (**110.**) The coefficient of x is an exact division of the absolute term. ∴ We try $+2$ for a root, and find that it satisfies the conditions of the equation, and is therefore a root. (**16.**) The equation is now reduced to an equation of the Eighth Degree, which we find no trouble in separating into two biquadratics:

$$(A) \qquad x^4 + 2x^3 + x^2 - 21 = 0,$$

and $$(B) \quad x^4 + 2x^3 + 17x^2 + 16x + 119 = 0.$$

(A) and (B) are readily resolved by the general method for the solution of such biquadratics. (A) contains two real roots, one +, and one −, and two imaginary roots; and (B) contains all imaginary roots; because

$$\left(17 - \frac{(2)^2}{4}\right)^2 = \left(\frac{2 \times 16}{2}\right)^2,$$

which is less than 4×119. That is,

$$(17 - 1)^2 - 4(119) = -200 = (z - y)^2.$$

Whence, $$z - y = \sqrt{-200}.$$

$\therefore$ Equation (r) contains six imaginary roots and three real roots.

REMARK. — The foregoing illustrations are really methods of *solutions*, rather than methods of locations of roots. *Our aim is to solve an equation without giving any attention to the signs and character of its roots, until they are determined by the solution.*

CUBIC EQUATIONS AND SOLUTIONS.

189. To find the roots of

$$(A) \quad x^3 - 2.5\,x^2 + \tfrac{31}{16}\,x - \tfrac{15}{32} = 0.$$

SOLUTION.

(1) $a^2 + b^2 + c^2 = 42.375 = (-2.5)^2 - 2(\frac{31}{16})$. (Th. II.)

(2) $\overline{ab}^2 + \overline{ac}^2 + \overline{bc}^2 = \frac{361}{256} = (\frac{31}{16})^2 - 2(-2.5 \times -\frac{15}{16})$. (Th. III.)

(3) $\therefore ac + bc - ab = \frac{19}{16} = (\frac{361}{256})^{\frac{1}{2}}$. (**114.**)

(4) $\therefore 2\,ab = \frac{12}{16}$, and $ab = \frac{6}{16}$. (Subtracting p_2 and (3).)

(5) Whence $\frac{15}{32} \div \frac{6}{16} = \frac{5}{4} = 1\frac{1}{4} = c$.

(6) $2.5 - 1\frac{1}{4} = a + b = 1.25$.

(7) $\therefore$ From $a + b = 1.25$ and $ab = \frac{12}{16}$, we readily find the other two roots to be $\frac{1}{2}$ and $\frac{3}{4}$.

(8) $\therefore$ The roots of (A) in the order of their magnitude are $\frac{1}{2}$, $\frac{3}{4}$, and $1\frac{1}{4}$, being all real and *plus*.

190. To find the roots of

$$(B) \quad x^3 - 2\,x^2 - 59\,x + 168 = 0.$$

SOLUTION.

(1) $a^2 + b^2 + c^2 = 122 =$ sum of [s] of roots. (Th. II.)

(2) $122 \times 3 = 366 = \square$ of sum of roots + sum [s] of diffs. (Th. II.)

(3) $(366)^{\frac{1}{2}} = 18 = a + b + c$. (19 being rejected (26).)

(4) $\therefore \dfrac{18 + -2}{2} = 8 =$ sum of *plus* roots in formation of equation; true sign $-$.

(5) $\dfrac{18-(-2)}{2} = 10 =$ sum of *minus* roots in formation of equation; true sign $+$.

(6) Either 8 or 10 must be a root of the equation, at least of the *Natural*, for the equation does not contain four roots. But it is seen by inspection that 8 is an exact divisor of the absolute term. -8 is tried, and it satisfies the equation, and is therefore a root. $122-(8)^2=58=a^2+b^2$, and $\frac{168}{8}=21=ab$. We now find the other roots to be 3 and 7. Therefore, the roots of (B) are 3, 7, and -8.

191. To find the roots of

$$(C)\quad x^3+7x-48=0.$$

SOLUTION. The second term is wanting, and the sign of third term $+$. $\therefore$ only one real $+$ root and a pair of imaginary roots. (**119** and **120**.) The sum of the squares of the roots

$$=-14=(\pm 0)-2(+7).\quad \text{(Th. II.)}$$

Change its sign and multiply by 3, and we have 42. The side of the greatest square in 42 whose side is integral is 6. $\therefore 6\div 2=3=c$, the greatest root (**26**), at least of the *natural*. 3 is tried and is found to satisfy the conditions of the equation, and is therefore a root. (**16**.) The other two roots are found from $a+b=3$ and $ab=16=\frac{48}{3}$, from which we find a or b to be $\frac{-3\pm\sqrt{-55}}{2}$.

192. To find the roots of

$$(D)\quad x^3-12x^2+72x-216=0.$$

SOLUTION.

(1) $a^2+b^2+c^2=0=(-12)^2-2(+72)$. (Th. II.)

(2) $(72)^2-2(-12\times -216)=0=\overline{ab}^2+\overline{ac}^2+\overline{bc}^2$. (Th. II.)

(3) $\therefore$ Only one real root, the $\sqrt[3]{216}=6$. (**122**.)

(4) $0-(6)^2=-36=a^2+b^2$, and $ab=\frac{216}{6}=36$.

(5) From (4) the other two roots are found to be $3\pm\sqrt{-27}$, or $3\pm 3\sqrt{-3}$.

193. To find the roots of

$$x^3+32x^2+319x+1008=0.$$

SOLUTION.

(1) $a^2+b^2+c^2=386=(32)^2-2(319)$. (Th. II.)

(2) $(\overline{ab}^2+\overline{ac}^2+\overline{bc}^2=37249=(319)^2-2(32\times 1008)$. (Th. III.)

(3) $(37249)^{\frac{1}{2}} = 193 = ac + bc - ab$. (**114.**)

(4) $\therefore \dfrac{193 + 319}{2} = ac + bc$, and $\dfrac{319 - 193}{2} = ab = 63$.

(5) $\therefore c = \frac{1008}{63} = 16$, and $32 - 16 = 16 = a + b$, and $[(a+b)^2 - 4\,ab]^{\frac{1}{2}} = a - b = 2$.

(6) $\therefore a = \dfrac{16 - 2}{2} = 6$, and $b = \dfrac{16 + 2}{2} = 8$.

(7) The terms are all plus, therefore we write for the roots of the equation, -6, -8, and -16. (**111.**)

194. To find the roots of

$$x^3 - 4\,x^2 + 9 = 0.$$

Solution.

(1) $a^2 + b^2 + c^2 = 16 = (-4)^2 - 2\,(\pm 0)$. (Th. II.)

(2) $\overline{ab}^2 + \overline{ac}^2 + \overline{bc}^2 = 72 = (\pm 0)^2 - 2\,(-4 \times +9)$. (Th. III.)

Here the third term is wanting, but Th. III. brings to light the sum of the squares of the products of the roots two and two.

(3) $3 \times 72 = 216 = \square$ of sum of products + sum of $\boxed{s}$ of differences of products. (Th. I.)

(4) $(216)^{\frac{1}{3}} = 6 = ab + ac + bc$. [216 being a perfect cube.]

(5) $\therefore \dfrac{6 + \pm 0}{2} = 3$ = sum of + products in the formation of equation; true sign $-$.

(6) $\therefore -9 \div -3 = 3 = c$.

(7) $16 - (3)^2 = 7 = a^2 + b^2$; and $7 \times 2 = 14 = \square$ of sum + sum $\boxed{s}$ of diffs. $\therefore 14 - (1)^2 = 13 = (a - b)^2$, whence,

(8) $a - b = \sqrt{13}$.

(9) $\therefore a = \dfrac{1 + \sqrt{13}}{2}$, and $b = \dfrac{1 - \sqrt{13}}{2}$.

195. To find the roots of

$$x^3 + 4\,x^2 - 9 = 0.$$

Solution the same as the above, and roots the same, but of *different signs.*

196. To find the roots of

$$x^3 - .8589\,x + .1411 = 0.$$

SOLUTION.

(1) $a^2 + b^2 + c^2 = 1.7178 = (\pm 0)^2 - 2(-.8589)$. (Th. II.)

(2) $1.7178 \times 3 = 5.1534 = \square$ of sum of roots + sum ⊡ of diffs. of roots. (Th. II.)

(3) $(5.1534)^{\frac{1}{2}} = 2 =$ sum of roots.

(The side of the greatest integral square being taken for sum of roots. This will give the true numerical sum, or it will be sufficient to locate the roots by determining the Natural.)

(4) $\therefore \dfrac{2 + \pm 0}{2} = 1 =$ sum + roots; true sign −.

(5) $\dfrac{2 - \pm 0}{2} = 1 =$ sum − roots; true sign +.

As the equation contains two + roots, from the signs of its terms, − 1 is tried and is found to satisfy the equation. It is therefore a root. (**16.**)

(6) Whence, $1.7178 - (-1)^2 = .7178 = a^2 + b^2$. Their product, $ab = .1411 = \dfrac{.1411}{1}$.

From (6) a and b are found to be respectively equal to .17 and .83. Therefore, we write for the roots of the equation, .17, .83, and − 1.

NOTE. — Should the absolute term of the above equation be greater or less than .1411, say less, and be .1410. The process discovers its Natural just as soon as − 1 becomes known. The Natural would be found to be the given equation. We find the roots of the Natural to be .17, .83, and − 1. Then should the equation read, $x^3 - .8589\,x + .1410 = 0$, the roots would be $< .17$, $> .83$, and < -1. (**112.**) Should the equation read, $x^3 - .8589\,x + .1412 = 0$, then the roots would be $> .17$, $< .83$, and > -1. The methods for solving an equation of the *third* degree, whose roots are approximate, are to be found under Art. **226**.

197. To find the roots of

$$x^3 + 2\,x^2 + 9 = 0.$$

SOLUTION.

(1) $a^2 + b^2 + c^2 = 4 = (2)^2 - 2(\pm 0)$. (Th. II.)

(2) $\overline{ab}^2 + \overline{ac}^2 + \overline{bc}^2 = -36 = (\pm 0)^2 - 2(+2 \times +9)$. (Th. III.)

(3) (Changing the sign). $2(36 \times 3)^{\frac{1}{3}} = 6 = ab + ac + bc$.

(4) $\therefore \dfrac{6 + \pm 0}{2} = 3 =$ sum $p_2 +$ roots ; true sign $-$;

and $\dfrac{6 - \pm 0}{2} = 3 =$ sum $p_2 -$ roots ; true sign $+$.

(5) $\therefore -9 \div -3 = 3 =$, say c, the greatest root. But the sum of [s] of p_2 is a *minus* quantity. $\therefore$ The equation contains but *one* real root. $+3$ satisfies all the conditions of the equation, and is therefore a root. (**16.**)

(6) $4 - (3)^2 = -5 = a^2 + b^2$; and $ab = \frac{9}{3} = 3$.

(7) $\therefore a + b = (a^2 + b^2 + 2\,ab)^{\frac{1}{2}} = (-5 + 6)^{\frac{1}{2}} = 1$,

and $a - b = (a^2 + b^2 - 2\,ab)^{\frac{1}{2}} = [-5 - (+6)]^{\frac{1}{2}} = \sqrt{-11}$.

(8) $\therefore a$ or $b = \dfrac{1 \pm \sqrt{-11}}{2}$.

198. To find the roots of

$$x^3 - 2\,x^2 - 9 = 0.$$

Solution same as above, and roots numerically the same, but of opposite signs.

199. To find the roots of

$$x^3 + x^2 - 10\,x + 8 = 0.$$

SOLUTION.

(1) $a^2 + b^2 + c^2 = 21 = (+1)^2 - 2(-10)$. (Th. II.)

(2) $21 \times 3 = 63 = \square$ of sum of roots + sum [s] of diffs. (Th. II.)

(3) $(63)^{\frac{1}{2}} = 7 = a + b + c$. (The side of the great integral square in 63 being taken for numerical sum of roots.)

(4) $\therefore \dfrac{7+1}{2} = 4 =$ sum $+$ roots; true sign *minus*;

and $\dfrac{7-1}{2} = 3 =$ sum $-$ roots; true sign *plus*.

(5) -4 is tried and it satisfies the equation, and is therefore a root. (**16.**)

(6) $\therefore 21 - (-4)^2 = 5 = a^2 + b^2$; and $8 \div 4 = 2 = ab$.

(7) $\therefore a + b = (a^2 + b^2 + 2\,ab)^{\frac{1}{2}} = [5 + (2 \times 2)]^{\frac{1}{2}} = 3$;

and $a - b = (a^2 + b^2 - 2\,ab)^2 = [5 - (2 \times 2)]^{\frac{1}{2}} = \sqrt{91} = 1$.

(8) $\therefore a = \dfrac{3+1}{2} = 2$, and $\dfrac{3-1}{2} = 1$.

(9) $\therefore$ The roots are 1, 2, and -4.

200. To find the roots of

$$x^3 + \frac{1}{30}x^2 - \frac{1}{5}x - \frac{1}{30} = 0.$$

SOLUTION.

(1) $a^2 + b^2 + c^3 = \frac{361}{900} = (\frac{1}{30})^2 - 2(-\frac{1}{5})$. (Th. II.)

(2) $\overline{ab}^2 + \overline{ac}^2 + \overline{bc}^2 = \frac{38}{900} = (-\frac{1}{5})^2 - 2(+\frac{1}{30} \times -\frac{1}{30})$. (Th. III.)

(3) $(\frac{38}{900} \times 3)^{\frac{1}{2}} = \frac{10}{30} = ab + ac + bc$. (The side of the greatest integral $\boxed{s}$ being taken from $\frac{114}{900}$ as the numerator and denominator of the fraction representing sum of p_2.)

(4) $\therefore (\frac{10}{30} + -\frac{1}{5}) \div 2 = \frac{2}{30}$ = sum of + products; true sign *minus*.

(5) $\therefore [\frac{10}{30} - (-\frac{1}{5})] \div 2 = \frac{8}{30}$ = sum of − products; true sign *plus*.

(6) $\frac{1}{30} \div \frac{2}{30} = \frac{1}{2} = a$. $\frac{1}{2}$ is tried and it satisfies the equation, and is therefore a root. (**16.**)

(7) $-\frac{1}{30} \div -\frac{1}{2} = \frac{2}{30} = \frac{1}{15} = bc$.

(8) $\frac{361}{900} - (\frac{1}{2})^2 = \frac{136}{900} = b^2 + c^2$.

(9) From (7) and (8) b and c are found to be, respectively, $-\frac{1}{3}$ and $-\frac{1}{5}$.

(10) $\therefore \frac{1}{2}, -\frac{1}{3}$, and $-\frac{1}{5}$ are the roots of the equation.

Again:

$$\frac{361}{900} \times 3 = \frac{1083}{900} = \square \text{ of sum} + \text{sum } \boxed{s} \text{ of diffs.}$$

The side of the greatest integral squares in 1083 and 900 is 32 and 30. The fraction $\frac{32}{30}$ is, however, rejected. (**26.**) $\frac{31}{30}$ is then taken as the numerical sum of roots.

$\therefore (\frac{31}{30} + \frac{1}{30}) \div 2 = \frac{16}{30}$ = sum + roots; true sign −;

and $(\frac{31}{30} - \frac{1}{30}) \div 2 = \frac{15}{30}$ = sum − roots; true sign +.

$\frac{15}{30} = \frac{1}{2} = a$, one of the roots. The other roots are obtained as in the prior solution.

201. To find the roots of

$$x^3 + x - 30 = 0.$$

SOLUTION.

(1) $a^2 + b^2 + c^2 = -2 = (\pm 0)^2 - 2(1)$. (Th. II.)

(2) $\therefore$ Only one real + root and a pair of pure imaginaries. (Arts. 24 and 100.)

(3) $x^3 + x = 30$. (Transposing absolute term.) The side of the greatest integral cube in 30 is 3, which satisfies the condition of the problem, and is therefore a root.

(4) $\therefore -2-(3)^2=-11=a^2+b^2$, and $ab=\frac{30}{3}=10$.

(5) $(a^2+b^2+2\,ab)^{\frac{1}{2}}=[-11+(2\times 10)]^{\frac{1}{2}}=3=a+b$.

(6) $(a^2+b^2-2\,ab)^{\frac{1}{2}}=[-11-(2\times 10)]^{\frac{1}{2}}=\sqrt{-31}=a-b$.

(7) $\therefore a \text{ or } b=\dfrac{-3\pm\sqrt{-31}}{2}$.

202. To find the roots of

$$x^3-\tfrac{403}{441}x+\tfrac{46}{147}=0.$$

SOLUTION.

(1) $a^2+b^2+c^2=\frac{806}{441}=(\pm 0)^2-2(-\frac{403}{441})$. (Th. II.)

(2) $\frac{806}{441}\times 3=\frac{2418}{441}=\square$ of sum of roots + sum $\boxed{s}$ of diffs.

(3) $(\frac{2418}{441})^{\frac{1}{2}}=\frac{46}{21}=a+b+c$. ($\frac{47}{21}$ being rejected (**26**).)

(4) $\therefore \frac{46}{21}\div 2=\frac{23}{21}=$ sum of + roots; true sign −; and $\frac{23}{21}=$ sum − roots; true sign +. $-\frac{23}{21}$ must be a root. It is tried and satisfies the equation, and is therefore a root. (**16**.) $\frac{806}{441}-(\frac{23}{21})^2=\frac{277}{441}=a^2+b^2$, and $\frac{46}{147}\div\frac{23}{21}=\frac{2}{7}=ab$. From sum of squares of a and b and their product we find $a=\frac{3}{7}$, $b=\frac{2}{3}$. $\therefore$ The roots of the equation are $\frac{3}{7}$, $\frac{2}{3}$, and $-\frac{23}{21}$.

203. To find the roots of the following cubics:

$$(l)\quad x^3-377\,x^2+36267\,x-900315=0.$$
$$(m)\quad x^3-373\,x^2+34767\,x-900315=0.$$
$$(n)\quad x^3-23\,x^2+142\,x-120=0.$$
$$(o)\quad x^3-21\,x^2+98\,x-120=0.$$
$$(p)\quad x^3-49\,x^2+658\,x-2640=0.$$
$$(q)\quad x^3-51\,x^2+758\,x-2640=0.$$

The foregoing cubics were suggested by Professor R. P. Baker, now president of Lamar College, Lamar, Missouri, in his criticism of the application of the *functions* of squares in determining the roots of equations, and he asks, What shall we do with this class of equations? *They do not differ in solution from that of any other equation.* In (l) and (m) the sum of the squares of the roots in each equation is equal to 69595, and their products are also equal.

Taking equation (l),

(1) $69595 \times 2 - 2(36267) = 66656$ = sum of squares of the differences of the roots. (**124**.)

Taking equation (m),

(2) $69595 \times 2 - 2(34767) = 69656$ = sum of squares of differences of roots.

We now see that the sum of the squares of the differences of the roots of (l) *and* (m) *are not the same; and while the product of the roots and the sum of the squares of the roots are the same in both equations, the sum of the roots and the sum of the squares of the differences of the roots of each equation are not the same. Should they be the same, the roots of each equation would be the same, in consequence of which two sets of roots could be found that would satisfy the conditions of the equations, and the whole theory of equations would fall to the ground.*

204. Hence we see that the sum of the squares of the roots of two equations may be the same, but the *sum of the roots, and the sum of the squares of the differences of the roots, will not be the same.*

From (l), $66656 \times 3 = 199968$ = □ of sum of diffs. of roots + sum of ⓢ of the diffs. of diffs. of roots. (Th. II.) If we take from 199968 one-half of the sum of their squares, we will obtain the square of the sum of their differences, nearly. It will be sufficiently close to determine the sum of the differences.

$199968 - \frac{66656}{2} = 166640$ = □ of sum of diffs. *nearly.* (Taking square root.)

16 66 40 | 408 $= 2c - 2a$. (**125**.) Whence $c - a = 204$.
16

808 66 40
64 64

We now readily find the roots of (l), as in (**143**), to be 39, 95, and 243.

In the same way we may arrive at the roots of the equations (m), (n), (o), (p), and (q).

205. Again, when the roots of equations are large and integral, which is readily discovered by the magnitude of the sum of squares of roots and size of absolute term, the roots are easily obtained by separating the equation into its prime factors.

To illustrate. Take absolute term of (l) or (m). The prime factors of

$$900315 = 5, \times 3, \times 3, \times 3, \times 3, \times 3, \times 3, \times 13, \times 19.$$

Taking the first and last factor we have $5 \times 19 = 95$, which we try in (l), and it proves to be a root. (**16.**) While $13 \times 19 = 247$ proves to be a root of (m). It would be a loss of time to solve either (l) or (m) by first finding the sum of the squares of its roots; but should the roots be *real* and *imaginary*, and approximate, the functions of squares is of great advantage: for should the absolute term of either (l) or (m) be 4,000,000, we will find, *mentally*, that (l) or (m) will then contain but one real root; for the sum of the squares of the products of its roots, taken two and two. is then a *minus* quantity. (**101.**) It will be shown further on, as we progress in the solution of cubics, that the easiest and simplest way to solve such an equation is to use our method of changing the cubic, and approximating the product of the imaginary roots.

SOLUTION OF CUBICS BY QUADRATICS.

206. Letting $x^3 + mx^2 + nx + q = 0$ always represent the *general equation* of the *third degree*, then, when

207. $$(A) \quad \frac{mn}{2} - \frac{m^3}{8} = q,$$

the equation can be reduced to a quadratic of the form

208. $(B)\ x^2 + \left(\frac{3m}{2} - \frac{2n}{m}\right)x + \left(\frac{m^2}{4} - \frac{2q}{m}\right) = 0.$

209. If (A) be true, then the solution of (B) will produce the greater real root, which can be no other than $\frac{m}{2}$: for when $\frac{mn}{2} - \frac{m^3}{8} = q$, the equation contains three roots so arranged in magnitude that the sum of the two smaller roots is equal to the greater or third root. This is also true when the cubic contains real and imaginary roots, in which case, the sum of the real parts of the imaginaries is equal to the real root.

210. *To illustrate.* Take the equation

$$x^3 - 8x^2 + 19.75x - 15 = 0.$$

(1) Then, $\frac{mn}{2} - \frac{m^3}{8} = q = \frac{8 \times 19.75}{2} - \frac{8^3}{8} = 15.$

(Changing signs.)

(2) $\frac{8 \times 19.75}{2} = 79$, and $\frac{8^3}{8} = 64.$

(3) $\therefore\ 79 - 64 = 15.$ Whence $\frac{8}{2} = 4$ is a root of the equation, say c. Then

$$a + b = 4 = (8 - 4), \text{ and } ab = 3.75 = \tfrac{15}{4}.$$

Whence $a = 1.5$, and $b = 2.5.$

211. To find the roots of

$$x^3 + 5x^2 + 7.5x + 3.125 = 0.$$

Applying the formula (A) (**207**), we have

(1) $$\frac{5 \times 7.5}{2} - \frac{5^3}{8} = 3.125.$$

(2) $$\frac{5 \times 7.5}{2} = 18.75.$$

(3) $$\frac{5^3}{8} = 15.625.$$

(4) $\therefore$ $18.75 - 15.625 = 3.125$. Whence $\frac{5}{2} = 2.5$ is one of the roots with its sign changed. $\therefore$ -2.5 is a root. (**16.**) $5 - 2.5 = 2.5 = a + b$, and $\frac{3.125}{2.5} = 1.25 = ab$. From this we find a or $b = -1.25 \pm \sqrt{.3125}$.

212. To find the roots of

$$x^3 - 6x^2 + 13.5x - 13.5 = 0.$$

Here we see by Th. II. that $(-6)^2 - 2(13.5) = 9$, the sum of ⊡ of roots, and that $3 \times 9 < (-6)^2$. $\therefore$ The equation contains imaginary roots. (**130.**) $\therefore$ Only one real root with sign $+$. (**110.**)

Applying the formula (A), we have

$$\frac{-6 \times 13.5}{2} - \frac{(-6)^3}{8} = -13.5.$$

$\therefore$ $\frac{6}{2} = 3 =$ one of the roots, say c. Then $a + b = 3$, and $ab = \frac{13.5}{3} = 4.5$. From $a + b$ and ab we find

$$a \text{ or } b = 1.5 \pm \sqrt{-2.25}.$$

213. It is evident from the foregoing (**211, 212**) that any equation of the Third Degree may be made to assume a quadratic form by the removal of its second term, and then substituting for the unknown quantity a new unknown quantity, which we will illustrate as we progress in the work.

REMOVING SECOND TERM IN CUBICS.

214. To remove the second term of the general equation of the Third Degree,

$$(E) \qquad x^3 + mx^2 + nx + q = 0,$$

we change the equation to the following form:

$$(F) \qquad y^3 + \left(\frac{m^2}{3} - n\right)y + \left[\left(\frac{2\,m^3}{27} + q\right) - \frac{mn}{3}\right] = 0.$$

215. *If* $\frac{m^2}{3} - n$ *is* $+$, *the coefficient of* y *will be minus; and if it be* $-$, *the coefficient of* y *will be plus. The coefficient of* y *being one-sixth of the sum of the squares of the differences of the roots in the equation to be changed, with its sign changed.*

216. Let it be required to remove the second term of

(*G*) $$x^3 + 12\,x^2 + 44\,x + 48 = 0.$$

Applying the formula (*F*) we write

(*H*) $$y^3 - 4\,y \pm 0 = 0.$$

(1) $$\left(\frac{m^2}{3} - n\right) = \frac{144}{3} - 44 = 4. \quad \therefore \quad -4\,y. \quad (\textbf{215.})$$

(2) $$\left(\frac{2 \times m^3}{27} + q\right) = \left(\frac{2 \times \overset{4}{\cancel{12}} \times \overset{4}{\cancel{12}} \times \overset{4}{\cancel{12}}}{\cancel{3} \times \cancel{3} \times \cancel{3}} + 48\right) = 176.$$

(3) $$\frac{mn}{3} = \frac{\overset{4}{\cancel{12}} \times 44}{\cancel{3}} = 176. \quad \therefore \; 176 - 176 = 0.$$

217. It is seen that the second term of (*G*) can be removed, and equation (*H*) formed, mentally. Were the terms of (*G*) alternately $+$ and $-$, the result would be the same.

218. We will now write equation (*G*) in this form:

$$x^3 + 12\,x^2 - 44\,x + 48 = 0.$$

Applying the formula (*F*) we write

$$y^3 - 92\,y + 352 = 0.$$

To illustrate.

(1) $$\left(\frac{m^2}{3} - n\right) = \frac{144}{3} - (-44) = +92. \quad \therefore \quad -92\,y. \quad (\textbf{215.})$$

(2) $$\left(\frac{2\,m^3}{27} + q\right) = \frac{2 \times \overset{4}{\cancel{12}} \times \overset{4}{\cancel{12}} \times \overset{4}{\cancel{12}}}{\cancel{3} \times \cancel{3} \times \cancel{3}} + 48 = 176.$$

(3) $$\frac{mn}{3} = \frac{\overset{4}{\cancel{12}} \times -44}{\cancel{3}} = -176. \quad \therefore \; 176 - (-176) = 352.$$

219. Let us now write the equation, thus:

$$x^3 - 12\,x^2 - 44\,x - 48 = 0.$$

From formula (F) we write the equation

$$y^3 - 92\,y - 352 = 0.$$

To illustrate.

(1) $\left(\dfrac{m^2}{3} - n\right) = \frac{144}{3} - (-44) = +\,92. \quad \therefore\ -\,92\,y.$ (**215.**)

(2) $\left(\dfrac{2\,m^3}{27} + q\right) = \left(\dfrac{2 \times -\overset{-4}{\cancel{12}} \times -\overset{-4}{\cancel{12}} \times -\overset{-4}{\cancel{12}}}{\cancel{3} \times \cancel{3} \times \cancel{3}} + -48\right) = -176.$

(3) $\dfrac{mn}{3} = \dfrac{-\overset{-4}{\cancel{12}} \times -44}{\cancel{3}} = +176. \quad \therefore\ -176 - (+176) = -352.$

220. To remove the second term in

$$x^3 - 2\,x^2 + 3\,x - 18 = 0.$$

From formula (F) we write

$$y^3 + 1\tfrac{2}{3}\,y - 16\tfrac{16}{27} = 0.$$

To illustrate.

(1) $\left(\dfrac{m^2}{3} - n\right) = (\tfrac{4}{3} - 3) = -\,1\tfrac{2}{3}. \quad \therefore\ +\,1\tfrac{2}{3}\,y.$ (**215.**)

(2) $\left(\dfrac{2\,m^3}{27} + q\right) = \left(\dfrac{2 \times -\,2 \times -\,2 \times -\,2}{3 \times 3 \times 3} + -\,18\right) = -\,18\tfrac{16}{27}.$

(3) $\dfrac{mn}{3} = \dfrac{-\,2 \times +\,3}{3} = -\,2. \quad \therefore\ -\,18\tfrac{16}{27} - (-\,2) = -\,16\tfrac{16}{27}.$

221. To remove the second term in

$$x^2 + 2\,x^2 + 5 = 0.$$

From the formula (F) we write

$$y^3 - 1\tfrac{1}{3}\,y + 5\tfrac{16}{27} = 0.$$

To illustrate.

(1) $\left(\frac{m^2}{3} - n\right) = \left(\frac{4}{3} - 0\right) = 1\frac{1}{3}. \quad \therefore \ -1\frac{1}{3}\,y.$ (**215.**)

(2) $\left(\frac{2\,m^3}{27} + q\right) = \frac{2 \times 2 \times 2 \times 2}{27} + 5 = 5\frac{16}{27}.$

(3) $\frac{mn}{3} = \frac{2 \times 0}{3} = 0. \quad \therefore \ 5\frac{16}{27} - 0 = 5\frac{16}{27}.$

222. To remove the second term in

$$x^3 + \tfrac{5}{8}\,x^2 + \tfrac{21}{15}\,x + 5 = 0.$$

From the formula (F) we write

$$y^3 + \tfrac{3657}{2880}\,y + 4\tfrac{3073}{3456} = 0.$$

To illustrate.

(1) $\left(\frac{m^2}{3} - n\right) = \left(\frac{\frac{25}{64}}{3} - \frac{21}{15}\right) = \frac{25}{192} - \frac{21}{15}$

$= \frac{375}{2880} - \frac{4032}{2880} = -\frac{3657}{2880}. \quad \therefore \ +\frac{3657}{2880}\,y.$

(2) $\left(\frac{2\,m^3}{27} + q\right) = 2 \times \frac{5}{8} \times \frac{5}{8} \times \frac{5}{8} \times \frac{1}{27} + 5 = 5\frac{250}{13824}.$

(3) $\frac{mn}{3} = \frac{\cancel{5}}{8} \times \frac{\overset{7}{\cancel{21}}}{\underset{3}{\cancel{15}}} \times \frac{1}{\cancel{3}} = \frac{7}{24}. \quad \therefore \ 5\frac{250}{13824} - \frac{7}{24} = 4\frac{3073}{3456}.$

223. To remove the second term in

$$x^3 + 327\,x^2 + 35643\,x - 2590058 = 0.$$

Applying the formula (F) we write

$$y^3 - 3885087 = 0.$$

To illustrate.

(1) $\left(\frac{m^2}{3} - n\right) = \left(\frac{\overset{109}{\cancel{327}} \times 327}{\cancel{3}} - 35643\right) = 0. \quad \therefore \ \pm 0\,y.$ (**215.**)

(2) $\left(\frac{2\,m^3}{27} + q\right) = \left(\frac{2 \times \overset{109}{\cancel{327}} \times \overset{109}{\cancel{327}} \times \overset{109}{\cancel{327}}}{\cancel{3} \times \cancel{3} \times \cancel{3}} + -2590058\right) = 0.$

$$(3)\quad \frac{mn}{3} = \frac{\overset{109}{\cancel{327}} \times + 35643}{\cancel{3}} = 3885087.$$

$$(4)\quad \therefore\ 0 - 3885087 = -\,3885087.$$

224. It may be remarked that, by application of the formula (F), the second term of any simple equation of the third degree may be removed, mentally, and the new equation written out in full. In our opinion it greatly excels in brevity that of the old method. The formula gives the coefficients of the new equation in terms of the coefficients of the equation to be changed. When the third term of the given equation is wanting, $\frac{mn}{3}$ is always a zero quantity, and $\left(\frac{2\,m^3}{27} + q\right)$ will be the absolute term of the new equation. If the reader will apply the formula to five or ten different equations, which he may form at random, he will become proficient in the application of the formula; and we do not doubt that he will prefer its use to that of the old method when he has occasion to remove the second term in a cubic equation. This method has, also, an important advantage over the old method in this: that while we are applying the formula, the *character* and *signs* of the roots become known; and thus does the application of the formula perform a double function.

225. *Examples.* — Remove the second term in the following equations, and then compare the labor with the old method:

$$(1)\quad x^3 - \tfrac{5}{8}\,x^2 + \tfrac{25}{128}\,x - 3 = 0.$$

$$(2)\quad x^3 - 2\,x^2 + 5\tfrac{17}{16}\,x - \tfrac{2}{3} = 0.$$

$$(3)\quad x^3 - 377\,x^2 + 36267\,x - 900315 = 0.$$

$$(4)\quad x^3 + \tfrac{11}{13}\,x^2 + \tfrac{17}{19}\,x + \tfrac{13}{21} = 0.$$

SOLUTIONS OF CUBICS. APPROXIMATE ROOTS.

226. Thus far have we been dealing with cubics containing, at least, one *integral* root. We will now take up a different class of cubic equations. The *condensed method* of approximating the real roots of cubic equations will be found to greatly excel in brevity that of any of the old methods; *but can only be applied when the roots of the equation are all real quantities.* We will also introduce, under this heading, the method for changing the cubic and approximating the product of the imaginary roots, — if such equation contains imaginary roots whose product is *incommensurable.* We also offer a method for the solution of cubic equations in the form of $x^3 \pm px \pm q = 0$. This method will be found to differ but little from the simple extraction of the cube root of a number, which can be found fully illustrated in any arithmetic.

227. To change an equation of the *third degree* into another cubic equation having for the *sum* of its roots the *sum of the products of the roots taken in pairs of two, or two and two,* of the given equation, let

$$(A) \qquad x^3 + mx^2 + nx + q = 0$$

be a *general cubic equation.* To change the equation, so that n, the coefficient of x, shall become the coefficient of x^2, we write an equation, thus:

$$(B) \qquad x'^3 + nx'^2 + mqx' + q^2 = 0.$$

This formula, (B), will be found to be correct; and, by Theorem III., the sum of the squares of the roots in (B) will be the same as the sum of the squares of the products of the roots, taken two and two, of the general equation (A). The *character* of the roots will be the same in both equations.

228. If n be wanting in (A, **227**), then we write for the changed equation,

(*C*) $$x'^3 \pm 0\,x'^2 + mqx' + q^2 = 0.$$

229. If m be wanting in (A, **227**), then we write for the changed equation,

(*D*) $$x'^3 + nx'^2 + q^2 = 0,$$

omitting the *third term*, because $0 \times q = 0$.

230. If m and n be both wanting in (A, **227**), we write

(*E*) $$x'^3 + q^2 = 0.$$

The roots of (E), when found, will be the separate products of the roots in

(*F*) $$x^3 + q = 0.$$

231. We will now illustrate how the "Horner method" can be used to advantage in cubics containing but one real root, if such root be approximate.

To illustrate. Take the equation

(*G*) $$x^3 - 6\,x^2 + 11\,x - 5 = 0.$$

This equation contains but one real root. ∴ Represent the roots by $a + \sqrt{-l}$, $a - \sqrt{-l}$, and b for the real root.

(1) By Th. II., $2\,a^2 + - 2\,l + b^2 = 14 = (-6)^2 - 2\,(11)$.

(2) By formula (B, **227**), the changed equation will be

(*H*) $$x'^3 - 11\,x'^2 + 30\,x' - 25 = 0.$$

(3) The only real root that (H) will contain, it is evident, must be that which is represented by

$$(a + \sqrt{-l}) \times (a - \sqrt{-l}) = a^2 + l.$$

(4) It is easily seen that when $a^2 + l$ becomes known, $a^2 + - l$ also becomes known; and that b is found by dividing the absolute term in (G) by the value of $a^2 + l$ in (H).

(5) By the Horner method we find $a^2 + l$ to be 7.4043 to four places of decimals.

(6) $\therefore\ b = \frac{5}{7.4043} = .675283 +$ to six places of decimals.

(7) $\therefore\ 6 - .675283 = 5.324717 = 2\,a$. Whence,

$$a = 2.6623585;\ \text{and } a^2 + l = 7.4043.$$

(8) Taking the square of b from the sum of their squares in (1), we obtain $2\,a^2 + - 2\,l$; and, dividing by 2, we obtain

$$a^2 + - l = 6.77199643+.$$

(9) $\therefore\ (a^2 + l) - (a^2 + - l) = 2\,l = .6323+$. Whence,

$$l = .31615;\ \text{and } \sqrt{-l} = \sqrt{-.31615}.$$

(10) $\therefore$ The roots of (G) are .675283, and

$$2.6623 + \pm \sqrt{-.3161+}.$$

232. To find the roots of

(I) $$x^3 - 2\,x - 5 = 0.$$

SOLUTION IN FULL.

(1) $a^2 + b^2 + c^2 = 4 = (+0) - 2(-2)$. (Th. II.)

(2) $\overline{ab}^2 + \overline{ac}^2 + \overline{bc}^2 = 4 = (-2)^2 - 2(\pm 0 \times -5)$. (Th. III.)

By substituting $\sqrt{4}$ or 2 in (A), the *Natural* equation is formed.

(I') $\therefore\ x^3 - 2\,x - 4 = 0 =$ the Natural of (I).

(3) $x^3 = 5 + 2\,x$. (From (A) by transposing.)

(4) $\therefore\ x = \sqrt[3]{5 + 2\,x}$. (From 3.)

(5) $x > 2$; $\therefore\ \sqrt[3]{5 + 2\,x} > \sqrt[3]{9}$. (6) $\therefore\ x = \sqrt[3]{9 + \text{inc. } 2\,x}$.

We now proceed to take the $\sqrt[3]{9 + \text{inc. } 2x}$. The process is as follows:

	$9 \mid 2.09455145$
$(2)^3 =$	8
$(2)^2 \times 300 = 1200$	1.000
	1.000000
120000	$.18 = \text{inc. } 2x = 2 \times .09$
$20 \times 9 \times 30 = 5400$	1.180000
$(9)^2 = 81$	1.120329
125481	.050671000
$(209)^2 \times 300 = 13104300$	$.008 = \text{inc. } 2x = 2 \times .004$
$209 \times 4 \times 30 = 25080$	.058671000
$(4)^2 = 16$	.052517584
13129396	.006153416000
	$.0010 = \text{inc. } 2x = 2 \times .0005$
$(2094)^2 \times 300 = 1315450800$	.007153416000
$2094 \times 5 \times 30 = 376920$	.006579138725
$(5)^2 = 25$	.000574277275000
1315827745	$.00010 = \text{inc. } 2x = 2 \times .00005$
	.000674277275000
$3(20945)^2 = (2094)^2 + 2(2094 \times 5)$	.000658055246375
$+ 5^2 = 131607907500$	.000016222028725
	$.000002 = \text{inc. } 2x = 2 \times .000001$
	.0000182+

The last two figures being found from the last divisor.

233. The foregoing process differs but little from the simple extraction of the cube root of a number $+ p$ times the *increment* of its root, *after the side of the greatest integral cube is taken from the number.*

234. Returning again to the solution of (I). Having found one of the roots, say $c = 2.09455145$, *to eight places of decimals,* we *immediately* discover that the other two roots will be imaginary, because $(2.09455145)^2 > 4$, *the sum of the squares of the roots.* This also became known as soon as one of the roots was found to be > 2, for the $(> 2)^2$ is > 4. The real parts of the imaginary will be $-$, and is $2.09455145 \div 2 = 1.047275+$. Their product will be $5 \div 2.09455145$

$= 2.3871+$. Therefore, the part affected by the radical will be

$$2.3871 - (1.04275)^2 = 1.29037+.$$

$$\therefore\ -1.047275 \pm \sqrt{-1.29037+}\ \textit{are the other two roots.}$$

235. Again: Applying formula (D), we have (**229**),

$$(x^3 - 2x - 5 = 0) = x^3 + 2x^2 - 25 = 0 = \text{the new equation.}$$

$$x^3 = 25 - 2x^2.$$

$$x = \sqrt[3]{25 - 2x^2}, \text{ as } x > 2,\ \sqrt[3]{25 - 2x^2} < \sqrt[3]{17}.$$

$$\therefore\ x = \sqrt[3]{17 - \text{inc. } 2x^2} = 2.3871+.$$

The labor is greatly lessened by the latter method, as can be verified by trial.

236. To find the roots of

$$(J) \qquad x^3 - 7x + 7 = 0.$$

SOLUTION.

(1) $a^2 + b^2 + c^2 = 14$.

(2) $14 \times 3 = 42 = \square$ of sum + sum [s] of diffs. (Th. II.)

The side of the greatest integral square in 42 is 6. $\therefore\ 6 \div 2 = 3$, and -3 introduced in (J) gives the *Natural*

$$(c) \qquad x^3 - 7x + 6 = 0.$$

The roots of (c) are 1, 2, and -3. Therefore, the roots of (J) will be > 1, < 2, and > -3 (**113**). We now approximate the roots to two places and obtain 1.3, 1.7, *nearly*, and 3.0. The sum of the squares of their differences is 4.73+, say 4.8. We now take the square root of 42 within the limit > 4.8 and < 4.9.

	42 | 6.0978+
	36
120	6.00
1209	6.0000
	1.0881
12187	4.911900
	.085309
121948	4.82559100
	.00975584
	4.81583516

$$\therefore \frac{6.0978}{2} = 3.0489. \quad \text{Whence, say } c = -3.0489.$$

$$\therefore a + b = 3.0489, \text{ and } a - b = \sqrt{(14 - (3.0489)^2 \times 2) - (3.0489)^2}$$
$$= a - b = .3351.$$

Whence, $a = 1.3569$, and $b = 1.6920$.

237. Returning to the solution of (J, **236**), we have, by transposition and changing sign of absolute term,

(b) $$x^3 = 7 + 7x.$$

Whence, $$x = \sqrt[3]{7 + 7x}.$$

As $x > 3$ in (b), $\sqrt[3]{7 + 7x} > \sqrt[3]{28}$. $\therefore x = \sqrt[3]{28 + \text{inc. } 7x}$.

Taking cube root of $28 + \text{inc. } 7x$ | 3.048917

$(3)^3 =$		27
$(3)^2 \times 300 =$	2700	1.000
		1.000000
	270000	$.28 = \text{inc. } 7x = 7 \times .04$
$30 \times 4 \times 30 =$	3600	1.280000
$(4)^2 =$	16	1.094464
	273616	.185536000
		$.056 = \text{inc. } 7x = 7 \times .008$
$(304)^2 \times 300 =$	27724800	.241536000
$304 \times 8 \times 30 =$	72960	.222382592
$(8)^2 =$	64	.019153408000
	27797824	$.0063 = \text{inc. } 7x = 7 \times .0009$
		.025453408000
$(3048)^2 \times 300 =$	2787091200	.025091228169
$3048 \times 9 \times 30 =$	822960	.000362179831000
$(9)^2 =$	81	$.00007 = \text{inc. } 7x = 7 \times .00001$
	2787914241	.000432179831000
		.0002787+
		.0001534
		$.000049 = \text{inc. } 7x = 7 + .000007$
		.0002024

Here we have $c = 3.048917$ *to six places of decimals.*

$$14 - (c)^2 = a^2 + b^2 = 4.7041478119.$$

$$\therefore [(4.7041478119) \times 2 - (c)^2]^{\frac{1}{2}} = a - b = .33513.$$

$$\therefore\ a = \frac{3.048917 - .33513}{2} = 1.35689+,$$

and
$$b = \frac{3.048917 + .33513}{2} = 1.69202+.$$

238. Remark. When the square of 300 is known, the square of the successive numbers 3.04, 3048, 30,489, 304,891, and 3,048,917, are readily found by the algebraic formula: $(a + b)^2 = a^2 + b^2 + 2\ ab$.

To illustrate. (1) $(304)^2 = (300 + 4)^2 = (300)^2 + (4)^2 + 2 \times 300 \times 4 = (a + b)^2 = a^2 + b^2 + 2 \times a \times b.$

(2) $(300)^2 = 90000$

(3) $(4)^2 = 16$

(4) $2 \times 300 \times 4 = 2400$

(5) $\text{Sum} = 92416 = (304)^2.$

Again: $(3048)^2 = (3040)^2 + (8)^2 + 2 \times 3040 \times 8.$

$$(3040)^2 = 100 \times 92416 = (10 \times 304)^2 = 9241600$$
$$(8)^2 = 64$$
$$2 \times 3040 \times 8 = 48640$$
$$\text{Sum} = 9290304$$

In the same way the square of 30,489, ⋯, may be found without much labor.

239. The method (**236**) given for solution of (J) excels all other methods in brevity; but it can only be applied in the solution of equations whose roots are all real quantities. The method, which we shall call *Condensed Approximation*, depends upon this fact: *If the roots of an equation are known to two places of decimals each, the square root of the sum of squares of roots, multiplied by the degree of the equation, taken within the limit of the sum of the squares of the differences of the roots to two places of decimals, will be the sum of the roots to four places of decimals; and taken within the limit of the sum of the squares of the differences of the roots to four places of decimals, will be the sum of the roots to eight places of decimals; and of eight places, to sixteen places; and so on, without limit.*

240. To find the roots of

$$(K) \qquad x^3 - 3x + 1 = 0.$$

SOLUTION. (1) Th. II., $a^2 + b^2 + c^2 = 6$.

(2) $6 \times 3 = 18 = \square$ of sum of roots + sum [s] of diffs. (Th. II.)
The side of the greatest $\square$ in 18, whose side is integral, is 4.

$\therefore 4 \div 2 = 2$. With -2 we build the Natural

$$(L) \qquad x^3 - 3x + 2 = 0.$$

The roots of (L) being 1, 1, and -2. $\therefore$ The roots of (J) will be < 1, > 1, and < -2 (**113**). This means that one root lies between 0 and 1, one between 1 and 2, and one between -1 and -2, but near -2.

$$(3) \qquad \therefore x^3 = 1 + 3x.$$

[Changing sign of absolute term and transposing.]

$$(4) \qquad x = \sqrt[3]{1 + 3x}.$$

As x in the transposed equation is > 1, and near 2, the $\sqrt[3]{1 + 3x} > \sqrt[3]{4}$. $\therefore x = \sqrt[3]{4 + \text{increment } 3x}$.

Taking the cubic root of (4 + increment $3x$), we have, as follows

	4 + inc. $3x$ | 1.87938
	1
300	3.000
$8 \times 1 \times 30 = 240$	2.4 = inc. $3x = 3 \times .8$
$(8)^2 = 64$	5.400
604	4.832
	.568000
$(18)^2 \times 300 = 97200$	.21 = inc. $3x = 3 \times .07$
$18 \times 7 \times 30 = 3780$	.778000
$(7)^2 = 49$	.707203
101029	.070797000
	.027 = inc. $3x = 3 \times .009$
$(1.87)^2 \times 300 = 10490700$	.097797000
$187 \times 9 \times 30 = 50490$	.094871439
$(9)^2 = 81$	.002925561000
10541271	.0009 = inc. $3x = 3 \times .0003$
	.003825561000
$(1879)^2 \times 300 = 1059182300$	.003178054257
$1879 \times 3 \times 30 = 169,110$	.000647506743
$(3)^2 = 9$	.00024 = inc. $3x = 3 \times .00008$
1059351419	.0008875+

The last figure of the root being obtained from the last divisor.

$\therefore$ The greater root, say c, $= -1.87938$, or $a + b$.

$$\therefore 6 - (c)^2 = a^2 + b^2 = 6 - (187938)^2;$$

and $$2\,[6 - (1.87938)^2] = (a + b)^2 + (a - b)^2. \quad \text{(41, Th. I.)}$$

$$a + b = 1.87938.$$

$$\therefore a - b = [(6 - \overline{1.87938}^2)\,2 - \overline{1.87938}^2]^{\frac{1}{2}} = 1.184788.$$

$$\therefore a = \frac{1.87938 - 1.184788}{2} = .347296;$$

and $$b = \frac{1.87938 + 1.184788}{2} = 1.532084.$$

We now submit the *condensed method* in full.

241. SOLUTION OF (K **240**) BY THE CONDENSED METHOD.

$$3 \times 6 = 18 = (a + b + c)^2 + (a - b)^2 + (a - c)^2 + (b - c)^2. \quad \text{(Th. II.)}$$

The roots found to two places of decimals each are:

$$a = .34,$$
$$b = 1.53,$$
$$c = 1.87.$$

$$\therefore 1.53 - .34 = 1.19, \text{ and } (1.19)^2 = 1.4161. \quad (1)$$
$$1.87 - .34 = 1.53, \text{ and } (1.53)^2 = 2.3409. \quad (2)$$
$$1.87 - 1.53 = .34, \text{ and } (.34)^2 = .1156. \quad (3)$$

Adding (1), (2), and (3), we have for the *sum of the squares of the differences of the roots to two places of decimals*, 3.8726.

Taking the square root of 3×6, or 18, within this limit, we obtain the sum of the roots as follows:

Limit 3.8726		18 | 3.7587
		9
	6.7	9.00
		4.69
	7.45	4.3100
		.3725
	7.508	3.937500
		.060064
	7.5167	3.87743600
		.00526169
		3.87217431

Why not .0006 for the fourth decimal place? The last divisor would then be 75166, and, multiplied by .006, gives .00450996, which, taken from the last remainder 3.87743600, gives 3.87292604. So we see that .0007 is the closest approximation to the limit 3.8726. Having the sum $= 3.7587$, one root, the greater, is $\frac{3.7587}{2} = 1.87935$. The other roots will be found as in the preceding solution.

REMARK. — (1) Find by trial the first root to two places of decimals, and (2) the last root, or greater, to two places of decimals; (3) their difference will be the middle or second root in magnitude to two places of decimals.

242. To find the roots of

$$(M) \qquad x^3 + x^2 - 500 = 0.$$

Here the sum of the $\boxed{s}$ of the roots $= 1 = (1)^2 - 2(+0)$. (Th. II.) The real root is + (**110**). The integral part of the real root must be the side of the greatest integral *cube* in 500. This we find to be 7. And as $(7)^2 > 1 \times 3$, the equation contains imaginary roots (**100**). $1 \times 3 = 3 = \square$ of sum of roots + sum of $\boxed{s}$ of diffs. of roots. And as one of the roots is > 7, its $\square$ is > 49. $\therefore\ 3 - > 49 = > -46$. Transposing terms, we have $x^3 = 500 - x^2$. Whence, $x = \sqrt[3]{500 - x^2}$, as $x > 7$. The $\sqrt[3]{500 - x^2} < \sqrt[3]{451}$. $\therefore\ x = \sqrt[3]{500 - \text{inc. } x^2}$.

	Taking the cube root of $500 - \text{inc. } x^2$ | 7.61728+
	$(7)^3 = 343$
$(7)^2 \times 300 = 14700$	157
$7 \times 6 \times 30 = 1260$	Less $49 = \text{inc. } x^2 = (7)^2$
$(6)^2 = 36$	108.000
15996	95.976
	12.024
$(76)^2 \times 300 = 1732800$	Less $8.76 = \text{inc. } x^2 = 2 \times 7 \times .6 \times (6)^2 = 8.76$
$76 \times 1 \times 30 = 2280$	3.264000
$(1)^2 = 1$	1.735081
1735081	1.528919
$(761)^2 \times 300 = 173736300$	Less $.1521 = \text{inc. } x^2 = 2 \times 7.6 \times .01 + (.01)^2 = 7521$
$761 \times 7 \times 30 = 159810$	1.376819000
$(7)^2 = 49$	1.217273113
173896159	.159545887

The other two figures of the root are found from the last divisor, *subtracting the increment of x^2 before multiplying.*

We now have the real root, say c, $= 7.61728$, and

$$\frac{500}{c} = a^2 + l = 65.64022853 + = (a + \sqrt{-l})(a - \sqrt{-l}).$$

$(a+\sqrt{-l})^2+(a-\sqrt{-l})^2+(c)^2=2\,a^2+-2\,l+c^2=1=$ sum of ☐ of roots.

$\therefore\ 1-(7.61728)^2=1-58.0229545984=-57.0229545984=2\,a^2+-2\,l.$

Whence, $$a^2 + - l = -28.5114772992.$$

$$(a^2 + - l) - (a^2 + l) = -2\,l = -94.1517058292.$$

Whence, $$-l = -47.0758529146.$$

$$\therefore\ \sqrt{-l} = \sqrt{-47.07585+}.$$

$\therefore$ The roots of (M) are 7.61728, and $-4.30864\cdots \pm \sqrt{-47.07585\cdots+}$.

243. To find the roots of

(N) $$x^3 - 7\,x + 1 = 0.$$

SOLUTION BY THE CONDENSED METHOD.

(1) Its Natural is $x^3 - 7\,x + 6 = 0$. (J, **236**.)

$\therefore$ Roots are all real, and < 1, > 2, and < -3. (**113**.)

(2) The sum of ☐ of roots $= 14$.

We now approximate the first and last root to two places of decimals each, and find .14 and 2.71. $\therefore$ 2.57 will be the middle root.

(3) $2.57 - .14 = 2.43$, and $(2.43)^2 = 5.9049$. (a)

(4) $2.71 - .14 = 2.57$, and $(2.57)^2 = 6.6049$. (b)

(5) $2.71 - 2.57 = .14$, and $(.14)^2 = .0196$. (c)

(6) $\therefore$ 12.5294. [Adding (a), (b), (c).]

(7) $14 \times 3 = 42$, and $(42)^{\frac{1}{2}}$ within the limit 12.5294, gives

(8) 5.42895 = *sum to five places of decimals.*

(9) $\therefore$ 2.71447 = c, the greater root, *to five places of decimals.*

[Dividing (8) by 2, the second term of (N) being wanting.]

(10) $\therefore\ 14 - (2.71447)^2 = a^2 + b^2$;

and $$(a^2 + b^2)\,2 = (a + b)^2 + (a - b)^2. \quad \text{(Th. I.)}$$

(11) $\therefore\ \{[14 - (2.71447)^2]\,2 - (2.71447)^2\}^{\frac{1}{2}} = a - b = 2.4280+.$

(12) $\therefore\ a = \dfrac{2.71447 - 2.4280}{2} = .14327+.$

(13) $\therefore\ b = \dfrac{2.71447 + 2.4280}{2} = 2.57120+.$

244. SECOND SOLUTION. $x^3 = 1 + 7\,x$. [Transposing terms and changing sign of absolute term of (N, **243**).]

REMARK. The reason for changing sign of absolute term is to render the greater root a + quantity.

(1) x has been located to be > 2, but < 3.

(2) $\therefore x = \sqrt[3]{1 + 7x} = \sqrt[3]{1 + 7 \times 2} = \sqrt[3]{15}$. But as $x > 2$, the $\sqrt[3]{1 + 7x} > \sqrt[3]{15}$. $\therefore x = \sqrt[3]{15 + \text{increment } 7x}$.

	$15 \,\vert\, 2.7144787$
$(2)^3 =$	8
$(2)^2 \times 300 = 1200$	7.000
$7 \times 2 \times 30 = 420$	4.9 = inc. $7x = 7 \times .7$
$(7)^2 = 49$	11.900
1669	11.683
	.217000
$(2.7)^2 \times 300 = 218700$	.07 = inc. $7x = 7 \times .01$
$27 \times 1 \times 30 = 810$	.287000
$(1)^2 = 1$	.219511
219511	.067489000
$(271)^2 \times 300 = 22032300$	.028 = inc. $7x = 7 \times .004$
$271 \times 4 \times 30 = 32520$	.095489000
$(4)^2 = 16$	.088259344
22064836	.007229656000
	.0028 = inc. $7x = 7 \times .0004$
$(2714)^2 \times 300 = 2209738800$	.010029656000
$2714 \times 4 \times 30 = 325680$	.008840257984
$(4)^2 = 16$	.001189398016000
2210064496	.00049 = inc. $7x = 7 \times .00007$
Using the last divisor and omitting all but six places of decimals in the quotient.	.001679+
	.001547
	.000132
	.000056 = inc. $7x = 7 \times .000008$
	.000188

Then c, the greatest root, $= -2.7144787$ to seven places of decimals. The other two roots, a and b, are now obtained as in (N, **243**) to be, respectively, .143277 and 2.571200.

245. To find the roots of

$$(O) \qquad x^3 + x - 9 = 0.$$

Solution. (1) The equation contains but one real + root and two imaginary roots which are *Pure*, and their real parts are $-$. (**104**, **100**.)

(2) By formula (D, **229**) we write

$$(P) \qquad x^3 - x^2 - 81 = 0.$$

The roots of (P) are evidently the products of the roots taken two and two in (O). As (O) contains but one *real root*, (P) will contain but one real root which is the product of the imaginary roots in (O). Transposing terms, $x^3 = 81 + x^2$. The side of the greatest integral cube in 81 is the integral part of the root x in (P). This is 4. $\therefore x > 4$. Whence

$$x = \sqrt[3]{97 + \text{inc. } x^2} = [(85 + 16) + \text{inc. } x^2]^{\frac{1}{3}}.$$

	$97. \mid 4.687072+$
$(4)^3 =$	64
	33.000
$(4)^2 \times 300 = 4800$	$5.16 = \text{inc. } x^2 = (4.6)^2 - (4)^2$
$4 \times 6 \times 30 = 720$	38.160
$(6)^2 = 36$	33.336
5556	4.824000
	$.7424 = \text{inc. } x^2 = 2 \times 4.6 \times .08 + \overline{.08}^2$
$(4.6)^2 \times 300 = 634800$	5.566400
$46 \times 8 \times 30 = 11040$	5.167232
$(8)^2 = 64$	$.399168000$
645904	$.065569 = \text{inc. } x^2 = 2 \times 468 \times .0007 + \overline{.0007}^2$
	$.464737000$
$(468)^2 \times 300 = 65707200$	$.460638703$
$468 \times 7 \times 30 = 98280$	$.004098297 + 4687 \times 2 \times .00007 + \overline{.00007}^2$
$(7)^2 = 49$	
65805529	

$\therefore$ Letting $a \pm \sqrt{-l}$ represent the imaginary roots in (O), their product will be $a^2 + l = 4.687072$; and $9 \div (a^2 + l) = 1.92017532694$, the *real* root of (O) *to eleven places of decimals*. The second term being wanting in (O), the sum of the + and − roots in the formation of the equation are *numerically* the same. $\therefore 1.92 \cdots 4 \div 2 = .96008766347$ is the real part of the imaginary with its sign changed; and $[(.9600 \cdots 7) + \sqrt{-l}][(.9600 \cdots 7) - \sqrt{-l}] = 4.687072$. Whence we find $+l = 3.76531+$.

$\therefore$ The roots of (O) are 1.92017532694, and

$$-.96008766347 \pm \sqrt{-3.76531+}.$$

Remark. $x^3 + x - 10 = 0$ may be taken as the *Natural* of $x^3 + x - 9 = 0$. The roots of the *Natural* being 2, and $-1 \pm \sqrt{-4}$.

246. To find the roots of

$$(Q) \qquad x^3 - 123\,x + 345 = 0.$$

SOLUTION.

$$(1) \qquad a^2 + b^2 + c^2 = 246.$$

(2) $246 \times 3 = 738 = \square$ of sum of roots + sum $\boxed{s}$ of diffs. (Th. II.)

The side of the greatest integral square in 738 is 27, which we reject. (**26.**) 26 is then taken, and $26 \div 2 = 13$; and substituting -13 in equation, we discover that 26 is not the true numerical sum of roots, being too great. 25 is rejected. (**26.**) 24 is then taken, and $24 \div 2 = 12$, and -12 substituted in the equation, the *Natural* is formed, being

$$(R) \qquad x^3 - 123\,x + 252 = 0.$$

$\therefore$ If we change sign of absolute term in (Q), the greater root will be $+$. The roots of (R) are 2.13+, 9.87+, and -12.

$\therefore$ The roots of (Q) will be > 2.13, < 9.87, and > -12.

Changing sign of absolute term and transposing, we have

$$x^3 = 345 + 123\,x.$$

Whence, $\qquad x = \sqrt[3]{345 + 123\,x}.$

As $x > 12$, the $\qquad \sqrt[3]{345 + 123\,x} > \sqrt[3]{1821}.$

$$\therefore\ x = \sqrt[3]{1821 + \text{inc. } 123\,x}.$$

$$\begin{array}{rl}
 & 1821\,|\underline{12.291023} \\
\underline{(12)^3} = & \underline{1728} \\
 & 93.000 \\
 & \underline{24.6} = \text{inc. } 123\,x = 123 \times .2 \\
 & 117.600 \\
 & \underline{87.848} \\
 & 29.752000 \\
 & \underline{11.07} = \text{inc. } 123\,x = 123 \times .09 \\
 & 40.822000 \\
 & \underline{40.483989} \\
 & .338011000 \\
 & \underline{.123} = \text{inc. } 123\,x = 123 \times .001 \\
 & .461011000 \\
 & \underline{.453169171} \\
 & .007841829000 \\
 & \underline{.00246} = \text{inc. } 123\,x = 123 \times .00002 \\
 & .01030 \\
 & .00906
\end{array}$$

$$\begin{array}{rr}
(12)^2 \times 300 = & 43200 \\
12 \times 2 \times 30 = & 720 \\
(2)^2 = & \underline{4} \\
 & \underline{\underline{43924}} \\
(122)^2 \times 300 = & 4465200 \\
122 \times 9 \times 30 = & 32940 \\
(9)^2 = & \underline{81} \\
 & \underline{\underline{4498221}} \\
(1229)^2 \times 300 = & 453132300 \\
1229 \times 1 \times 30 = & 36870 \\
(1)^2 = & \underline{1} \\
 & \underline{\underline{453169171}}
\end{array}$$

The last two figures of the root being obtained by the last divisor, adding the increment of $123\,x$ each time before multiplication.

$\therefore$ The greater root in (P) is $-\ 12.291023$ *to six places of decimals.*

Letting a, b, and c represent the roots in order of magnitude, c will be the greater root. Then $a+b=c$, the second term of the equation being wanting.

(1) $a^2+b^2+c^2=246. \quad \therefore\ 246-(12.291023)^2$

(2) $\qquad =246-151.069246386529$

(3) $\qquad = 94.930753613471=a^2+b^2$, and multiplied by 2

$\qquad\qquad 2$

(4) $\qquad =189.861507226942=(a+b)^2+(a-b)^2.$ (**41** — Th. I.)

(5) $\quad (a+b)^2=151.069246386529$; and subtracted,

(6) $\qquad = 38.792260840413=(a-b)^2$; and taking square root,

(7) $\qquad = \ 6.228343=a-b.$

(8) $$\therefore\ a=\frac{12.291023-6.228343}{2}=3.031340 \text{ ; and}$$

(9) $$b=\frac{12.291023+6.228343}{2}=9.259683.$$

Therefore the roots of the equation (Q) are all real, being two *plus* roots and one *minus* root.

PROBLEMS.

Find the roots of the following equations:

1. $x^3-3\,x+7=0.$

2. $x^3+3\,x-7=0.$

3. $x^3-27\,x^2+54\,x-216=0.$

4. $x^3+27\,x^2-54\,x+216=0.$

5. $x^3-11\,x^2+17\,x-22=0.$

6. $x^3-11\,x^2+17\,x+22=0.$

7. $x^3-12\,x^2+72\,x-144=0.$

8. $x^3+12\,x^2+72\,x+144=0.$

9. $x^3-3\,x^2-3\,x-4=0.$

10. $x^3+3\,x^2+3\,x+4=0.$

11. $x^3-5\,x^2-5\,x-4=0.$

12. $x^3+5\,x^2+5\,x+4=0.$

13. $x^3-1421\,x^2+5684=0.$

14. $x^3+1421\,x+5684=0.$

15. $x^3+23\,x^2+13\,x+13=0.$

16. $x^3+23\,x^2+13\,x-13=0.$

17. $x^3-10\,x^2+31\,x-30=0.$

18. $x^3+10\,x^2+31\,x-30=0.$

19. $x^3+17\,x^2+20\,x+1=0.$

20. $x^3-17\,x^2+20\,x-1=0.$

Apply formula (A, **227**) to the following equations:

(a) $x^3 - 17x^2 + 54x - 350 = 0$.
(b) $x^3 - 4x^2 + 6x - 5 = 0$.
(c) $x^3 + 6x - 21 = 0$.
(d) $x^3 + \frac{11}{16}x - \frac{3}{4} = 0$.
(e) $x^3 - \frac{11}{16}x + \frac{3}{4} = 0$.

Find the value of x in each of the following expressions:

(f) $[\ 9 + \text{increment}\ 3x]^{\frac{1}{3}}$. $x > 2, < 3$.
(g) $[\ 28 + \text{increment}\ 6x]^{\frac{1}{3}}$. $x > 3, < 4$.
(h) $[127 + \text{increment}\ 20x]^{\frac{1}{3}}$. $x > 5, < 6$.
(i) $[\ 16 + \text{increment}\ 3x]^{\frac{1}{3}}$. $x > 2, < 3$.

BIQUADRATICS AND SOLUTIONS.

247. To find the roots of

(A) $$x^4 + 4x^3 - 19x^2 - 46x + 120 = 0.$$

SOLUTION.

(1) $a^2 + b^2 + c^2 + d^2 = 54 = (4)^2 - 2(-19)$. (Th. II.)

(2) $54 \times 4 = 216 = \square$ of sum of roots + sum $\boxed{s}$ of diffs. (Th. II.)

The side of the greatest integral square in 216 is 14.

(3) $\therefore \frac{14 + 4}{2} = 9 =$ sum of *plus* roots in formation of equation; true sign $-$.

(4) $\therefore \frac{14 - 4}{2} = 5 =$ sum of *minus* roots in formation of equation; true sign $+$.

From algebraic sum and signs of the terms of the equation, there are two + roots and two − roots. $\therefore$ We write the quadratics

(p) $$x^2 + 9x + y = 0.$$

(q) $$x^2 - 4x + e = 0.$$

The product of (p) and (q) will be

(B) $$x^4 + 4x^3 + (e + y + - 45)x^2 + (9e + - 5y)x + ey = 0.$$

The coefficients of (B) are evidently equal to the coefficients of (A), at least in the *Natural*.

(5) $\therefore e + y + -45 = -19.$ Whence,

(6) $e + y = 26.$

(7) $ey = 120.$ [From the absolute terms of (A) and (B)].

Solving (6) and (7), we find $e = 6$ and $y = 20$. We now complete the quadratics of (p) and (q), which solved gives for the roots of (A), 2, 3, and -4, -5.

The roots of (A) may also be found from $a + b = 5$ and $c + d = 9$, and $abcd = 120$.

248. To find the roots of

$$(C) \qquad x^4 + x^3 + .5\,x^2 - 5\,x + 25 = 0.$$

SOLUTION.

(1) $a^2 + b^2 + c^2 + d^2 = 0 = (+1)^2 - 2(.5).$ (Th. II.)

(2) $\overline{abc}^2 + \overline{abd}^2 + \overline{acd}^2 + \overline{bcd}^2 = 0 = (-5)^2 - 2(.5 \times 25).$ (Th. II.)

$\therefore$ The equation contains all imaginary roots; for in equations of the *fourth degree*, unless a few "reciprocal equations," when the sum of squares of roots and sum of squares of products of roots taken *three* and *three* are in *both cases* a zero *quantity*, the equation must contain all imaginary roots. Such imaginary roots must be equal conjugate imaginaries, in which the square of the *real part* of the imaginary must be *numerically* equal to *that part of the root affected by the radical;* or the equation must contain *Pure* and *Real* imaginaries, the sum of whose squares are numerically equal, but having opposite signs, in consequence of which, cancel each other, or become *zero*. Equation (C) having one of its terms affected by a *minus* sign, the real parts of the imaginaries will have opposite signs, one pair being + and one pair −. We now represent the roots of (C), algebraically, as follows:

$$a \pm \sqrt{-a^2}, \text{ and } b \pm \sqrt{-b^2}.$$

Their product will be $4\,a^2b^2 = 25$. Whence $ab = 25$.

From their algebraic sum we write $2\,b - 2\,a = 1$. Whence $b - a = .5$.

$\therefore a + b = [(a-b)^2 + 4\,ab]^{\frac{1}{2}} = \sqrt{10.25} = 3.201562 +$ *to six places of decimals.*

$\therefore a = \dfrac{3.201562 - .5}{2} = 1.350781+$, and $b = \dfrac{3.201562 + .5}{2} = 1.850781+$.

$\therefore$ The roots of (C) will be

$$1.350781 \pm \sqrt{-(1.350781)^2}, \text{ and } -1.850781 \pm \sqrt{-(1.850781)^2}.$$

249. We now write the equation

$$(D) \qquad x^4 + x^3 + .5\,x^2 + 5\,x + 25 = 0.$$

It will be noticed that (D) differs from (C, **248**) only in that of the sign of the fourth term. The sum of squares of roots, and sum of squares of products of roots taken three and three, are in both cases a *zero* quantity. ∴ The equation contains imaginary roots, one pair being *Pure* and one pair *Real.* The signs of the *real* parts will not be changed, one being + and the other –. We now write for the roots the algebraic expressions,

$$a \pm \sqrt{-l}, \text{ and } -b \pm \sqrt{-m}.$$

$2\,a^2 + -2\,l$ represents the sum of the squares of one pair, and $2\,b^2 + -2\,m$ represents the sum of the squares of the other pair of imaginaries. ∴ $(2\,a^2 + -2\,l) + (2\,b^2 + -2\,m) = 0$. (Th. II.)

If $2\,a^2 = 2\,l$, then will $2\,b^2 = 2\,m$, and the roots would be the same as in (C, **248**). But this we know cannot be the case, for no two equations can have the same roots if the signs of its terms are different. The last term is a perfect square, therefore we may write the quadratics,

$$(p) \qquad x^2 + 2\,b + 5 = 0, \text{ and}$$

$$(q) \qquad x^2 - 2\,a + 5 = 0.$$

If (p) and (q) be the true quadratics, their product must be equation (D). This product we find to be

$$(E)\ x^4 + (26 + -2\,a)x^3 + (10 + -4\,ab)x^2 + (10\,b + -10\,a)x + 25 = 0.$$

The coefficients of (E) are, therefore, equal to the coefficients of (D). ∴ $26 - 2\,a = 1$. Whence $b - a = .5$, and $10 + -4\,ab = .5$; whence $4\,ab = 9.5$, and $10\,b - 10\,a = 5$; whence $b - a = .5$.

∴ $a + b = [(a-b)^2 + 4\,ab]^{\frac{1}{2}} = (9.75)^{\frac{1}{2}} = 3.122498+$, *to six places of decimals.*

$$\therefore\ a = \frac{3.122498 - .5}{2} = 1.311249, \text{ and } b = \frac{3.122498 + .5}{2} = 1.811249.$$

Having found the real parts of the imaginaries, we now proceed to find $\pm\sqrt{-l}$, and $\pm\sqrt{-m}$. We may now write the imaginaries thus:

$$1.311249 \pm \sqrt{-l}, \text{ and } 1.811249 \pm \sqrt{-m}.$$

The sum of the squares of these expressions will be:

$$(1.31249)^2 2 \pm 2(\sqrt{-l})^2 = 3.43874788 + -2\,l. \qquad (e)$$

$$(1.81124)^2 2 \pm 2(\sqrt{-m})^2 = 6.56124588 + -2\,m. \qquad (c)$$

(1) $\therefore 0 = 4.99999688 + - l + - m$. [Adding (*e*) and (*c*) and dividing by 2.]

This last expression may be written for solution

(2) $5 + - l + - m = 0$.

(3) $\therefore l + m = 5$, or $4.99999688+$.

(4) $(a + \sqrt{-l})(a - \sqrt{-l}) = a^2 + l$.

(5) $(b + \sqrt{-m})(b - \sqrt{-m}) = b^2 + m$.

(6) $\therefore a^2 + b^2 + l + m =$ the sum of their products.

(7) As $l + m = 5$, $m = 5 - l$. $(a^2 + l)(b^2 + m) = \overline{ab}^2 + a^2m + b^2l + lm = 25$.

(8) It has been found that $4\,ab = 9.5$, whence $ab = 2.375$. $\therefore$

(9) $a^2b^2 = (2.375)^2 = 5.640625$, which we now substitute in $(a^2 + l)(b^2 + m)$.

(10) $\therefore 5.640625 + a^2m + b^2l + lm = 25$, and subtracting 5.640625 from both sides we have

(11) $a^2m + b^2l + lm = 19.359375$.

(12) $\therefore l^2 - 6.561249\,l = - 10.7625053$. [Substituting in (11) a^2 and b^2, and putting $m = 5 - l$.]

(13) $\therefore l = 3.28062294$, and $\pm\sqrt{-l} = \pm\sqrt{-3.28062294}$.

(14) (m) now becomes known, and $\pm\sqrt{-m} = \pm\sqrt{-1.71937394}$.

Remark. — It is seen that in the solution of (D) we have arrived at roots in the form of $a \pm \sqrt{-b^2}$, and $b \pm \sqrt{-a^2}$; and in the solution of (C), roots in the form of $a \pm \sqrt{-a^2}$, and $b \pm \sqrt{-b^2}$. In both cases the sum of the squares of the roots, and the sum of the squares of the products of the roots, taken three and three, are *zero* quantities; and we will find this to be true of all equations of the *fourth degree*, having the sum of squares of roots and sum of squares of products, taken three and three, a *zero* quantity. There are, however, a few "reciprocal equations" of the fourth degree that may be found to contain two real roots and two imaginary roots. $x^4 + 2\,x^3 + 2\,x^2 + 2\,x + 1 = 0$ is an equation of the latter class, usually called a "reciprocal" or "recurring" equation.

Referring again to solution of (D), the numerical sum of roots is found to be $6.244996+$.

$\therefore \frac{6.244996+1}{2}=3.622498=$ sum of $+$ roots in formation of equation; true sign $-$; and $\frac{6.244996-1}{2}=2.622498=$ sum of *minus* roots in formation of equation; true sign $+$. $\therefore$ The roots of (D) are

$$1.311249 \pm \sqrt{-3.28062294},$$

and $$-1.811249 \pm \sqrt{-1.71937394}.$$

250. To find the roots of

$$(E) \qquad x^4 - x^3 + .5\,x^2 - 5\,x + 25 = 0.$$

SOLUTION. (1) $a^2+b^2+c^2+d^2=0=(-1)^2-2(.5)$. (Th. II.)

(2) $\overline{abc}^2+\overline{abd}^2+\overline{acd}^2+\overline{bcd}^2=0=(-5)^2-2(.5\times 25)$. (Th. IV.)

$\therefore$ The roots are imaginary (**132**). We now write the quadratics:

$$(e) \qquad x^2 - \tfrac{1}{2} + \sqrt{(l)}x + 5 = 0, \text{ and}$$

$$(f) \qquad x^2 - \tfrac{1}{2} - \sqrt{(l)}x + 5 = 0.$$

Their product will be

$$(F) \qquad x^4 - x^3 + (10 + \tfrac{1}{4} - l)x^2 - 5\,x + 25 = 0.$$

The coefficients of (F) are evidently equal to the coefficients of (E). $\therefore 10\tfrac{1}{4} - l = .5$. Whence, $l = 9.75$, and $\sqrt{l} = \sqrt{9.75} = 3.122498$. We now complete the quadratics (e) and (f).

$$(g) \qquad x^2 - 3.622498\,x + 5 = 0, \text{ and}$$

$$(h) \qquad x^2 + 2.622498\,x + 5 = 0.$$

Solving (g) and (h), the roots of (E) are obtained, being numerically the same as the roots of (D, **249**), but of opposite signs in the real parts of the imaginaries.

REMARK.—It will be found that if we desired to solve (D, **249**) by quadratics, we would simply change the signs of the coefficients of x in (g) and (h); and, in which case, the equations would be for the solution of (D, **249**)

$$(i) \qquad x^2 + 3.622498\,x + 5 = 0, \text{ and}$$

$$(j) \qquad x^2 - 2.622498\,x + 5 = 0.$$

The solutions of (i) and (j) would be the roots of (D, **249**), and would be a great saving in time and labor.

251. To find the roots of

$$(G) \qquad x^4 + 22\,x^3 + 75\,x^2 - 662\,x - 2224 = 0.$$

SOLUTION. (1) $a^2 + b^2 + c^2 + d^2 = 334 = (22)^2 - 2(75)$. (Th. II.)

(2) $334 \times 4 = 1336 = \square$ of sum of roots + sum $\boxed{s}$ of diffs. of roots. (Th. II.) The terms of the equation not being all +, or alternately + and −, the numerical sum of p_2 is not known. ∴ We take from 1336, $(22)^2 - 2(-75)$ or 634. This will be the sum of the squares of the differences, *nearly;* sufficiently near to obtain the numerical sum of roots, and to find its Natural, at least. $1336 - 634 = 702 = \square$ of sum, *nearly*, according to our hypothesis. The side of the greatest square in 702 whose side is integral is 26. ∴ $\frac{26+22}{2} = 24$ = sum + roots; true sign −. $\frac{26-22}{2} = 2$ = sum − roots; true sign +. We now form the quadratics:

$$(p) \qquad x^2 + 24\,x + y = 0, \text{ and}$$

$$(q) \qquad x^2 - 2\,x - z = 0.$$

The product of (p) and (q) is

$$(H) \quad x^4 + 22\,x^3 + (-z + y + -48)x^2 + (-242 + -2\,y)x - zy = 0.$$

The coefficients of (H) are equal to those of (G).

(1) ∴ $-z + y + -48 = 75$. Whence, $y - z = 123$.

(2) $zy = 2224$. [From absolute terms of (G) and (H) by changing sign.]

(3) ∴ $[(z-y)^2 + 4\,zy]^{\frac{1}{2}} = 155 = z + y$.

(4) ∴ $z = \frac{155 - 123}{2} = 16$; and $y = \frac{155 + 123}{2} = 139$.

Substituting the values of z and y in (p) and (q) and solving by quadratics, we find for the roots of (G), $1 \pm \sqrt{17}$, and $-12 \pm \sqrt{5}$.

252. To find the roots of

$$(J) \qquad x^4 - 5\,x^3 + 5\,x^2 - 5\,x + 1 = 0.$$

SOLUTION.

(1) $a^2 + b^2 + c^2 + d^2 = 15 = (-5)^2 - 2(5)$. (Th. II.)

(2) $\overline{abc}^2 + \overline{abd}^2 + \overline{acd}^2 + \overline{bcd}^2 = 15 = (-5)^2 - 2(5 \times 1)$. (Th. IV.)

We now have an equation which is generally called "recurring" or "reciprocal." When the coefficients of such equations equally distant from the *extreme* terms of the equation have the same sign, they may be reduced to an equation of half that degree by dividing the equation by x^2.

Dividing (J) by x^2, and collecting terms, we have

$$(K)\qquad \left(x^2+\frac{1}{x^2}\right)-5\left(x+\frac{1}{x}\right)+6=0.$$

Substituting y for $x+\frac{1}{x}$, and y^2-2 for $x^2+\frac{1}{x^2}$,

$$y^2-5\,y+4=0.$$

Whence,
$$y=4, \text{ or } 1.$$

$$\therefore\ x+\frac{1}{x}=4, \text{ whence } x=2\pm\sqrt{3};$$

and when
$$x+\frac{1}{x}=1,\ x=\tfrac{1}{2}(1\pm\sqrt{-3}).$$

253. It will now be our object to render the solutions of all such equations much more simple and direct.

To do this we write for such equations the general (special) equation

$$(L)\qquad x^4+mx^3+nx^2+mx+1=0.$$

We now write for the equation (L) the quadratics

$$(p)\qquad x^2+ax+1=0.$$

$$(q)\qquad x^2+bx+1=0.$$

Their product will be

$$(M)\qquad x^4+(a+b)x^3+(ab+2)x^2+(a+b)x+1=0.$$

Examining the coefficients of (L), we at once discover the relations of the terms to that of (J). The coefficients of (M) are evidently equal to the coefficients of (L). We notice that the coefficients of x^3 and x are the same; while the coefficient of x^2 is made up of the product ab + the sum of the products of the quadratics (p) and (q), $a+b$ being the sum of the roots of the quadratics that enter into the formation of equation (M). It is also easily seen that this law of formation will hold good as long as the coefficients of x^3 and x in (L) remain the same, and its absolute term *a perfect square.*

254. To solve (J, **252**),

(1) $a + b = 5,\ ab + 2 = 6,\ ab = 4.$

(2) $ab = 4.$

(3) $[(a + b)^2 - 4\,ab]^{\frac{1}{2}} = a - b = 3.$

(4) $\therefore\ a = \frac{5 - 3}{2} = 1$; and $b = \frac{5 + 3}{2} = 4.$

Substituting the values of a and b in (p) and (q), we have

(r) $x^2 - x + 1 = 0.$

(s) $x^2 - 4\,x + 1 = 0.$

Solving (r), $x^2 - (\ ) + 4 = 3.$

$$x - 2 = \sqrt{3}.$$

$$x = 2 \pm \sqrt{3}.$$

Solving (s), $x^2 - (\ ) + \frac{1}{4} = -\frac{3}{4},$

$$x - \tfrac{1}{2} = \frac{\sqrt{-3}}{2},$$

$$x = \frac{1 \pm \sqrt{-3}}{2}.$$

$\therefore$ The roots of (J) are $2 \pm \sqrt{3}$, and $\frac{1 \pm \sqrt{-3}}{2}$; being two real and two imaginary.

[As indicated by the radicals, it is seen that two of the roots will be +, and two −.]

255. We now write the equation

(P) $x^4 + 5\,x^3 + 5\,x^2 + 5\,x + 1 = 0.$

Here the terms are all +; and the sum of the squares of the roots, and sum of square of products of roots taken three and three are the same. The coefficients of x^3 and x are the same. Therefore we write the equation, algebraically, as follows:

(P') $x^4 + (a + b)\,x^3 + (ab + 2)\,x^2 + (a + b)\,x + 1 = 0.$

The quadratics of (P') being

(t) $$x^2 + ax + 1 = 0, \text{ and}$$

(u) $$x^2 + bx + 1 = 0.$$

SOLUTION.

(1) $a + b = 5.$

(2) $ab = 3 = ab = 5 - 2 = ab + 2.$

(3) $[(a+b)^2 - 4\,ab]^{\frac{1}{2}} = a - b = 13 = (5)^2 - 4(3).$

(4) $\therefore\ a = \dfrac{5 - \sqrt{13}}{2} = 2.5 - \sqrt{3.25};$

and $b = \dfrac{5 + \sqrt{13}}{2} = 2.5 + \sqrt{3.25}.$

We now complete the quadratics (t) and (u) by substituting the numerical values of a and b. We then have

(t') $$x^2 + (2.5 - \sqrt{3.25})x + 1 = 0.$$

(u') $$x^2 + (2.5 + \sqrt{3.25})x + 1 = 0.$$

Solving (t').

$$x^2 + (\ ) + (1.25 - \sqrt{.8125})^2 = -1 + (1.25 - \sqrt{.8125})^2 = .375 - 2.5\sqrt{.8125}.$$

$$x + 1.25 - \sqrt{.8125} = \sqrt{.375 = 2.5\sqrt{.8125}}.$$

$$\therefore\ x = -1.25 \pm \sqrt{.375 - 2.5\sqrt{.8125}}.$$

256. Let us now take the equation

(N) $$x^4 + 6\,x^3 + 6\,x^2 - 6\,x + 1 = 0.$$

SOLUTION. (1) $a + b = 6$, and $-(a+b) = -6$; and -1 becomes the absolute term of the quadratics. $\therefore\ ab - 2 = 6$. Whence, $ab = 8$. To illustrate more plainly, we write the quadratics for (N), as follows:

(p') $$x^2 + ax - 1 = 0,$$

(q') $$x^2 + bx - 1 = 0.$$

The product of (p') and (q') will be the biquadratic,

(M') $$x^4 + (a+b)\,x^3 + (ab - 2)\,x^2 - (a+b)\,x + 1 = 0.$$

(2) $\therefore\ [(a+b)^2 - 4\,ab] = a - b = 2 = [(6)^2 - 4(8)]^{\frac{1}{2}} = 2.$

(3) $\therefore\ a = \dfrac{6-2}{2} = 2$, and $b = \dfrac{6+2}{2} = 4.$

We now complete (p') and (q'), and we have,

(r') $$x^2 + 2x = 1,$$

(s') $$x^2 + 4x = 1.$$

Solving (r'), $$x^2 + (\ \ ) + 1 = 2,$$
$$x + 1 = \sqrt{2}.$$
$$x = -1 \pm \sqrt{2}.$$

Solving (s'), $$x^2 + (\ \ ) + 4 = 5,$$
$$x + 2 = \sqrt{5},$$
$$x = -2 \pm \sqrt{5}.$$

$\therefore$ The roots of (N) are $-1 \pm \sqrt{2}$, and $-2 \pm \sqrt{5}$, being all real and minus.

257. Let us now write the equation

(S) $$x^4 + 5x^3 + 5x + 1 = 0.$$

Writing the biquadratic

(S') $$x^4 + (a+b)x^3 + (ab+2)x^2 + (a+b)x + 1 = 0.$$

The middle term in (S) is wanting; therefore, $ab + 2 = 0$. Whence, $ab = -2$; or if ab is $+$, 2 is $-$.

Solution. (1) $a + b = 5$.

(2) $ab = -2$.

(3) $[(a+b)^2 - 4ab]^{\frac{1}{2}} = a - b = \sqrt{33} = (5)^2 - 4(-2)$.

(4) $\therefore a = \dfrac{5 - \sqrt{33}}{2}$, and

(5) $b = \dfrac{5 + \sqrt{33}}{2}$.

We now complete the quadratics (t) and (u) (**255**),

(t'') $$x^2 + \left(\frac{5 - \sqrt{33}}{2}\right)x + 1 = 0,$$

(u'') $$x^2 + \left(\frac{5 + \sqrt{33}}{2}\right)x + 1 = 0.$$

Solving (t'), $$x^2 + (\ \ ) + \frac{\overline{5 - \sqrt{33}}^2}{4} = \frac{42 \mp \sqrt{33}}{16}$$
$$x + \frac{5 - \sqrt{33}}{4} = \frac{(42 - \sqrt{33})^{\frac{1}{2}}}{4}.$$
$$\therefore x = -\tfrac{5}{4} \pm \tfrac{1}{4}[\sqrt{33} \pm (42 \mp \sqrt{33})^{\frac{1}{2}}].$$

258. The reader will readily admit by an examination of the preceding articles (**252–256**) that the method greatly excels in brevity and simplicity that of the old method (**252**, K).

259. To find the roots of

$$(T) \qquad x^4 + 5x^3 + 8.25x^2 + 5x + 1 = 0.$$

SOLUTION. (1) $a + b = 5$; $ab + 2 = 8.25$; $ab = 6.25$.

(2) $[(a+b)^2 - 4ab]^{\frac{1}{2}} = a - b = 0 = (5)^2 - 4(6.25)$.

(3) $a = \frac{5+0}{2} = 2.5$; and $b = 25 = \frac{5-0}{2}$.

∴ The quadratics that solve the equation are:

$$x^2 + 2.5x + 1 = 0,$$

and

$$x^2 + 2.5x + 1 = 0.$$

Their product will be equation (T).

260. Now we will change the absolute term, making the equation read,

$$(T') \qquad x^4 + 5x^3 + 8.25x^2 + 5x + 17 = 0.$$

Now, this equation cannot be solved by the old method of reducing the equation to an equation of half the degree. Dividing the equation by x^2 it becomes

$$x^2 + 5x + 8.25 + \frac{5}{x} + \frac{17}{x^2} = 0.$$

Collecting terms we have

$$x^2 + \frac{17}{x^2} + 5\left(x + \frac{1}{x}\right) + 8.25 = 0.$$

Here $\left(\frac{1}{x}\right)^2$ differs very materially from $\frac{17}{x^2}$. Thus we see that we cannot apply the old method. The only method for the solution of (T'), contained in any prior work, is the Horner or Newton methods of approximation, which is long and tedious; and, the introduction of a fractional coefficient renders the solution of (T') still more difficult and tedious by either the Newton or Horner method. However, it will be seen that the equation is easily solved by our method (**186**).

We will now lay down the following *immutable law* for the solution of a certain class of *biquadratics* by *quadratics*.

261. *Letting* $x^4 + mx^3 + nx^2 + ox + q = 0$ *always represent a general equation of the Fourth Degree, when* $n - \frac{m^2}{4} = \frac{2\,o}{m}$, *a solution of the biquadratic by quadratics lies; because* $n - \frac{m^2}{4}$, *and* $\frac{2\,o}{m}$, *are each, respectively, equal to the sum of the absolute terms of the quadratics that enter into the formation of the biquadratic; and, therefore,* $n - \frac{m^2}{4}$, *or* $\frac{2\,o}{m}$, *is equal to the true sum of the quadratic factors of the absolute term of the biquadratic.*

It now becomes important to know the meaning of the term *quadratic factors*, for which we adduce the following definition.

262. Quadratic Factors are the absolute terms of any two quadratics whose product forms a biquadratic, and are, therefore, true factors of the absolute term of the biquadratic.

263. Referring again to the solution of (T', **260**), we have (**261**) the following

SOLUTION.

(1) $$8.25 - \frac{25}{4} = 2 = z + y = \frac{2 \times 5}{5}.$$

(2) $$zy = 17.$$

(3) $$\therefore\ [(z + y)^2 - 4\,zy]^{\frac{1}{2}} = 8\sqrt{-1} = [(2)^2 - 4(17)]^{\frac{1}{2}},$$

(4) $$\therefore\ z = \frac{2 + 8\sqrt{-1}}{2} = 1 + 4\sqrt{-1},\ \text{and}$$

(5) $$y = \frac{2 - 8\sqrt{-1}}{2} = 1 - 4\sqrt{-1}.$$

∴ The quadratics are

(a) $$x^2 + 2.5\,x + 1 + 4\sqrt{-1} = 0.$$

(b) $$x^2 + 2.5\,x + 1 - 4\sqrt{-1} = 0.$$

The product of (a) and (b) will be (T', **260**); and by the solution of either (a) or (b), we arrive at the roots of the equation

$$x^4 + 5\,x^3 + 8.25\,x^2 + 5\,x + 17 = 0.$$

264. It will be noticed by an examination of the equation

(T'') $$x^4 + 5\,x^3 + 8.25\,x^2 + 5\,x + 17 = 0,$$

that $z + y = 2$, no matter what the absolute term becomes, *so long that it does not become zero.* Should the sign of the absolute term be *minus,* the solution will be the same; but if the terms of the equation are all *minus* (except the first term), the solution will be different than that of the solution of (T'', **260**).

265. To find the roots of

(A) $$x^4 - 5\,x^3 - 5\,x^2 - 5\,x - 6 = 0.$$

By inspection we write for the roots of the equation

$$6,\ -1, \text{ and } \pm 0 \pm \sqrt{-1}. \quad (\textbf{133.})$$

266. To find the roots of

(B) $$x^4 - 5\,x^3 - 5\,x^2 - 5\,x - 5 = 0.$$

Here, $(-5)^2 - 2(-5) = 35 = a^2 + b^2 + c^2 + d^2.$ (Th. II.)

$(-5)^2 - 2(-5 \times -5) = -25 =$ sum of $\boxed{s}$ of p_3. (Th. IV.)

The last term is negative. ∴ Two real roots of opposite sign. (**103.**) Hence, the sum of the squares of the products of the roots taken three and three being a *minus* quantity, the equation contains but two real roots and two imaginary roots. (**101.**) We may now write the roots, algebraically, as follows:

$$a,\ b, \text{ and } c \pm \sqrt{-l}.$$

If we examine (A, **265**), we will find that it is the *Natural* of (B). The roots of (A) may be written, algebraically,

$$a,\ b, \text{ and } \pm \sqrt{-l}.$$

Let us now take the equation (*A*, **265**), and apply Ths. II. and IV.

(1) Sum of □ of roots = 35.

(2) Sum of □ of $p_2 = -25$.

(3) Sum of □ of $p_3 = -35$.

Applying Ths. II. and IV. to equation (*B*), we have

(1) Sum of [s] of roots = 35.

(2) Sum of [s] of $p_2 = -25$.

(3) Sum of [s] of $p_3 = -25$.

The sum of the squares of the roots, and the sum of the squares of the products of the roots taken *two* and *two*, have remained unchanged; while the sum of the squares of the products of the roots taken *three* and *three* have been reduced. But the *character* of the roots of each equation are the same, being two *real* roots and two *purely imaginary*. Should the absolute term of (*B*) become -1, the signs and coefficients of the other terms of the equation remaining permanent, the equation would still contain two real and two imaginary roots.

We now lay down this rule prior to the solution of (*B*):

267. *When the equation $x^4 + m^3 + nx^2 + ox + q = 0$ contains real and imaginary roots in the form of a, b, and $\pm\sqrt{-l}$, $m = a + b$, and $+l = (\sqrt{-l})(-\sqrt{-l}) = \frac{o}{m}$; and in consequence of which the roots of the biquadratic are readily obtained.*

Referring again to (*B*, **266**), let us represent the roots by $-a$, $+b$, and $\pm\sqrt{-l}$ in its formation, being the algebraic expressions of the roots in the formation of the *Natural* (*A*, **265**). If (*B*) contains roots in this form, then $-abl = -5$; and $a + b = -5$, and $-ab + l = -5$. We now have the equations, by changing signs,

$$(1)\ a - b = 5;\ (2)\ ab - l = 5;\ (3)\ abl = 5.$$

From the above equations we find the first two figures for the values of a and b. $a = 5.9$, $b = .92$, and $l = .90$.

From this, by the *Condensed Method*, the roots are found to be 5.9961+ and $-.9218+$. And having found the real roots, the imaginary roots are readily found to be $-.03715 \pm \sqrt{-.90323}$.

268. We will now introduce the method for changing an equation of the *Fourth Degree* to an equation of the *Sixth Degree,* in which the sum of the products of the roots of the biquadratic shall be the sum of the roots of the *Sixth Degree* equation.

To change the general equation

$$(C) \qquad x^4 + mx^3 + nx^2 + ox + q = 0,$$

we write the equation

$$(D) \quad y^6+ny^5+(mo-q)y^4+[(m^2-2n)q+2nq+(o^2-2nq)]y^3 + [q(om-4q)+3q^2]y^2+nq^2yx+q^3=0.$$

To illustrate. Take the equation

$$(E) \qquad x^4 - 7x^3 + 20x^2 - 32x + 24 = 0.$$

Applying the formula, we have

$$(F) \quad y^6-20y^5+200y^4-1240y^3+4800y^2-11520y+13824-0.$$

The *sixth* will contain the same *character* of roots as the *fourth;* that is, if the roots of the *fourth* are *real* and *imaginary,* the *sixth* will contain *real* and *imaginary* roots; *but if the fourth contains all imaginary roots, the sixth will contain two real roots, which will be the separate products of the imaginary roots of the biquadratic. The real roots of the sixth will then be the* **Quadratic Factors** *of the absolute term of the biquadratic.*

To solve (E).

(1) $(-7)^2 - 2(20) = 9 = a^2 + b^2 + c^2 + d^2$. (Th. II.)

(2) $9 \times 4 = 36 = \square$ of sum of roots + sum $\boxed{s}$ of diffs. (Th. II.)

(3) As $36 < (-7)^2$, the equation contains imaginary roots. (**130**.)

(4) $(-32)^2 - 2(20 \times 24) = 64 =$ sum of $\boxed{s}$ of p_3. (Th. IV.)

In both (1) and (4) the sum of $\boxed{s}$ is a perfect $\square$. $\therefore \sqrt{9} = 3 =$ one of the roots, and $\sqrt{64} = 8 = 2(a^2 + l) =$ twice the product of the imaginary roots. $\therefore \frac{8}{2} = 4 = a^2 + l$; and $3 \times 4 = 12$, and $24 \div 12 = 2$, the other real root.

The sum of the squares of the roots may be written

$$a^2 + b^2 + 2\,a^2 + - 2\,l = 9. \qquad (t)$$

$$(a^2 + b^2) = (2)^2 + (3)^2 = a^2 + b^2 = 13. \qquad (s)$$

$$\therefore\ 2\,a^2 + - 2\,l = - 4. \quad \text{[Taking } (s) \text{ from } (t).] \qquad (u)$$

$$a^2 + - l = - 2. \quad \text{[Dividing } (u) \text{ by } (2).] \qquad (v)$$

But

$$a^2 + l = 4. \qquad (w)$$

$$\therefore\ 2\,a^2 = 2. \quad \text{Whence } a^2 = 1, \text{ and}$$

$$\therefore\ a = 1.$$

$\therefore$ The roots of (E) are 2, 3, and $1 \pm \sqrt{-3}$.

269. The question that will naturally arise in the mind of the reader is this: *Does it simplify the solution of an equation of the Fourth Degree to change it to an equation of the Sixth Degree?*

Our answer is this:

There are a certain class of biquadratics in which a solution is obtained more easily and readily by changing the equation, and especially is this true when the roots of the biquadratic are all approximate imaginaries. By applying formula (D, **268***), the roots can be readily arrived at by the Horner method.*

To illustrate. Take the equation

$$(A) \qquad x^4 - 6\,x^3 + 18\,x^2 - 26\,x + 20 = 0.$$

The roots of this equation are all *approximate* imaginaries. The roots of its *Natural* are $1 \pm \sqrt{-2}$, and $2 \pm \sqrt{-3}$; and these roots will satisfy all the conditions of (A) but that of its absolute term. Applying formula (*D*, **268**), we obtain

$$(B) \quad y^6 - 18\,y^5 + 136\,y^4 - 676\,y^3 + 2720\,y^2 - 7200\,y + 8000 = 0.$$

As (A) contains all imaginary roots, (B) will contain two *real roots* representing the *quadratic factors* of the *absolute term* of (A). The product of the imaginary roots of (A) may be represented, algebraically, by $a^2 + l$ and $b^2 + m$, and the sum of the squares of the roots by

$$2\,a^2 + 2\,b^2 + - 2\,l + - 2\,m = 0 = (-6)^2 - 2\,(18).$$

It is evident that to solve (A) we have but to find either $a^2 + l$, or $b^2 + m$. $a^2 + l = 3 = (1 + \sqrt{-2})(1 - \sqrt{-2})$ in the *Natural*, the absolute term of which is 21, being the product of $1 \pm \sqrt{-2}$ and $2 \pm \sqrt{-3}$. The absolute term of (A) has been reduced, so we begin to find $a^2 + l$, which we know to be < 3 and > 2.

We find from (B), by the Horner method, $a^2 + l = 2.99512+$.

Whence $b^2 + m = 6.67661 = \frac{20}{2.99512}$. We now have the equations:

(1) $2a^2 + 2b^2 + -2l + -2m = 0 = (-6)^2 - 2(18)$, (Th. II.) = the sum of the squares of the roots of (A).

(2) $a^2 + b^2 + -l + -m = 0$. [Dividing (1) by 2.]

(3) $a^2 + l = 2.99512$.

(4) $b^2 + m = 6.67661$.

(5) $a^2 + b^2 + l + m = 9.67173$. [Adding (3) and (4).]

(6) $2a^2 + 2b^2 = 9.67173$. [Adding (5) and (2).]

(7) $\therefore 9.67173 = (a + b)^2 + (a - b)$. (Th. I.)

(8) $2a + 2b = 6$. [From equation (A).]

(9) $a + b = 3$.

(10) $(a - b)^2 = .67173$. [Taking $(a + b)^2$ from (7).]

(11) $\therefore a - b = .8195 = \sqrt{.67173}$.

(12) $\therefore a = \frac{3 - .8195}{2} = 1.09025$, and

(13) $b = \frac{3 + .8195}{2} = 1.90975$.

(14) $l = 1.80648$. [Taking a^2 from (3).]

(15) $m = 3.02947$. [Taking b^2 from (4).]

The roots of (A) are

$$1.09025 \pm \sqrt{-1.80658}, \text{ and}$$

$$1.90975 \pm \sqrt{-3.02947}.$$

REMARK. — Find the roots of (A) by the old method, and then compare it with the foregoing solution. We have no doubt but what you will prefer the method which we have just offered.

270. To find the roots of

$$(L) \qquad x^4 - 14x^3 + 79x^2 - 210x + 250 = 0.$$

SOLUTION.

(1) $a^2 + b^2 + c^2 + d^2 = 38 = (-14)^2 - 2(79)$. (Th. II.)

(2) $38 \times 4 = 152 = \square$ of sum of roots + sum of $\boxed{s}$ of diffs. of roots. (Th. II.)

(3) As $152 < (-14)^2$, the equation contains imaginary roots. (**130.**)

(4) $79 - \frac{(14)^2}{4} = \frac{2 \times -210}{-14} = 30 = z + y$. (**261.**)

(5) $zy = 250$.

(6) $[(30)^2 - 4(250)]^{\frac{1}{2}} = \sqrt{-100}$.

(7) $\therefore z = 15 + \sqrt{-25}$, and

(8) $y = 15 - \sqrt{-25}$.

We now form the quadratics,

$$(p) \qquad x^2 - 7x + 15 + \sqrt{-25} = 0.$$

$$(q) \qquad x^2 - 7x + 15 - \sqrt{-25} = 0.$$

Their product equals (L); (p) solved gives

$$3.5 \pm \sqrt{-2.75 - \sqrt{-25}};$$

and (q) solved gives $3.5 \pm \sqrt{-2.75 + \sqrt{-25}}$.

We now meet with an entirely different class of biquadratics in (L) than that of any of the prior equations which we have given and solved. We notice that the *quadratic factors* of (L) are a pair of conjugate imaginaries; and we can readily see that if we change (L) to an equation of the *Sixth Degree* that it will contain all imaginary roots, and we cannot, therefore, approximate the roots by the Horner method. If we try to find the roots of such an equation by the Horner method, or by any of the old methods, we will come to the conclusion that any of such methods are very unsatisfactory. The easiest and most ready method for the solution of such equations will be found to be that explained in Arts. **186** and **261**.

271. To find the roots of

$$(M) \qquad x^4 + 2x^2 - 4x - 2 = 0.$$

SOLUTION.

(1) $a^2 + b^2 + c^2 + d^2 = 4 = (2)^2 - 2(\pm 0)$. (Th. II.)

(2) $\overline{abc}^2 + \overline{abd}^2 + \overline{acd}^2 + \overline{bcd}^2 = 16 = (-4)^2 - 2(\pm 0 \times -2)$. (Th. IV.)

In both cases the theorems give perfect squares.

(3) $\overline{ab}^2+\overline{ac}^2+\overline{ad}^2+\overline{bc}^2+\overline{bd}^2+\overline{cd}^2=12=(\pm 0)^2-2[(2\times -4)-(-2)]$.

We may now safely conclude that the roots are all real. The middle term being wanting, we let $z+y=2$, and $zy=-2$, which, solved, gives $z=1+\sqrt{3}$, and $y=1-\sqrt{3}$. We now form the quadratics,

$$(p) \qquad x^2+2.73205\,x+2.73025=0,$$

$$(q) \qquad x^2-\ .73205\,x-\ .73025=0.$$

Their product will be the equation (M). Or we may write for the quadratics,

$$(p') \qquad x^2+(1+\sqrt{3})x+1+\sqrt{3}=0,$$

$$(q') \qquad x^2+(1-\sqrt{3})x+1-\sqrt{3}=0.$$

From (p') and (q') the roots of (M) may be accurately expressed in the form of *irrational fractions* and *imaginary quantities*, we having now discovered, by inspection of the quadratics (p) and (p'), that the equation *does not contain all real roots, as first suggested;* but that (M) contains two real roots of opposite signs and a pair of imaginary roots.

We now see that the **Quadratic Factors** of a *biquadratic* may be *whole numbers, irrational fractions in pairs*, or a *pair* of *conjugate imaginaries*. In (p') the absolute term, $(1+\sqrt{3})$, is made up of the product of a pair of conjugate imaginaries. Should we change (M) to an equation of the *Sixth Degree*, we can obtain the product of the imaginaries expressed in the form of an *incommensurable root.*

272. To find the roots of

$$(N) \qquad x^4-8\,x^3+14\,x^2+4\,x-8=0.$$

SOLUTION.

(1) Sum of ⓢ of roots $=36=(-8)^2-2\,(14)$.

(2) $36\times 4=144=\square$ of sum of roots + sum of ⓢ of diffs. of roots.

(3) Sum of ⓢ $p_3=240=(4)^2-2(14\times -8)$.

The terms of the equation not being alternately + and −, and the last term −, the equation contains at least two real roots of opposite signs. As the equation contains both + and − roots, 8 is not the true numerical sum of roots. ∴ The true sum is >8.

We now find by synthetic division two of the roots to two places of decimals, and from this we find the other two roots to two places; and the sum of the squares of the differences of the roots thus far found we find to be 54.4+. We now take the square root of 4×36, or 144 within this limit.

	144 | 9.4641 = sum of roots
	81
184	63.00
	7.36
1886	55.6400
	1.1316
18924	54.508400
	.059696
189281	54.44870400
	.00189281

$\therefore \dfrac{9.4641 + -8}{2} = .73205$ = sum of + roots in formation of equation; true sign −; and $\dfrac{9.4641 - (-8)}{2} = 8.73205$ = sum of −roots in formation of equation; true sign +.

$-.73205$ is found to be the negative root. 2.73205 is also a root. The other two roots are then found from their sum and product.

Again: It is now seen that equation (N) is more easily solved, and that we can separate it into two quadratics. The factors of the absolute term (and the only ones) are 1 and 8 and 2 and 4. But the previous solution shows us that 2 and 4 are the proper factors. We now write the quadratics

(p) $\qquad x^2 - ax - 2 = 0$, and

(q) $\qquad x^2 - bx + 4 = 0$.

Their product will be

(N') $\quad x^4 - (a + b)x^3 + (ab + 4 - 2)x^2 + (2b - 4a)x - 8 = 0.$

If this be the true equation, the coefficients of (N) will be equal to the coefficients of (N'). We now have the equations

(1) $a + b = 8$, $\qquad$ (2) $ab = 14 - (4 - 2) = 12.$

From (1) and (2) we find $a = 2$ and $b = 6$, which substituted in (p) and (q) gives

(p') $\qquad x^2 - 2x - 2 = 0$, and

(q') $\qquad x^2 - 6x + 4 = 0$.

The solution of (p') gives $1 \pm \sqrt{3}$, and the solution of (q') $3 \pm \sqrt{5}$. They are the true roots of the biquadratic (N), and can be easily approximated, if required, to any degree of accuracy. It will be noticed that if we apply formula (**261**) *that it will fail to render the roots. A universal general solution for biquadratics will be given later.*

273. To find the roots

$$(M') \qquad x^4 + x^3 - 195.5\,x^2 - 234\,x + 139.5 = 0.$$

Solution. (1) $a^2 + b^2 + c^2 + d^2 = 392 = \square$ of sum of roots + sum of $\boxed{s}$ of diffs. of roots.

(2) $392 \div 2 = 196$. ∴ The roots of the equation are the sides of two rt. triangles constructed in a circle whose diameter is the square root of 196. (**136**.)

We may now represent the roots of the equation, as follows:

$$\begin{cases} a + \sqrt{l} \\ a - \sqrt{l} \\ b + \sqrt{m} \\ b - \sqrt{m} \end{cases}$$

If the sides are integral, l and m will be found to be *zero*. From algebraic sum we write

(1) $2\,a - 2\,b = 1$; whence, $a - b = .5$.

(2) $a^2 + b^2 + l + m = 196$, one-half sum $\boxed{s}$.

(3) $2\,a^2 + 2\,l = 196$. [Sum $\boxed{s}$ in both cases being equal.]

(4) ∴ $2\,b^2 + 2\,m = 196$.

(5) $392 \times 4 = 1568 = \square$ of sum + sum $\boxed{s}$ diffs.

(6) ∴ $1568 - 2(195.5) = 1177 = \square$ of sum of roots, *nearly;* at least, sufficiently near to determine numerical sum of roots. The side of the greatest integral square in 1177 is 34, which is rejected. (**26**.) 33 is then taken, and we have

$$\frac{33+1}{2} = 17 = \text{sum of + roots, true sign } -;$$

and

$$\frac{33-1}{2} = 16 = \text{sum of } - \text{ roots, true sign } +.$$

$$2\,a + 2\,b = 33;\ \text{whence, } a + b = 16.5.$$

$$\therefore\ a = \frac{16.5 - .5}{2} = 8;\ \text{and } b = \frac{16.5 + .5}{2} = 8.5.$$

$\therefore\ a^2+l=98=l=98-(8)^2=34.\quad \therefore\ 8\pm\sqrt{34}$ for two of the roots; and $b^2+m=98=m=98-(8.5)^2=25.75.\quad \therefore\ -8.5\pm\sqrt{25.75}$ are the other two roots; and, as they will satisfy all the conditions of the problem, they are, therefore, the true roots of the equation (M').

273 *a*. To find the roots of

$$(A)\qquad x^4-27x^3+261.91x^2-1075.41x+1563=0.$$

[Submitted for solution by Professor J. B. Young, of Safford, Arizona.]

SOLUTION. Applying formula under (**186**), we discover that this difficult equation is easily solved.

$$(1)\ 261.91-\frac{(27)}{4}=\frac{2\times -1075.41}{27}=79.66=z+y.$$

$$(2)\ zy=1563.$$

$$(3)\ z=39.83+\sqrt{23.4289},\text{ and}$$

$$(4)\ y=39.83-\sqrt{23.4289}.\quad \text{[Solving (1) and (2).]}$$

The quadratics then will be

$$(p)\qquad x^2-13.5x+39.83+\sqrt{23.4289}=0,\text{ and}$$

$$(q)\qquad x^2-13.5x+39.83-\sqrt{23.4289}=0.$$

Solving the quadratics (p) and (q), we obtain for the roots

$$6.75\pm[(6.0625)+\sqrt{23.4289}]^{\frac{1}{2}},\text{ and}$$

$$6.75\pm[(6.0625)-\sqrt{23.4289}]^{\frac{1}{2}}.$$

REMARK. — It will take fully four hours' time to find the roots to four places of decimals each by the Horner method.

274. To find the roots of

$$(A)\qquad x^4+30x^3+325x^2+489x+2478=0.$$

SOLUTION.

(1) $a^2+b^2+c^2+d^2=250=$ sum of [s] of roots. (Th. II.) The terms of the equation are all +. $\therefore$ No real + roots. (**111.**) By inspection we see that Theorem IV. will give largely a plus quantity for sum of [s] of roots taken *three* and *three*, and *two* and *two*. We now represent the roots by

$$a+\sqrt{l},$$
$$a-\sqrt{l},$$
$$b+\sqrt{m},$$
$$b-\sqrt{m}.$$

If the roots are integral, l and m will be *zero*.

(2) $\therefore\ 2a^2 + 2b^2 + 2l + 2m = 250.$

(3) $a^2 + b^2 + l + m = 125.$

(4) $250 \times 4 = 1000 = \square$ of sum + sum $\boxed{s}$ of diffs. of roots. (Th. II.)

(5) $\therefore\ 1000 - (30)^2 = 4a^2 + 4b^2 - 8ab + 8l + 8m = 100.$

(6) $a^2 + b^2 - 2ab + 2l + 2m = 25.$ [Dividing (5) by 4.]

Now factor absolute term into its prime factors. $2478 = 2 \times 3 \times 7 \times 59.$ Put

(7) $(a + \sqrt{l})(a - \sqrt{l}) = a^2 - l = 2 \times 3 \times 7$, or 59.

(8) $(b + \sqrt{m})(b - \sqrt{m}) = b^2 - m = 59$, or $2 \times 3 \times 7$.

(9) $a^2 + b^2 - l - m = 101.$

(10) $\therefore\ 2a^2 + 2b^2 = 226.$ (Adding (3) and (9).)

(11) $\sqrt{226} = 15 = (a + b) + (a - b)^2.$ (Th. II.)

(12) $\therefore\ a - b = 1.$

(13) $\therefore\ a = \dfrac{15 + 1}{2} = 8;\ b = \dfrac{15 - 1}{2} = 7.$

(14) $(a + \sqrt{l})(a - \sqrt{l}) = a^2 - l.$

(15) $(b + \sqrt{m})(b - \sqrt{m}) = b^2 - m.$

(16) $(a^2 - l)(b^2 - m) = \overline{ab}^2 + lm - a^2m - b^2l = 2478.$

Substituting in (15) and (16) the values of $\overline{ab}^2$ and a^2, b^2, and collecting terms we have

(17) $685 + lm - 64m - 49l = 0.$

Substituting in (6) the values of a^2, b^2, and $2ab$, we have

(18) $l + m = 12$, whence $m = 12 - l.$

Substituting in (17) the value of (m), and transposing and collecting terms, we have

(19) $l^2 - 27l = -110$, from which we find

(20) $l = 5.\ \therefore\ m = 7 = (12 - 5).$

(21) $\therefore$ The roots of the equation are $-8 \pm \sqrt{5}$, and $-7 \pm \sqrt{7}$.

275. To find the roots of

$$(B) \qquad x^4 + 14x^3 + 96x^2 + 368x + 768 = 0.$$

SOLUTIONS.

(1) $a^2 + b^2 + c^2 + d^2 = 4 = (14)^2 - 2(96).$ (Th. II.)

(2) $\overline{abc}^2 + \overline{abd}^2 + \overline{acd}^2 + \overline{bcd}^2 = -12032 = (368)^2 - 2(14 \times 768).$

$\therefore$ The equation contains imaginary roots. (**101**.)

Factoring absolute terms, we have

$$768 = 2 \times 2 \times 2 \times 2 \times 2 \times 2 \times 2 \times 2 \times 3.$$

Trial of the combinations of these factors show that 24 and 32 are the true *quadratic factors* of the absolute term. (3) $a^2+b^2+l+m=56$. The sum of squares may be represented by $2a^2+2b^2-2l-2m$, which, divided by 2, gives (4) $a^2+b^2-l-m=2$, which, added to (3), gives $2a^2+b^2=58$. Whence $a+b=7$, and $a-b=3$.

And subtracting (3) and (4), $l+m=\frac{56-2}{2}=24$. We now readily write for the roots $-5 \pm \sqrt{-7}$ and $-2 \pm 2\sqrt{-5}$. (See the *universal general solution for biquadratics.*)

276. To find the roots of

$$x^4+8x^3-3x^2-206x-520=0.$$

SOLUTION.

(1) $a^2+b^2+c^2+d^2=70=(8)^2-2(-3)$. (Th. II.)

(2) $70 \times 4 = 280 = \square$ of sum of roots + sum of $\boxed{s}$ of diffs. of roots. (Th. II.) The side of the greatest integral $\square$ in 270 is 16. Therefore,

$$\frac{16+8}{2}=12=\text{sum of + roots; true sign }-;$$

and $$\frac{16-8}{2}=4=\text{sum of -- roots; true sign }+.$$

The last term is negative, ∴ two real roots of opposite sign. We try 4, and find that 16 is not the true numerical sum of roots. 17 is rejected. (**26.**) [The numerical sum being > 16, because the root 4 is found to be *too small.*] 18 is then taken, and we have

$$\frac{18+8}{2}=13=\text{sum of + roots; true sign }-;$$

and $$\frac{18-8}{2}=5=\text{sum of }-\text{ roots; true sign }+.$$

5 is tried, and it satisfies the condition of the problem, and 18 is therefore the true numerical sum of roots. We have now discovered that the equation contains a pair of imaginary roots, because $270 < (18)^2$. (**130.**) $13-5=9$ and $9-5=4$. ∴ -4 is a root. The other two roots are now readily found to be $-4.5 \pm \sqrt{-5.75}$.

277. To find the roots of

$$x^4 + q = 0.$$

Solution. The equation is of even degree, and the sign of its last term +. The *second*, *third*, and *fourth* terms are wanting, therefore, the sum of squares of roots, and sum of squares of roots taken *three* and *three*, will, in either case, be a *zero* quantity; and Th. IV gives for sum of squares of products of roots taken *two* and *two*, $+2q$. ∴ The equation contains all imaginary roots, the real part of one pair being +, and the other, −. The roots may be represented algebraically, by

$$\pm a \pm \sqrt{-a^2}.$$

By an algebraic process we arrive at the following formula for the roots of such an equation:

$$\pm\left(\frac{q}{2}\right)^{\frac{1}{2}} \pm \left(\frac{q}{2}\right)^{\frac{1}{2}}.$$

If $q = 1$, the roots will be $\pm\sqrt{.5} \pm \sqrt{-.5}$; which factored, gives $\pm\sqrt{.25 \times 2} \pm \sqrt{+.25 \times -2} = \pm\frac{1}{2}\sqrt{2} \pm \frac{1}{2}\sqrt{-2}$.

278. To find the roots of

$$x^4 + 8 = 0.$$

Solution. Applying formula (**186**), the quadratics are

(p) $$x^2 + 0x \pm 0 + \sqrt{-8} = 0.$$

(q) $$x^2 + 0x \pm 0 - \sqrt{-8} = 0.$$

Solving either (p) or (q) the roots of the biquadratic are obtained.

279. To find the roots of

$$x^4 - 20x^3 + 140x^2 - 400x + 19 = 0.$$

Solution.

(**186**) $$\begin{cases} (1)\ 140 - \dfrac{(-20)^2}{4} = \dfrac{2 \times -400}{-20} = z + y = 40. \\ (2)\ zy = 19. \\ (3)\ \begin{cases} x^2 - 10x + z = 0, \\ x^2 - 10x + y = 0. \end{cases} \end{cases}$$

From (1) and (2) we find z and y to be, respectively, $20+\sqrt{381}$ and $20-\sqrt{381}$. We now complete the quadratics (3)

(p) $$x^2 - 10x + 20 + \sqrt{381} = 0.$$

(q) $$x^2 - 10x + 20 - \sqrt{381} = 0.$$

Solving either (p) or (q) the roots of the biquadratic are found to be

$$5 \pm (5 \pm \sqrt{381})^{\frac{1}{2}}.$$

280. To find the roots of

$$x^4 + 2x^3 + 3x^2 + 2x - 11 = 0.$$

SOLUTION.

(**186**) $$\begin{cases} (1)\ 3 - \dfrac{(2)^2}{4} = \dfrac{2 \times 2}{2} = 2 = z + y. \\ (2)\ zy = -11. \\ (3)\ \begin{cases} x^2 + x + y = 0, \\ x^2 + x + z = 0. \end{cases} \end{cases}$$

From (1) and (2) we find z and y to be, respectively, $1+\sqrt{12}$ and $1-\sqrt{12}$, which substituted in (3) we have

(p) $$x^2 + x + 1 + \sqrt{12} = 0.$$

(q) $$x^2 + x + 1 - \sqrt{12} = 0.$$

Solving either (p) or (q) we obtain for the roots of the biquadratic,

$$-\tfrac{1}{2} \pm (-.75 \mp \sqrt{12})^{\frac{1}{2}}.$$

Taking + sign in radical we have two real roots, and taking − sign, two imaginary roots.

281. To find the roots of

$$x^4 + 20x^3 + 100x^2 + 17 = 0.$$

SOLUTION.

(**186**) $$\begin{cases} (1)\ 100 - \dfrac{(20)^2}{4} = \dfrac{2 \times \pm 0}{20} = 0 = z + y. \\ (2)\ zy = 17. \\ (3)\ \begin{cases} x^2 + 10x + y = 0, \\ x^2 + 10x + z = 0. \end{cases} \end{cases}$$

From (1) and (2) we find z or $y = \pm 0 \pm \sqrt{-17}$, which we substitute in (3) and obtain

$$(p) \qquad x^2 + 10x \pm 0 + \sqrt{-17} = 0.$$

$$(q) \qquad x^2 + 10x \pm 0 - \sqrt{-17} = 0.$$

Solving either (p) or (q) we obtain for the roots of the biquadratic,

$$-5 \pm \sqrt{25 + \sqrt{-17}},$$

and

$$-5 \pm \sqrt{25 - \sqrt{-17}}.$$

282. To find the roots of

$$x^4 - 2x^3 + 71x^2 - 70x + 23 = 0.$$

SOLUTION.

$$(\mathbf{186}) \quad \begin{cases} (1)\ 71 - \dfrac{(-2)^2}{4} = \dfrac{2 \times -70}{-2} = z + y = 70. \\ (2)\ zy = 23. \\ (3)\ \begin{cases} x^2 - x + y = 0, \\ x^2 - x + z = 0. \end{cases} \end{cases}$$

From (1) and (2) we find z and y to be, respectively, $35 + \sqrt{1202}$ and $35 - \sqrt{1202}$, which substituted in (3) gives

$$(p) \qquad x^2 - x + 35 + \sqrt{1202} = 0, \text{ and}$$

$$(q) \qquad x^2 - x + 35 - \sqrt{1202} = 0.$$

Solving (p) or (q) the roots of the biquadratic are found to be

$$\tfrac{1}{2} \pm \sqrt{-34.75 \pm \sqrt{1202}}.$$

283. To find the roots of

$$x^4 + \tfrac{6}{7}x^3 + \tfrac{3}{7}x^2 + \tfrac{36}{343}x + 2 = 0.$$

SOLUTION.

$$\begin{cases} (1)\ \dfrac{3}{7} - \dfrac{(\frac{6}{7})^2}{4} = \dfrac{2 \times \frac{36}{343}}{\frac{6}{7}} = z + y = \tfrac{12}{49}. \\ (2)\ zy = 2. \\ (3)\ \begin{cases} x^2 + \frac{3}{7}x + y = 0, \\ x^2 + \frac{3}{7} + z = 0. \end{cases} \end{cases}$$

From (1) and (2) we find z and y to be, respectively,

$$\frac{6 + \sqrt{-4766}}{49}, \text{ and } \frac{6 - \sqrt{-4766}}{49}.$$

We now complete the quadratics (3),

(p) $$x^2 + \tfrac{3}{7}x + \frac{6 + \sqrt{-4766}}{49} = 0, \text{ and}$$

(q) $$x^2 + \tfrac{3}{7}x + \frac{6 - \sqrt{-4766}}{49} = 0.$$

Solving (p) or (q) we obtain for the roots of the biquadratic,

$$\tfrac{1}{14}(-3 \pm (-15 \pm 4\sqrt{-4766})^{\frac{1}{2}}).$$

REMARK. — *The reader will now be able to see the importance of the formula* (**186**).

284. Solve the following *Biquadratics* by the formula (**186**):

(1) $x^4 - 2x^3 + 5x^2 - 4x + \frac{2}{3} = 0.$

(2) $x^4 - 2x^3 - 13x^2 + 14x + 17 = 0.$

(3) $x^4 + 2x^3 + 15x^2 + 14x + 27 = 0.$

(4) $x^4 - 2x^3 - 10x^2 + 11x + 24 = 0.$

(5) $x^4 - 2x^3 - 2x^2 + 3x - 119 = 0.$

(6) $x^4 + 2x^3 + x^2 + 1\frac{2}{3} = 0.$

(7) $x^4 - 2x^3 + x^2 - 21 = 0.$

(8) $x^4 + 13x^3 + 75x^2 + 219\frac{3}{8}x + 2111 = 0.$

(9) $x^4 + 13x^3 + 13x^2 - 190\frac{1}{8}x + 2111 = 0.$

(10) $x^4 - 2x^3 + 7x^2 - 5x + 23 = 0.$

(11) $x^4 + 2x^3 + 17x^2 + 16x + 119 = 0.$

(12) $x^4 + 14x^3 + x^2 - 336x + 16 = 0.$

(13) $x^4 + 114x^3 + 11x^2 - 178695x + 1601 = 0.$

(14) $x^4 - 756x^3 + 428652x^2 - 108020304x + 22170267 = 0.$

(15) $x^4 + 756x^3 + 142884x^2 + 5000 = 0.$

(16) $x^4 - 17x^3 + 101x^2 - 247x + 200 = 0.$

(17) $x^4 - x^3 - 43x^2 - 21.625x + 117 = 0.$

(18) $x^4 - 11x^3 + 41x^2 - 59.125x + 31 = 0.$

(19) $x^4 - 1728x^3 + 746500x^2 - 3456x - 741317 = 0.$

(20) $x^4 + 3x^3 + \frac{5}{9}x^2 - 2\frac{1}{2}\frac{3}{4}x + 5 = 0.$

To solve any of the foregoing equations by the "Sturm Theorem" and the "Horner Method," the task is difficult.

THE QUINTIC AND SOLUTIONS.

285. To find the roots of

$$(A) \qquad x^5 - q = 0.$$

SOLUTION.

(1) Sum of squares of roots $= 0$. (Th. II.)

(2) Sum of squares of products of roots $p_4 = 0$. (Th. V.)

(3) $\therefore$ Only one real root with sign contrary to sign of absolute term.

(4) The real root is $(q)^{\frac{1}{5}}$.

(5) The other roots are equal to conjugate imaginaries.

(6) $(x^5 - q) \div x - (q)^{\frac{1}{5}} =$

$$(B) \qquad x^4 + (q)^{\frac{1}{5}}x^3 + (q^2)^{\frac{1}{5}}x^2 + (q^3)^{\frac{1}{5}}x + (q^4)^{\frac{1}{5}} = 0.$$

The formula for the solution of (B) is

$$(p) \qquad x^2 + \left(\frac{(q)^{\frac{1}{5}} + \sqrt{5(q^2)^{\frac{1}{5}}}}{2}\right)x + (q^2)^{\frac{1}{5}} = 0.$$

$$(q) \qquad x^2 + \left(\frac{(q)^{\frac{1}{5}} - \sqrt{5(q^2)^{\frac{1}{5}}}}{2}\right)x + (q^2)^{\frac{1}{5}} = 0.$$

To illustrate numerically, we take the equation

$$(C) \qquad x^5 - 3 = 0.$$

(1) The real root is $(3)^{\frac{1}{5}}$, and $(x^5 - 3) \div x - (3)^{\frac{1}{5}} =$

$$(D) \qquad x^4 + (3)^{\frac{1}{5}}x^3 + (9)^{\frac{1}{5}}x^2 + (27)^{\frac{1}{5}}x + (81)^{\frac{1}{5}} = 0.$$

The quadratics for the solution of (D) will then be

$$(p') \qquad x^2 + \left(\frac{(3)^{\frac{1}{5}} + \sqrt{5(3^2)^{\frac{1}{5}}}}{2}\right)x + (9)^{\frac{1}{5}} = 0.$$

$$(q') \qquad x^2 + \left(\frac{(3)^{\frac{1}{5}} - \sqrt{5(3^2)^{\frac{1}{5}}}}{2}\right)x + (9)^{\frac{1}{5}} = 0.$$

NOTE. — See **Universal Solution.**

286. To find the roots of

$$(E) \qquad x^5 + 4\,x^4 - 61\,x^3 - 76\,x^2 + 1068\,x - 1440 = 0.$$

SOLUTION.

(1) $a^2 + b^2 + c^2 + d^2 + e^2 = 138 = (+4)^2 - 2(-61)$. (Th. II.)

(2) $138 \times 5 = 690 = \square$ of sum of roots + sum of $\boxed{S}$ of diffs. of roots. (Th. II.)

(3) $690 - 61 = 629 = \square$ of sum *nearly;* sufficiently near to determine its *Natural.*

(4) The side of the greatest $\square$ in 629 whose side is integral is 25, which is rejected (**26**); 24 is then taken for numerical sum of roots, and we have

(5) $\dfrac{24 + 4}{2} = 14 =$ sum of *plus* roots in formation of equation; true sign $-$.

(6) $\dfrac{24 - 4}{2} = 10 =$ sum of *minus* roots in formation of equation; true sign $+$.

(7) From algebraic sum and signs of terms we see that the equation contains three + roots and two − roots. We now write the *cubic* and *quadratic.*

$$(p) \qquad x^3 - 10\,x^2 + ax - y = 0.$$

$$(q) \qquad x^2 + 14\,x + z = 0.$$

The product of (p) and (q) is

$$(F) \qquad x^5 + 4\,x^4 + (a + z + - 140)\,x^3 + [14\,a - (e + y)]\,x^2$$
$$+ (az + - 14\,y)\,x - zy = 0.$$

If (F) be the true equation, the coefficients of (E) and (F) are equal.

(8) $a + z = 79$. [From third terms.]

(9) $\therefore\ a = 79 - z$. [Transposing (z) in (8).]

(10) $a = \dfrac{10\,z + y - 76}{14}$. [From fourth terms.]

(11) $\therefore\ 79 - z = \dfrac{10\,z + y - 76}{14}$. [From (9) and (10).]

(12) Whence $24\,z + y = 1182$. [Multiplying (11) by 14, and collecting terms.]

(13) $zy = 1440$. [From absolute terms, changing signs.]

(14) $\therefore\ z = 48$ and $y = 30$. [Solving (12) and (13).]

Substituting the values of z and y in the cubic (p) and quadratic (q), we have

(p') $$x^3 - 10x^2 + 31x - 48 = 0.$$

(q') $$x^2 + 14x + 30 = 0.$$

Solving (p') and (q'), we obtain 2, 3, 5, and -6, -8.

2 satisfies equation (E); they are, therefore, the true roots of the equation.

287. To find the roots of

(G) $$x^5 + 25x^4 + 250x^3 + 1250x^2 + 3125x + 3125 = 0.$$

SOLUTION.

(1) $(25)^2 - 2(250) = 125 = a^2 + b^2 + c^2 + d^2 + e^2$. (Th. II.)

(2) $125 \times 4 = 2(250)$. $\therefore$ The roots are equal at least in the Natural. (**138**.) $\therefore\ 25 \div 5 = 5$, and the roots are -5, -5, -5, -5, -5. As they will satisfy the equation, they are therefore the true roots. Should the equation read

(H) $$x^5 + 25x^4 + 250x^3 + 1250x^2 + 3125x + 243 = 0,$$

the real root of (H), and the only one, will be

$$-[5 - \sqrt[5]{(3125 - 243)}].$$

The other four roots of the equation will be found from a biquadratic. Should the absolute term be 3157, then the real root will be

$$-[5 + \sqrt[5]{(3157 - 3125)}] = -7.$$

288. To find the roots of

(I) $$x^5 + 7x^4 + 20x^3 - 30x^2 - 216x - 432 = 0.$$

SOLUTION.

(1) $a^2 + b^2 + c^2 + d^2 + e^2 = 9 = (7)^2 - 2(20)$. (Th. II.)

(2) $\overline{abcd}^2 + \cdots + \overline{bcde}^2 = 20736 = (-216)^2 - 2(-30 \times -432)$. (Th. V.)

(3) Both these results are perfect squares, and we therefore try the square root of 9 (or 3) for the real root. As 3 satisfies the conditions of the equation, it is a root. The square of 3 taken from the

sum of the squares of the roots leaves 0 for the sum of the squares of the remaining roots. $\therefore$ The equation contains imaginary roots. How many? Dividing the equation by $x - 3$ (by synthetic division), we find that the sum of the squares of the roots p_3 of the biquadratic is 0. $\therefore$ *The equation contains four imaginary roots* (**132**), *and only one real + root.*

The roots of the biquadratic may be represented algebraically by $a \pm a\sqrt{-1}$, and $b \pm b\sqrt{-1}$. Their product will be

$$(a \pm a\sqrt{-1})(b \pm b\sqrt{-1}) = 4\,\overline{ab}^2 = \tfrac{432}{3} = 144.$$

Whence, $2\,ab = 12$, and $ab = 6$. Their sum $= +7 - (-3) = 10$.

From $a + b = 10$ and $ab = 6$ the roots are obtained as in the solution of biquadratics.

289. To find the roots of

$$(J) \qquad x^5 + x^4 - 26\,x^3 - 12\,x^2 + 134\,x + 119 = 0.$$

[Submitted for solution by W. M. H. Woodward, United States Interior Department, Santa Fe, N.M.]

SOLUTION IN FULL.

(1) $\quad a^2 + b^2 + c^2 + d^2 + e^2 = 53 = (1)^2 - 2(-26)$. (Th. II.)

To locate roots, and, if possible, to find its Natural.

(2) $53 \times 5 = 265 = \square$ of sum of roots + sum $\boxed{s}$ of diffs. of roots. The side of the greatest integral square in 265 is 16, which is rejected (**26**). 15 is then taken, and we have,

(3) $\dfrac{15+1}{2} = 8 =$ sum of + roots; true sign $-$.

(4) $\dfrac{15-1}{2} = 7 =$ sum of $-$ roots; true sign $+$.

(5) $265 - (15)^2 = 40 =$ sum of $\boxed{s}$ of diffs. of roots.

(6) $40 \times 10 = 400 = \square$ of sum of diffs. + sum of $\boxed{s}$ of the diffs. of diffs. 400 is a perfect square.

$\therefore$ (7) $(400)^{\frac{1}{2}} = 20 =$ sum of diffs. $= (4\,E + 2\,d) - (4\,a + 2\,d)$. (**125**)

We now readily find 1, 2, 3, 4, and 5 for the roots. From algebraic sum and sign of absolute term the equation contains three minus roots and two plus roots. With $-1, -2, -5$, 3, and 4 we build the

Natural

$$(K) \qquad x^5 + x^4 - 27\,x^3 - 13\,x^2 + 134\,x + 120 = 0.$$

(8) $\therefore$ The roots of (J) will be < -1, > -2, $< +3$, $> +4$, < -5.

With the roots of the Natural we find the products of the roots taken *four* and *four*, and locate the roots as in [(1), (**184**)]. We find the sum of the squares of the differences of the roots to two places of decimals to be 44.44+. We now take the square root of the sum of squares of roots multiplied by the degree of the equation within this limit. $53 \times 5 = 265$.

Limit 44.44+

	265. | 14.8512 = sum of roots.
	196.
28.8	69.00
	23.04
2965	45.9600
	1.4825
29701	44.477500
	.029701
297022	44.44779900
	594044
	44.44185856

$$\therefore \frac{14.8512 + 1}{2} = 7.9256 = \text{sum of } + \text{ roots; true sign } -.$$

$$\frac{14.8512 - 1}{2} = 6.9256 = \text{sum } - \text{ roots; true sign } +.$$

We can now separate the equation into a *cubic* and *quadratic*, which solved gives for the roots of the equation

$$-.98770+, \ -2.05745+, \ -4.88055+, \text{ and } 3.4628, 3.4628.$$

290. To find the roots of

$$(L) \qquad x^5 - x^4 - 68\,x^3 - 60\,x^2 + 1160\,x + 2419 = 0.$$

[Submitted for solution by Professor J. B. Young, Safford, Arizona.]

First Solution.

(1) $a^2 + b^2 + c^2 + d^2 + e^2 = 137 = (-1)^2 - 2(-68)$. (Th. II.)

(2) $137 \times 5 = 685 = \square$ of sum of roots + sum $\boxed{s}$ of diffs.

(3) The side of the greatest integral square in 685 is 26, which is rejected. (**26.**) 25 is then taken, and we have

(4) $\frac{25 + - 1}{2} = 12 =$ sum + roots; true sign $-$.

(5) $\frac{25 - (-1)}{2} = 13 =$ sum $-$ roots; true sign $+$.

The digits that will satisfy these numbers are readily found to be 3, 4, 5, 6, and 7; and from sign of absolute term and algebraic sum it is seen that three of the roots are *minus*, and two *plus*.

The product of 3, 4, 5, 6, and 7 is 2520, > 2419. $\therefore$ The roots of (L) will be

$$<-3, \; >-4, \; <-5, \text{ and } >6, \text{ and } <7. \quad (\mathbf{113.})$$

We now write the cubic and quadratic,

(p) $$x^3 + 12x^2 + ax + y = 0.$$

(q) $$x^2 - 13x + z = 0.$$

Their product will be

(M) $$x^5 - x^4 + (z + a + -156)x^3 + (12z + y + -13a)x^2 + (az + -13y)x + zy = 0.$$

The coefficients of (M) are equal to the coefficients of (L).

(1) $\therefore z + a + -156 = -68$. Whence $z + a = 88$, and $a = 88 - z$.

(2) $12z + y - 13a = -60$. Whence $a = \frac{60 + 12z + y}{13}$.

(3) $\therefore \frac{60 + 12z + y}{13} = 88 - z = 25z + y = 1084$.

(4) $\therefore z = \frac{1084 - y}{25}$.

(5) $z = \frac{2419}{y}$. (From absolute terms.)

(6) $\therefore \frac{1084 - y}{25} = \frac{2419}{y}$.

(7) $y^2 - 10849 = -60475$. [Reducing (6).]

(8) $y = 59$. [Solving (7).]

(9) $z = 41 = \frac{2419}{59}$.

We now complete the cubic and quadratic by introducing the values of a, z, and y, and we have

(p') $$x^3 + 12x^2 + 47x + 59 = 0.$$

(q') $$x^2 - 13x + 41 = 0.$$

Solving (q'), we obtain for two of the roots

$$6.5 \pm .5\sqrt{5}.$$

Letting $x = y - 4$, and applying formula (F, **214**), to (p'), we have

$$(N) \qquad y^3 - y - 1 = 0.$$

y is >1. $\therefore\ y = \sqrt[3]{2 + \text{increment } y} = 1.324717950\dot{5}$.

$\therefore\ x = 1.3247179505 + -4 = -2.6752820495$.

The other two roots of (p') are now easily found to be

$$-4.66235897525 \pm \sqrt{-.06615823338455+}.$$

$\therefore$ Equation (L) contains two real $+$ roots, and one real $-$ root, and a pair of real imaginaries.

Second Solution for (L).

(1) When we discover that the sum of roots is 25, and that the roots of the *Natural* are

$$-3,\ -4,\ -5,\ 6, \text{ and } 7,$$

we see that the only change has been in that of the absolute term. If we should approxmate the sum of the roots, we cannot find a closer approximation than 24.99999 to five places of decimals. We may, therefore, at once write

(1) $24.99999 = \text{sum of roots}$.

(2) $\therefore\ \dfrac{24.99999 + -1}{2} = 11.999995 = \text{sum of } + \text{ roots}$; true sign $-$.

(3) $\dfrac{24.99999 - (-1)}{2} = 12.99999 = \text{sum of } - \text{ roots}$; true sign $+$.

We may now form the cubic and quadratic,

$$(p') \qquad x^3 + 11.99999x + ax + y = 0.$$

$$(q') \qquad x^2 - 12.99999x + z = 0.$$

We can readily see the labor that is required to solve (p') and (q'), and that the first solution is the most ready method.

Remark. — *The solution of $y^3 - y - 1 = 0$ is, practically, the solution of the cubic $x^3 - 6x^2 + 11x - 7 = 0$; and by no other method can any of the roots of the equation (L) be accurately expressed except by the method which we offer in the first solution; and the character (real or imaginary) and the signs of the roots are developed by the solution. The "Horner Method," the "Sturm Theorem," and "Descartes' Rule of Signs" are wholly disregarded.*

DISCUSSION OF THE WANTZEL THEOREM ON THE ALGEBRAICAL SOLUTION OF EQUATIONS OF A DEGREE HIGHER THAN THE FOURTH.

(By W. M. H. Woodward, United States Interior Department, Santa Fe, N. M.)

291. I will give at length Wantzel's demonstration of the impossibility of the algebraical solution of such equations, as it appears in Serret's "Cours d'Algebre Superieure," with such comments as seem proper from time to time.

"Let
$$f(x) = 0$$
be an equation of the mth degree, of which the coefficients are not determined, and designate by
$$x_1,\ x_2,\ \cdots,\ x_m,$$
its m roots, which we will suppose may be expressed algebraically in functions of the coefficients.

If the equation, $f(x) = 0$, is satisfied by the value x_1 of x, whatever may be its coefficients, we must reproduce identically x_1 in substituting in the expression the rational function corresponding to each root, since the roots of the equation are then entirely arbitrary. Likewise, every relation between the roots must be identical, and not cease to exist if we replace these roots by each other in any manner whatever.

Designate by y the first radical which enters in the value of x_1, in following the order of calculation, and let
$$y^n = p;$$
p will depend immediately upon the coefficients of $f(x) = 0$, and will be expressed by a symmetrical function of the roots, $F(x_1, x_2, x_3, \cdots)$; y will be a rational function, $\phi(x_1, x_2, x_3, \cdots)$, of the same roots.

Since the function ϕ is not symmetrical, unless the nth root of p can be extracted exactly, it must change whenever we transpose two roots, x_1, x_2, for example; but the relation

$$\phi^n = F$$

will always be satisfied. Besides, the function F being invariable by this transposition, the values of ϕ are the roots of the equation $y^n = F$, and we have

$$\phi(x_2, x_1, x_3, \cdots) = \alpha\phi(x_1, x_2, x_3, \cdots),$$

α being an nth root of unity."

It now becomes important to know the definition of a symmetrical function.

"Whenever a function of several quantities does not change when we exchange, between themselves, in every possible manner, the quantities which it embraces, this function is called symmetrical" (Serret's "Cours d'Algebre Superieure," 170). According to this definition, if a function changes at all when two of the quantities which it involves are exchanged, it is not symmetrical, although it may not change when another two are exchanged. For example, take the function, $ab + ac + ad + bc + bd$, of the quantities a, b, c, and d. If we exchange a and b, we have $ba + bc + bd + ac + ad$, which is identical with the first function. Also, if we exchange c and d, the resulting function is identical with the first. But if we exchange a and c, we have

$$cb + ca + cd + ba + bd,$$

in which we have cd where we at first had ad. In like manner, if we exchange a and d, we have a function with cd in place of ac. If we exchange b and c, the resulting function replaces bd with cd. Also, if we exchange b and d, we see that bc is replaced with cd. From this we know that because a function is not symmetrical, it does not necessarily follow that its value changes whenever two of the quantities which it involves are exchanged. Although it is not proven, it appears that in this particular case the function actually does change its value with each interchange of the roots of the equation.

Resuming the demonstration: "If we transpose the roots x_1 and x_2 there comes

$$\phi(x_1, x_2, x_3, \cdots) = \alpha\phi(x_2, x_1, x_3, \cdots),$$

from which, on multiplying in order,

$$\alpha^2 = 1.$$

This result proves that the number n, supposed prime, is necessarily equal to 2. *Then the first radical which occurs in the value of the unknown must be of the second degree.* This is what happens, in fact, for the equations which we know how to solve.

The function ϕ having only two values, changes with every transposition, and will not be changed (No. 493, Serret's "Cours d'Algebre Superieure") by a circular substitution of three or of five letters, because each of these substitutions is equivalent to an even number of transpositions."

Since the mere fact that a function is not symmetrical does not necessarily prove that it will change in value by every exchange of two letters, it is allowable, till the contrary is proved, to suppose that possibly some of the transpositions do not change the value of the function. If this is the case, it may be changed by a circular substitution of three letters, if two of the letters by being exchanged do not affect the value of the function, although the function admits of only two values.

Returning to Wantzel's demonstration:

"Continue the series of operations indicated to form the value x_1 of x.

We will combine the first radical with the coefficients of $f(x) = 0$, or the function ϕ with some symmetrical functions of the roots, with the aid of the first operations of algebra, and we will thus obtain a function of the roots susceptible of two values, and, consequently, invariable by the circular substitution of three letters."

That a function is susceptible of two values does not necessarily prove that it changes its value with every transposition of the letters involved, and if by some interchange its value does not change, it is not necessarily invariable by the circular substitution of three letters.

"The subsequent radicals will be able to give still some functions of the same kind, if they are of the second degree. Suppose that we let α be a radical for which the equivalent rational function is not invariable by these substitutions; designating it always by

$$y = \phi(x_1, x_2, x_3, \cdots).$$

In the equation $y^n = p$

we still make $p = F(x_1, x_2, x_3, \cdots)$;

this function will not be symmetrical, but only invariable by the circular substitution of three letters. If we replace

$$x_1, x_2, x_3$$

by

$$x_2, x_3, x_1$$

in ϕ, the relation $\phi^n = F$

will always remain; and, since F does not change by this substitution, we have

$$\phi(x_2, x_3, x_1, x_4, \cdots) = \alpha\phi(x_1, x_2, x_3, x_4, \cdots),$$

α designating an nth root of unity.

"By making in this equation the circular substitution

$$(x_1, x_2, x_3),$$

and by repeating this substitution, we will have

$$\phi(x_3, x_1, x_2, x_4, \cdots) = \alpha\phi(x_2, x_3, x_1, x_4, \cdots),$$
$$\phi(x_1, x_2, x_3, x_4, \cdots) = \alpha\phi(x_3, x_1, x_2, x_4, \cdots);$$

then, by multiplying together the three preceding equations, we will conclude that

$$\alpha^3 = 1.$$

Thus, n will be equal to 3.

If the number of the quantities $x_1, x_2, x_3, x_4, \cdots$ is greater than four, or if the equation $f(x) = 0$ is of a degree higher than the fourth, we will be able to effect in ϕ a circular substitution of five letters, for example,

$$(x_1, x_2, x_3, x_4, x_5);$$

the function F will not change by this substitution, and we will have

$$\phi(x_2, x_3, x_4, x_5, x_1, \cdots) = \alpha\phi(x_1, x_2, x_3, x_4, x_5, \cdots);$$

then in repeating from another part the same substitution,

$$\phi(x_3, x_4, x_5, x_1, x_2, \cdots) = \alpha\phi(x_2, x_3, x_4, x_5, x_1, \cdots),$$

. . . .

By multiplication we obtain

$$\alpha^5 = 1,$$

which involves $\alpha = 1$, since α is a cube root of unity."

It has been shown that F was invariable by the circular substitution of three letters. Since

$$\phi^2 = F,$$

in order that F may be invariable by the circular substitution of five letters in ϕ, it is necessary that by this circular substitution of five letters, α cannot take more than three values. Until the contrary is proved, it is allowable to suppose that it is possible for α to take more than three values. And since a number can have only three cube roots, $F(=\phi^2)$ will then be variable when we make in ϕ a circular substitution of five letters.

If α is equal to 1, then ϕ must be invariable by the circular substitution of five letters. But there is nothing in the hypothesis to indicate that such is the case. If ϕ is not invariable, then α is one of the imaginary fifth roots of unity, and cannot be at the same time a cube root of unity. If, by hypothesis, α is a cube root of unity, then it is not shown that the equations given above are true. There being five members of equations, each of which is equal to some other multiplied by α, and itself divided by α is equal to one of the others shows that the α used in this case is either unity or an imaginary fifth root of unity. If it be unity, α is invariable by the circular substitution of five letters, and if it be an imaginary fifth root of unity, it cannot involve $\alpha = 1$. If the F here used is the same as the symmetrical function F used in the earlier part of the demonstration, then the only condition we can put on α is that it is a fifth root of unity. Also we will have

$$\phi(x_1, x_2, x_3, x_4, x_5, \cdots) = \alpha\phi(x_2, x_3, x_4, x_5, x_1, \cdots)$$
$$= \beta\phi(x_3, x_4, x_5, x_1, x_2, \cdots) = \gamma\phi(x_4, x_5, x_1, x_2, x_3, \cdots)$$
$$= \delta\phi(x_5, x_1, x_2, x_3, x_4, \cdots),$$

where 1, α, β, γ, δ are the fifth roots of unity. From this we see that α cannot be equal to 1, and therefore is not a cube root of unity, and ϕ is not invariable by the circular substitution of five letters.

"Then, if the degree of the equation is greater than 4, the function ϕ is invariable by the circular substitution of three letters, which is contrary to our hypothesis."

The function ϕ cannot be invariable by the circular substitution of three letters unless $\alpha = 1$, which, *ut supra demonstravimus*, is not the case.

"Then, all the radicals involved in the expression of a root of a general equation of a degree greater than four must be equal to rational functions of the roots, which functions are invariable by the circular substitution of three roots."

This conclusion is based upon the supposition that $\alpha = 1$, which, as we have before shown, is not the case.

"By substituting these functions in the expression x_1, we arrive finally at an equality of the form

$$x_1 = \psi(x_1, x_2, x_3, x_4, x_5, \cdots),$$

which must be identical; but this is impossible, since the second member renders invariable when we replace x_1, x_2, x_3 by x_2, x_3, x_1, while the first member evidently changes."

If α is not equal to one, the second member may change with each exchange of the quantities x_1, x_2, x_3, $\cdots$. If some of these quantities are equal to each other, then no change will be caused in either member by interchanging those equal.

"Then, it is impossible to solve by radicals the general equation of the fifth degree, or of a degree higher than five."

If we should accept his demonstration as true, we would be forced to the conclusion that the general equation of a degree higher than four was destitute of roots. The conclusion of Wantzel that the roots cannot be indicated in algebraical language is equivalent to saying that there are no roots, since it is absurd to say that finite quantities exist which cannot be expressed in any function or other finite quantities, which are themselves symmetrical functions of the first, however complicated. Cauchy has demonstrated that an equation of the mth degree has precisely m roots. While we have not learned how to form these functions, still they must exist.

NOTE.—The above has particular reference to an equation of the fifth degree, where it is stated that α must be one of the fifth roots of unity. nth should be substituted for fifth in that and similar places. It is proved, though not stated, that when a circular substitution of five letters takes place, n is equal to five. Since in an equation of the fifth degree it is impossible to have a circular substitution of more than five roots, the degree of the highest radical is not greater than five, or, generally, the degree of the highest radical is not greater than five, the degree of the equation.

INTERPRETATION OF IMAGINARY QUANTITIES.

292. General Theorem of Imaginary Quantities. — *An Imaginary Quantity is the indicated square root of the difference of the squares (with its sign changed) of the bases of two right triangles having a common perpendicular which is the radius of a circle; two of such triangles lying wholly within the semicircle, and two partly within and partly without the semicircle.*

Dem. — Let $ABCE$ be a ⊙. Draw AC, its diameter. Let AC, bisected in O, be the centre. Draw $OE \perp$ to AC. Then draw the lines or chords EA and EC; and the line EF to meet OA extended in F; and the line EG to meet OC extended in G. Then we have by construction four rt. ⊿s:

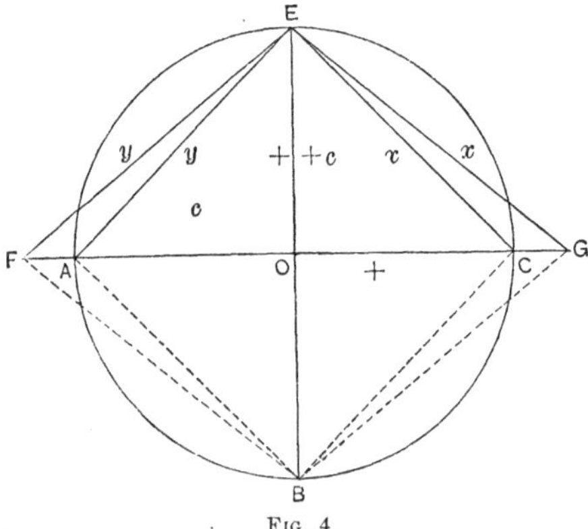

Fig. 4.

two in the upper right-hand quadrant, one being wholly within and the other partly within and without the quadrant; and two equivalent ⊿s in the upper left-hand quadrant.

Designate *distance* above and to the right of the centre O, $+$; and to the left and below the centre O, $-$.

Let $AC = 2c$, *a real quantity.* Then will OE and OC be each equal to $+c$; and OA and OB be each equal to $-c$. Then will the lines EA, EC, EF, and EG be $+$, being above the centre O; and by changing the $\triangle$ to the lower semi-circle the lines are *minus;* and the lines FA and CG remain unchanged in sign, FA being *minus* and CG *plus.*

Designate all lines by x to the left and y to the right.

Then, from the rt. $\triangle$ EOA and EOC, we have the equation

(1) $$x^2 + y^2 = 4\,c^2.$$

As EA and EC are equal by construction, and drawn in the semicircle AEC, their rectangle will equal one-half the square of AC. As $AC = 2\,c$, $\overline{AC}^2 = 4\,c^2$. Therefore,

(2) $$xy = 2\,c^2.$$

From (1) and (2) we find $x = \sqrt{2\,c^2}$, and $y = \sqrt{2\,c^2}$.

Let us now increase the rectangle xy by any real quantity, say b, letting (x^2+y^2) always remain permanent $(4\,c^2)$. Then

(3) $$xy = 2\,c^2 + b.$$

From (1) and (3) we find

$$x = (2\,c^2 + \tfrac{1}{2}\,b)^{\frac{1}{2}} + (-\tfrac{1}{2}\,b)^{\frac{1}{2}},$$

and $$y = (2\,c^2 + \tfrac{1}{2}\,b)^{\frac{1}{2}} - (-\tfrac{1}{2}\,b)^{\frac{1}{2}}.$$

We now meet with this so-called "imaginary," which, while it may be seen, we are wont to call it (only and at best) an optical illusion, a kind of "plug," as our early mathematicians would call it, "to fill a vacuum so much abhorred by nature."

We will now proceed to demonstrate that this imaginary quantity, $\pm\sqrt{-\tfrac{1}{2}\,b}$, and all like expressions of quantity, are such as is claimed for it in the definition (**22**), upon which the foregoing theorem is based.

(1) We have shown that $EA = \sqrt{2\,c^2}$. Let us assume that $EF = \sqrt{2\,c^2 + \tfrac{1}{2}\,b}$. Then, to find OF, we have

$$\overline{EF}^2 - \overline{EO}^2 = \overline{OF}^2 = (\sqrt{2\,c^2 + \tfrac{1}{2}\,b})^2 - (c)^2$$
$$= (2\,c^2 + \tfrac{1}{2}\,b) - c^2 = c^2 + \tfrac{1}{2}\,b = \overline{OF}^2.$$

If we take from $\overline{OF}^2$, $\overline{OA}^2$, we will have the difference of the squares of the bases of the two rt. $\triangle$ *EOA* and *EOF*. Therefore,

$$(\overline{OF}^2 - \overline{OA}^2) = (c^2 + \tfrac{1}{2}b) - c^2 = \tfrac{1}{2}b;$$

and changing its sign, on reversing the subtraction, we have $-\frac{1}{2}b$, the differences of the squares of the bases of the two rt. $\triangle$ *EOA* and *EOF*.

Indicating the square root of $-\frac{1}{2}b$, we have $\sqrt{-\frac{1}{2}b}$; and it being left of the centre *O*, its sign is *minus* by hypothesis. Therefore, $-\sqrt{-\frac{1}{2}b}$ is the indicated square root of the difference of the squares of the bases of the two rt. $\triangle$ *EOA* and *EOF*; and the line $EF = \sqrt{2c^2 + \frac{1}{2}b}$. Again: As the $\triangle$ *EOG* and *EOC* are equivalent by construction to the $\triangle$ *EOA* and *EOF*, the line $EC = \sqrt{2c^2}$, and the line $EG = \sqrt{2c^2 + \frac{1}{2}b}$, while the line *GC* represents $+\sqrt{-\frac{1}{2}b}$.

Therefore, in the expression $\sqrt{2c^2 + \frac{1}{2}b} \pm \sqrt{-\frac{1}{2}b}$ the imaginary part, $(-\frac{1}{2}b)$, affected by the radical *is*, and simply means, the indicated square root of the difference of the squares, with its sign changed, of the bases of two right triangles, having a common perpendicular, the radius of a circle.

By reversing the triangles to the lower semicircle, we have the imaginary, $-\sqrt{2c^2 + \frac{1}{2}b} \pm \sqrt{-\frac{1}{2}b}$, which is represented by the dotted lines *BF* and *BG*, the only change being that of the sign of the real part of the imaginary.

Hence the theorem, "An Imaginary Quantity," etc.

293. The real part of an imaginary quantity is either plus or minus; and in this respect it does not differ from real quantities: the sign of its real part being determined by the position it occupies from an assumed point called the centre.

294. The product of a pair of conjugate imaginaries is a *plus quantity.* This is the old rule, and it is true; *but the reason given for the rule is false.*

295. Imaginary quantities are added, subtracted, and divided the same as real quantities; but with respect to multiplication the general law governing the functions of the signs *plus* and *minus* have been reversed when we consider the product of a pair of imaginary quantities. *This is a grave mistake. Why should there be an exception?* Should there be an exception to the universal law, *that the product of a plus and minus quantity is other than a minus quantity, the whole theory of algebraic operations must fall to the ground.* But, happily, there is no exception to the universal law governing the functions of the signs plus and minus in algebraic operations. There is no reason for the old rule "*that the product of two imaginary terms is real, with the sign before the radical, as by the common rule reversed.*"

296. *We will now give some practical illustrations.*

Let it be required to find the product of

$$a+\sqrt{-b}, \text{ and } a-\sqrt{-b}.$$

The operation in full will be,

(1) $\qquad a+\sqrt{-b}$

(2) $\qquad a-\sqrt{-b}$

(3) $\qquad a^2+a\sqrt{-b}$, multiplying (1) by a in (2).

(4) $\quad -a\sqrt{-b}-(-b)$, multiplying (1) by $-\sqrt{-b}$ in (2).

Adding (3) and (4), we have

(5) $\qquad a^2-(-b)=$

(6) $\qquad a^2+b.$

In (5), $-(-b)$ changes its sign in accordance with the law governing the sign $-$, as used in algebraic operations.

Again, $(a+\sqrt{-b})^2+(a-\sqrt{-b})^2=2\,a^2+-2\,b$.

The process in full will be,

(1) $(a+\sqrt{-b})^2=a^2+2\,a\sqrt{-b}+-b$.

(2) $(a-\sqrt{-b})^2=a^2-2\,a\sqrt{-b}+-b$.

Adding (1) and (2), we have $2\,a^2+-2\,b$, the middle terms having the same numerical value, but of opposite signs, cancel each other in the process of addition.

297. If we multiply $\sqrt{-a}$ by $\sqrt{-b}$, the common rule is still in force, as illustrated in the following process:

(1) $+\sqrt{-a}=\sqrt{a}\times\sqrt{-1}$,

(2) $+\sqrt{-b}=\sqrt{b}\times\sqrt{-1}$,

(3) $\sqrt{a}\times\sqrt{b}=\sqrt{ab}$,

(4) $(\sqrt{-1})(\sqrt{-1})=-1$.

(5) $\therefore\ -1\times\sqrt{ab}=-\sqrt{ab}$.

The $\sqrt{-1}$ may be taken as the universal factor, and its square is always ~~a~~ -1. Properly speaking, $(+\sqrt{-1})^2=+-1$; but the real part of the imaginary is 0, and being 0, $0+-1=-1$. We therefore omit the sign + in the operation. The product of $+1+\sqrt{-1}$ by itself is equal to its square. That is,

$$(1+\sqrt{-1})^2=(1+\sqrt{-1})(1+\sqrt{-1})$$
$$=1+2\sqrt{-1}+-1=+2\sqrt{-1},$$

— the numerals $+1$, and -1, cancel one another in the process of addition; and the *law* of the signs + and −, as used in algebraic operations, is the same as the application of the signs to real quantities. *Then there is no exception to the universal rule, and imaginary quantities are added, subtracted, multiplied, and divided the same as real quantities.*

298. The square root of a binomial surd in the form of $a \pm \sqrt{b}$ may be found when $a^2 - b$ is a perfect square; in which case the root may be expressed in the form of another binomial surd.

299. Returning again to the interpretation of an imaginary quantity, we notice that the sum of the squares of $\sqrt{2\,c^2 + \frac{1}{2}\,b} + \sqrt{-\frac{1}{2}\,b}$ and $\sqrt{2\,c^2 + \frac{1}{2}\,b} - \sqrt{-\frac{1}{2}\,b}$ is a *plus quantity*, which is equal to the square of the diameter AC of the circle, Fig. 4. The sum of the squares being a plus quantity, the imaginary is Real (**24**). We will thus conclude that we have accounted for all Real Imaginaries.

300. We will now take up the other class, known as Pure Imaginaries. To do so, let us take the imaginaries $\sqrt{2\,c^2 + \frac{1}{2}\,b} \pm \sqrt{-\frac{1}{2}\,b}$, which are real according to the definition, and let us begin to decrease this imaginary by *reducing* the sum of the squares of the pair. Let us write

(1) $$\sqrt{c^2 + \tfrac{1}{2}\,b} + \sqrt{-\tfrac{1}{2}\,b}, \text{ and}$$

(2) $$\sqrt{c^2 + \tfrac{1}{2}\,b} - \sqrt{-\tfrac{1}{2}\,b}.$$

Where are we now? To answer this question let us find the sum of the squares of (1) and (2).

(3) $$(\sqrt{c^2+\tfrac{1}{2}b}+\sqrt{-\tfrac{1}{2}b})^2 = c^2+\tfrac{1}{2}b+2\sqrt{c^2+\tfrac{1}{2}b}\sqrt{-\tfrac{1}{2}b}+-\tfrac{1}{2}b.$$

(4) $$(\sqrt{c^2+\tfrac{1}{2}b}-\sqrt{-\tfrac{1}{2}b})^2 = c^2+\tfrac{1}{2}b-2\sqrt{c^2+\tfrac{1}{2}b}\sqrt{-\tfrac{1}{2}b}+-\tfrac{1}{2}b.$$

Adding the results of (3) and (4), we have

(5) $$x^2 + y^2 = 2\,c^2.$$

As $2\,c^2$ is a real quantity, we are still in the field of the Real Imaginary.

Let us now write the imaginaries

(6) $$\sqrt{\tfrac{1}{2}\,b} + \sqrt{-\tfrac{1}{2}\,b},$$

(7) $$\sqrt{\tfrac{1}{2}\,b} - \sqrt{-\tfrac{1}{2}\,b}.$$

What have we now?

(8) $(\sqrt{\tfrac{1}{2}b}+\sqrt{-\tfrac{1}{2}b})^2=\tfrac{1}{2}b+2\sqrt{\tfrac{1}{2}b}\sqrt{-\tfrac{1}{2}b}+-\tfrac{1}{2}b.$

(9) $(\sqrt{\tfrac{1}{2}b}-\sqrt{-\tfrac{1}{2}b})^2=\tfrac{1}{2}b-2\sqrt{\tfrac{1}{2}b}\sqrt{-\tfrac{1}{2}b}+-\tfrac{1}{2}b.$

Adding the results of (8) and (9), we have

(10) $$x^2+y^2=0.$$

The real parts of the imaginaries have been reduced to such an extent that the sum of the squares has become zero. The circle has been swept away, in consequence of which the *inner* and *outer* triangles have disappeared, and the only tangible quantity remaining being the indicated square root, *with its sign changed, of the difference of the squares of the bases of before existing triangles,* and its numerically equivalent real parts. *We are now in the field of the Imaginary Origin, which is the dividing line between the Real and the Pure.*

301. Referring to Fig. 4, we can readily see, letting the expressions $(-\sqrt{-\tfrac{1}{2}b})$ and $(+\sqrt{-\tfrac{1}{2}b})$ remain permanent, that as the circle grows smaller, the lines *EF*, *EG*, *EA*, and *EC* gradually grow less, while the lines *FA* and *GC* continually approach the centre *O*. The angles *EFO* and *EGO* become smaller as the *difference between the intercepted arcs which determines their magnitude* is diminished. When the circle disappears, the angles disappear, and *FA* and *CG* come together at the centre, and the lines *EF* and *EG* become the lines *FO* and *GO*, for the point *E* has become merged in the point *O*. They maintain, however, their original signs.

302. The sum of the squares and the angles of an Imaginary Origin are each equal to zero, and the magnitude of the imaginary expression $\pm\sqrt{-b}$ is immediately determined by changing its sign and extracting the square root.

303. Let us now take the numerical imaginary $2 \pm \sqrt{-4}$. The sum of the squares is 0. It is, therefore, an Imaginary Origin, and its unit is $1 \pm \sqrt{-1}$. Let us decrease its real part so that the imaginary will read $1 \pm \sqrt{-4}$.

What kind of an imaginary have we now?

(1) $$(1+\sqrt{-4})^2 = 1 + -4 + 2\sqrt{-4}.$$

(2) $$(1-\sqrt{-4})^2 = 1 + -4 - 2\sqrt{-4}.$$

Adding (1) and (2), we have

(3) $$x^2 + y^2 = -6.$$

304. The sum of the squares is a *minus* quantity, and we are, therefore, *in the field of the Pure Imaginary according to our definition.*

305. If the imaginary, $a \pm \sqrt{-b}$, be *Real,* then the magnitude of the imaginary part, $\pm \sqrt{-b}$ is a variable quantity; and if it be an *Imaginary Origin* or a *Pure Imaginary,* then is $\pm \sqrt{-b}$ a definite and fixed quantity, because its numerical magnitude is found by changing its sign and extracting its square root.

306. We will now conclude that we have accounted for all kinds and classes of *conjugate imaginaries.* The question that will now arise in the mind of the thoughtful student is this: *What shall be done with the general imaginary,* $a + b\sqrt{-1}$?

307. The **General Imaginary,** $a + b\sqrt{-1}$, is the product of a pair of conjugate imaginaries; and the imaginary part $(b\sqrt{-1})$ may be defined to mean the indicated square root, with its sign changed, of the difference of the squares of the perpendiculars of two right triangles having a common base which is the radius of a circle. In this respect the general imaginary does not differ from the conjugate imaginary from which it is derived. The following theorem may be used in the demonstration and illustration of the general imaginary.

308. Proposition. Theorem VI. *If a secant, drawn from either terminus of the diameter of a circle, be produced to meet another line proceeding from the centre of the circle, and perpendicular to its diameter, then twice the square of the secant, diminished by twice the difference between the square of the whole perpendicular and the radius of the circle, is equal to the square of the diameter.*

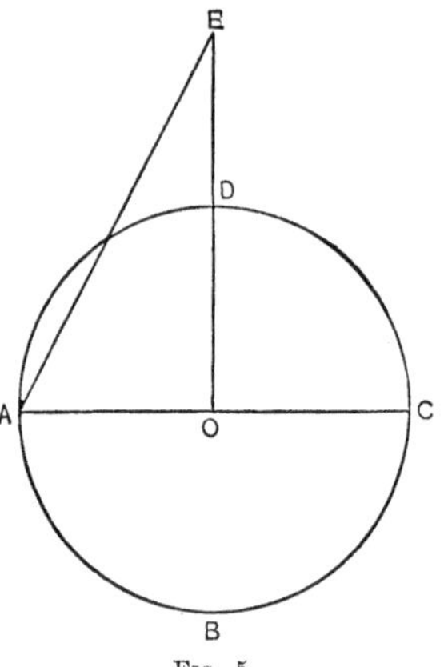

Fig. 5.

For demonstration.

Let $ABCD$ be such circle. Let AC be its diameter, bisected in O. Let AE be such secant, and OE the whole perpendicular. Then prove that

$$2\overline{AE}^2 - 2[\overline{OE}^2 - \overline{OD}^2] = \overline{AC}^2.$$

In the demonstration let the line AE represent the real part of the general imaginary, and the line DE the imaginary part.

309. The general imaginary is *Real* when the square of the real part is numerically or algebraically greater than the square of its imaginary; and when the square of the real part is less than the square of the imaginary part, it is *Pure;* and when they are equal, a *general origin.*

310. The signs + and −, occurring in general or conjugate imaginaries, are the result of position from an assumed point called the *centre* or *origin.*

THE UNIVERSAL SOLUTION.

We will now introduce what shall hereafter be called the *Universal Solution*, and for which we advance the following definition:

311. The **Universal Solution** is a method by which the roots of any *numerical* or *literal* equation can be expressed in terms of the coefficients of such equation.

REMARK. — *General solutions* for equations of a degree *higher* than *four* have been looked upon as a discovery to be hoped for, rather than expected; *but no one ever dreamed that a solution, not only general, but universal in its application, would be discovered. Able* demonstrated, we are told, that if an equation, containing *literal* coefficients, be of a degree higher than *four*, *it could not be solved;* and, later, *Wantzel*, in that elegant French work, Serret's "Cours d'Algèbre Supérieure," gives a rather plausible demonstration of the impossibility to solve by radicals *any* equation higher than the *fourth degree*. But, when *truths* are *hidden*, by assuming a *false* hypothesis, the truth is made to assume and partake the nature of such hypothesis; and, if the hypothesis be true, by false reasoning we arrive at incorrect conclusions. We will not attempt to demonstrate the possibility of a *general*, or *universal* solution, *but we will proceed at once to that which is higher — the actual solution itself.*

GENERAL SOLUTION OF THE FOURTH DEGREE.

312. We will begin the universal solution with a general solution of the *fourth degree*, — it being correctly considered that a general solution of the *Cubic* has been accomplished. General solutions are claimed for the *fourth* by Descartes, Euler, Simpson, and others, — some of them requiring the removal of the second term, while others do not. None of them, however, are of much practical use, as they do not *simplify* the solution, *and will not render the roots unless certain relations exist between them.*

313. It may not be out of place, at this time, to remark that general solutions for equations of *any* degree, requiring the removal of the second term, are *not* discoveries of the relations that exist between the roots and the coefficients of the equation, but fitful inventions that do not satisfy the mind of the thoughtful and progressive student of mathematics. Such methods are simply *devices*, applicable when certain relations exist between the roots, and are not based upon the relations of the roots to the coefficients. If we possess the knowledge of such existing relations, there is no need to apply the device.

314. We will now take up Cardan's method, and interpret the meaning of the imaginary expressions in what is generally known as the "irreducible" case. Take the general equation $x^3 + mx^2 + nx + q = 0$, which becomes, on removal of the second term, either

$$(A) \qquad x'^3 - px' \pm q = 0,$$

$$\text{or } (B) \qquad x'^3 + px' \pm q = 0.$$

Letting $x' = z + \frac{p}{3z}$, A becomes, by Cardan's formula,

$$(C) \qquad z^6 \pm qz^3 = \frac{-p^3}{27}.$$

Solving (C) by quadratics, we have

$$x' = \left(\frac{-q}{2} + \sqrt{\frac{q^2}{4} + \frac{p^3}{27}}\right)^{\frac{1}{3}} + \left(\frac{-q}{2} - \sqrt{\frac{q^2}{4} + \frac{p^3}{27}}\right)^{\frac{1}{3}}.$$

Now, by letting $x = x' + \frac{m}{3}$, the roots of the general or original equation are obtained.

When the roots of (A) are all *real*, and two of them equal, there is no need to apply Cardan's formula; because $\left(\frac{p}{3}\right)^{\frac{1}{2}}$ renders one of the equal roots, $\frac{-p}{3}$ being always a perfect square when two of the roots are real and equal.

Representing the roots of (A) by a, a, and $-2a$, then

$$(x-a)(x-a)(x+2a)=x^3-3a^2+2a^3=0.$$

Putting $-3a^2=-p$, changing signs, and taking the square root of both members, we have $a=\sqrt{\frac{p}{3}}$. When two of the roots are imaginary we may represent them algebraically by $a+\sqrt{-l}$, $a-\sqrt{-l}$, and $-2a$, or the signs of the real parts may be reversed. Then on multiplying together

$$(x-a+\sqrt{-l})(x-a-\sqrt{-l})(x+2a),$$
$$=x^3\pm(3a^2+l)x+2a(a^2+l)=0.$$

When l is numerically greater than $4a^2$, the coefficient of x will be *plus;* and when $4a^2>l$, the coefficient will be *minus.*

Letting $x^3-(3a^2+l)x+2a(a^2+l)=x^3-px+q=0$, l may be found in terms of p and q; and p and q in terms of l. By an algebraic process we arrive at the formula

(D) $$6p\sqrt{l}+8l\sqrt{l}=\sqrt{27q^2-4p^3}.$$

D gives us a formula by which l may be found as a real quantity, which may be illustrated by the solution of

(E) $$x^3-2x-5=0.$$

E containing two imaginary roots, applying formula (D), we have

(F) $$12\sqrt{l}+8l\sqrt{l}=\sqrt{643}.$$

Squaring both sides of (F), and dividing by 64, we have

(G) $$l^3+3l^2+\tfrac{9}{4}l=\tfrac{643}{64}.$$

(1) l is found from (G) to be 1.290359+.

(2) $\therefore\ 3a^2-1.290359=2$. Whence

(3) $a=\sqrt{\frac{3.290359}{3}}=1.047275+$.

(4) $\therefore\ 2a=2.09455+$.

(5) $\therefore$ The roots of (E) are 2.09455+, and

$$-1.047275\pm\sqrt{-1.290359}.$$

315. When $27q^2 + 4p^3$ is *minus*, the roots are *all real*, but *unequal;* and when *plus*, only one real root, and two imaginary roots; and when *zero*, the roots are *all real* and *two* of them *equal*. This will be found to be true of all cubic equations in the form of $x^3 \pm px \pm q = 0$.

It is, therefore, evident that when $\frac{q^2}{4} + \frac{p^3}{27}$ in Cardan's formula is +, only one real and two imaginary roots; and when *minus*, the roots are all *real*, but unequal; and when *zero*, all real, and two of them equal.

316. It now being known that the roots of any cubic equation can be expressed in terms of its coefficients, that if we can change an equation of the *Fourth Degree*, or an equation of any degree *higher than four*, to an equation of the *third degree*, that the roots of the given equation, whether it be of the *fourth degree*, or of a degree higher than four, can likewise be expressed in terms of the coefficients of the given equation. Then, *to evolve a general solution of the fourth degree*, we must change it to an equation of the *third degree* whose coefficients are functions of *all* the coefficients of the *fourth*. That is, the coefficients of the *third* must be made up from true combinations of the coefficients of the *fourth*. A failure to thus reduce the *fourth* to an equation of the *third* degree must necessarily give us a formula as faulty as the old, — for *none* of the old methods for solving the *fourth* are *true;* and they cannot and will not render the roots in all cases. Four quantities are to be considered in a general solution of the *fourth degree*. These four *quantities* are its *coefficients*, which are functions of its roots and of each other. All the old methods, *as well as the one we shall offer*, depend upon the solution of a cubic. If the old methods produce a true cubic, then they will render the roots of the fourth. If the student will take the time to change the following biquadratics to a cubic by any of the old methods, and then find the roots of such cubic by the Horner method, and with these roots the roots of the *fourth*, he will come to the conclusion that none of the old methods will form a *true* cubic in all cases. Take, for such trial, the numerical equations,

$$(1)\quad x^4 + 7x^3 + 16x^2 + 26.25x + 11 = 0.$$

$$(2)\quad x^4 - 22x^3 + 151x^2 - 352x + 217 = 0.$$

$$(3)\quad x^4 + 17x^3 - 22x^2 - 117x - 11 = 0.$$

317. We will now proceed to a general solution of the *fourth degree*, which will be found to be *true* and *universal* in its application to all kinds and classes of equations of the fourth degree. Our aim shall be to bring it within the comprehension of all who understand the formation of equations.

318. Let, for convenience, the quantities a, b, c, and d represent the roots of the general equation of the fourth degree, which is

$$(H)\qquad x^4 + mx^3 + nx^2 + ox + q = 0.$$

The following relations of the roots to the coefficients are known to exist:

$$(1)\qquad a + b + c + d = -m.$$

$$(2)\qquad ab + ac + ad + bc + bd + cd = +n.$$

$$(3)\qquad abc + abd + acd + bcd = -o.$$

$$(4)\qquad abcd = +q.$$

From (2) we can form the following quadratics:

$$(e)\qquad y^2 + (ab + cd)y + q = 0,$$

$$(f)\qquad y^2 + (ac + bd)y + q = 0,$$

$$(g)\qquad y^2 + (ad + bc)y + q = 0.$$

Letting $ab + cd = s$, $ac + bd = t$, $ad + bc = u$, and substituting these values in ($\dot{e}$), (f), and (g), on multiplying the three quadratics together, we have

$$(I) \quad y^6 + (s+t+u)y^5 + [(st+su+tu)+3q]y^4 + [2q(t+s+u)+tsu]y^3 + [q(ts+tu+su)+3q^2]y^2 + q^2(s+t+u)y + q^3 = 0.$$

By Th. IV. [Art. 178 — Functions of Squares] we form this equation of the sixth degree, having for the sum of its roots the products of the roots taken *two* and *two*, and represented by ab, ac, ad, bc, bd, cd:

$$(J) \quad y^6 + ny^5 + (mo-q)y^4 + [(m^2-2n)q + 2nq + (o^2-2nq)]y^3 + [q(om-4q)+3q^2]y^2 + q^2ny + q^3 = 0.$$

The roots of (I) and (J) being equal, on comparing term by term with each other, we have

(1) $\quad s+t+u = n.$

(2) $\quad st + su + tu = (mo - 4q) = (mo - q) - (+3q).$

(3) $\quad stu = [(m^2 - 2n)q + (a^2 - 2nq)]$
$\quad = [(m^2-2n)q + 2nq + (o^2 - 2nq)] - 2nq.$

From (1), (2), and (3), we form the cubic

$$(K) \quad y^3 + ny^2 + (mo-4q)y + (m^2-2n)q + (o^2-2nq) = 0.$$

All the coefficients of the general equation (H) are represented in the formula (K). The roots of (K) are readily seen to be no other than the sums of ($ab + cd$), ($ac + bd$), and ($ad + bc$). When these sums are found from (K), by substituting their values in the quadratics (e), (f), and (g), the quantities ab, ac, ad, bc, bd, and cd become known by the solutions of the quadratics. Then,

$$x = \left\{\frac{ac \times ad}{cd}\right\}^{\frac{1}{2}}, \left\{\frac{bc \times bd}{cd}\right\}^{\frac{1}{2}}, \cdots,$$

for the quantities a, b, c, d, or x_1, x_2, x_3, and x_4.

REMARK.—It requires no course of reasoning to convince the reader that (K) is a true formula for all equations of the fourth degree.

319. Again: Let $a'n = ab + cd$; $b'n = ac + bd$; $c'n = ad + bc$.

Then $$(y + a'n)(y + b'n)(y + c'n) =$$

$$(L)\quad y^3 + n(a' + b' + c')y^2 + n^2(a'b' + a'c' + b'c')y + n^3a'b'c' = 0.$$

The coefficients of (L) and (K) being equal, we have

$$(M)\quad y^3 + y^2 + \frac{(mo - 4q)}{n^2}y + \frac{(m^2 - 2n)q + (o^2 - 2nq)}{n^3} = 0.$$

The roots of (M) being represented by a', b', c', which, when obtained from (M), by multiplying, respectively, by n, renders the quantities $(ab + cd)$, $(ac + bd)$, and $(ad + bc)$, either (K) or (M) may be used, but in our opinion (K) has the preference.

320. K and L are not the only formulas that may be used in a general solution of the fourth degree.

$$(H')\quad x^4 + mx^3 + nx^2 + ox + q = 0.$$

By Th. IV., we have, letting o represent the sum of the roots,

$$(N)\quad x^4 + ox^3 + nqx^2 + mq^2x + q^3 = 0.$$

Multiplying (H') and (N) together, we have (writing y for x),

$$(O)\quad y^8 + (m + o)y^7 + (n + mo + nq)y^6 + (o + on + mnq + mq^2)y^5 + (q + o^2 + n^2q + m^2q^2 + q^3)y^4 + (oq + onq + nmq^2 + mq^2)q^3 + (nq^2 + omq^2 + nq^3)y^2 + q^3(m + o)y + q^4 = 0.$$

From the relations of the roots to the coefficients (Art. 318. 1, 3) we can form the following quadratics:

$$(1)\quad y^2 + (a + bcd)y + q = 0.$$

$$(2)\quad y^2 + (b + acd)y + q = 0.$$

$$(3)\quad y^2 + (c + abd)y + q = 0.$$

$$(4)\quad y^2 + (d + abc)y + q = 0.$$

Letting the quantities s, t, u, and v represent, respectively, the coefficients of y in the quadratics, by substitution and multiplication, we have

$$(P)\ y^8 + (s + t + u + v)\,y^7 + (4\,q^2 + p_2)\,y^6 + (3\,q^2p_1 + p_3)\,y^5$$
$$+ (6\,q^2 + 2\,qp_2)\,y^4 + \cdots + q^3(s + t + u + v)\,y + q^4 = 0,$$

The coefficients of (O) and (P) being equal, we can form by comparison the following biquadratic:

$$(Q)\ y^4 + (m + o)\,y^3 + [(n + om + nq) - 4\,q]\,y^2$$
$$+ [(o + on + mnq + mq^2) - 3\,q^2]\,y$$
$$+ [(q + o^2 + n^2q + m^2q^2 + q^3)]$$
$$- \{6\,q^2 + 2\,q[(o + on + mnq + nq) - 3\,q\,(m + o)]\} = 0.$$

(Q) may now be reduced to a *cubic* by formula (K) (Art. 318). The roots of the cubic will be

$$\begin{cases} (1)\ ab + ac + cd\,(a^2 + b^2) + ab\,(c^2 + d^2) + q\,(ab + cd). \\ (2)\ ac + bd + bd\,(c^2 + a^2) + ac\,(b^2 + d^2) + q\,(ac + bd). \\ (3)\ ad + bc + bc\,(a^2 + d^2) + ad\,(c^2 + b^2) + q\,(ad + bc). \end{cases}$$

The sum of these quantities is represented by

$$(n + mo + nq) - 4\,q$$

of the general equation.

Letting the quantities A, B, C, and D represent the coefficients of y^3, y^2, y^1, and y^0 in (Q), we have, by application of the formula (K),

$$(R)\ \ y'^3 + By'^2 + [AC - 4\,D]y' + (A^2 - 2\,B)D + (C^2 - 2\,BD) = 0.$$

It is now seen that the quantities represented in (1), (2), and (3), complex as they really are, can be separately expressed in terms of the coefficients of the general equation; and finally, the quantities $a + bcd$, $b + acd$, $\cdots$; and lastly, a, bcd, b, acd, $\cdots$, can be separately expressed.

321. We will now give a few practical illustrations of the application of formula (K) in the solution of numerical equations of the *fourth degree*.

Take the following equations:

$$\text{(i.)}\quad x^4 + 2x^3 + 2x^2 + 2x + 1 = 0.$$
$$\text{(ii.)}\quad x^4 + 4x^3 + 7x^2 + 7x + 6 = 0.$$
$$\text{(iii.)}\quad x^4 + 6x^3 + 18x^2 + 36x + 36 = 0.$$
$$\text{(iv.)}\quad x^4 - 7x^3 + 24.5x^2 + 14x + 4 = 0.$$
$$\text{(v.)}\quad x^4 - \tfrac{2}{3}x^3 + \tfrac{2}{9}x^2 + \tfrac{4}{9}x + \tfrac{4}{9} = 0.$$
$$\text{(vi.)}\quad x^4 - 1 = 0.$$
$$\text{(vii.)}\quad x^4 - 14x^3 + 71x^2 - 154x + 111 = 0.$$
$$\text{(viii.)}\quad x^4 - 11x^3 - 5x^2 - x - 1 = 0.$$

. . . .

From (i.) we have the cubic

$$(e)\qquad y^3 + 2y^2 \pm 0y \pm 0x \pm 0 = 0.$$

Dividing by y^2, we have

$$y + 2 = 0.$$

Whence, $y = -2$, and ± 0, and ± 0, and the three quadratics will be

$$y^2 + 2y + 1 = 0,$$
$$y^2 \pm 0y + 1 = 0,$$
$$y^2 \pm 0y + 1 = 0.$$

It is seen that the roots of simple equations, like (1), can be solved mentally, when desired.

From (ii.) we have the cubic

$$(f)\qquad y^3 + 7y^2 + 4y - 23 = 0.$$

Solving (f), we have 1.431+ for one of the roots, and one of the quadratics will be, the root being real,

$$y^2 - 1.431y + 6 = 0.$$

The other two roots of (f) can be found from a quadratic.

From (iii.) we have the cubic

$$(g) \qquad y^3 + 18\,y^2 + 72\,y \pm 0 = 0.$$

Dividing by y, we have

$$y^2 + 18\,y + 72 = 0.$$

Therefore, one of the quadratics will be

$$y^2 \pm 0\,y + 36 = 0.$$

The other two being obtained from the solution of the quadratic,

$$y^2 + 18\,y + 72 = 0.$$

From (iv.) we have the cubic

$$(h) \qquad y^3 + 24.5\,y^2 + 82\,y \pm 0 = 0$$

$$\text{(dividing by } y) \qquad = y^2 + 24.5\,y + 82 = 0.$$

From (v.) we have the cubic

$$(i) \qquad y^3 + \tfrac{2}{9}\,y^2 - \tfrac{56}{27}\,y \pm 0 = 0$$

$$\text{(by division)} \qquad = y^2 + \tfrac{2}{9}\,y - \tfrac{56}{27} = 0.$$

From (vi.) we have the cubic

$$(j) \qquad y^3 \pm 0\,y^2 + 4\,y \pm 0 = 0$$

$$\text{(by division)} \qquad = y^2 + 4 = 0.$$

From (vii.) we have the cubic

$$(k) \qquad y^3 - 71\,y^2 + 1712\,y - 13948 = 0.$$

The biquadratic (vii.) may be more easily solved by separating the equation into the following quadratics:

$$x^2 - 7\,x + 11 + \sqrt{10} = 0,$$

$$x^2 - 7\,x + 11 - \sqrt{10} = 0.$$

(Art. 186, Functions of Squares.)

It is seen that when $(m^2 - 2n)$ and $(o^2 - 2nq)$ are each, respectively, 0, the formula reduces the biquadratic immediately to an equation of the second degree. It will also be noticed that no attention is given to signs and character (real or imaginary) of the roots till they are developed by the solution.

GENERAL SOLUTIONS HIGHER THAN THE FOURTH DEGREE.

322. We have shown that an equation of the fourth degree may be changed to an equation of the *sixth degree*, and to an equation of the *eighth degree;* and that the coefficients of the *sixth* and *eighth* are functions of the coefficients of the *fourth*. As the same universal law enters into the formation of equations of all degrees, the same universal relation exists between the roots and the coefficients of equations of *all* degrees. Then, any equation higher than the *fourth* may also be changed to an equation *higher* or *lower* than the given equation. An equation of the *fifth* degree contains *five* roots, and *no more*. The greatest number of combinations of these roots entering the equation, and taken in pairs of *two* and *two*, is *ten*. The same number of combinations is found when the roots are taken *three* and *three*. Therefore, letting a, b, c, d, e, represent the roots of the *fifth*, $ab, ac, ad, ae, bc, bd, be, cd, ce$, and de will represent the product of these roots taken *two* and *two*. There being *ten* of such quantities, we can form an equation of the *tenth degree;* also, an equation of the same degree from the product of the roots taken *three* and *three*. These two equations can be multiplied together, and we will have an equation of the twentieth degree, the coefficients of which will be functions of the coefficients of the *fifth*. We may also form an equation of the tenth degree by combining each root with each product of the roots taken *four* and *four*.

Thus: $a + bcde$, $b + acde$, $c + abde$, $d + abce$, and $e + abcd$. This will give the following quadratics:

$$x^2 + (a + bcde)x + q = 0,$$
$$x^2 + (b + acde)x + q = 0,$$
$$x^2 + (c + abde)x + q = 0,$$
$$x^2 + (d + abce)x + q = 0,$$
$$x^2 + (e + abcd)x + q = 0.$$

On multiplying together we have an equation of the *tenth* degree, built by the product of *five quadratics*. It will be shown that the coefficients of the new equation are combinations or functions of the coefficients of the *fifth*. In the same way we deal with equations of the *sixth* degree, *seventh* degree, and so on.

323. *Even degree equations, higher than the second, can be separated into the quadratic equations that enter into their formation.*

324. The absolute terms of the quadratics that enter into the formation of *even* degree equations are *quadratic factors* of the equation from which they are derived. An equation of the *fourth degree* has *two* quadratic factors; the *sixth degree, three;* the *eighth degree, four;* the *tenth degree, five;* the *twelfth degree, six;* and so on, for even degree equations.

325. The quadratic factors of the *fourth* will form a *quadratic;* the quadratic factors of the *sixth* will form a *cubic,* and the cubic can be changed to a quadratic; the quadratic factors of the eighth will form a *biquadratic,* which can be changed to a cubic, and the cubic to a quadratic; the quadratic factors of the *tenth* will form a *fifth,* which can be raised to a sixth, and the sixth changed to a cubic; the quadratic factors of the *twelfth* will form a sixth, and the sixth can be changed to a cubic. This is the process by which we are to arrive at general solutions for equations as high as the *twelfth degree.*

326. The great labor required to obtain a formula, by which *odd* degree equations, higher than *three*, can be separated into a cubic and quadratic, or changed to a *cubic*, and the unsatisfactory results of such a formula (as will appear further on) leads us to include the *fifth* in a general solution of the *sixth;* and the *seventh,* in a general solution of the *eighth.*

GENERAL SOLUTION OF THE SIXTH DEGREE.

327. We shall now proceed to a general solution of the sixth degree. The general equation is

$$(S) \qquad x^6 + mx^5 + nx^4 + ox^3 + px^2 + tx + q = 0.$$

Let (S) be built by the product of the following quadratics:

$$\text{(i.)}\quad x^2 + \frac{m}{a}x + y = 0,$$

$$\text{(ii.)}\quad x^2 + \frac{m}{b}x + z = 0,$$

$$\text{(iii.)}\quad x^2 + \frac{m}{c}x + w = 0.$$

On multiplying together the three preceding quadratics, we obtain:

$$(T)\quad x^6 + m\left(\frac{1}{a}+\frac{1}{b}+\frac{1}{c}\right)x^5 + \left[y+z+w+m^2\left(\frac{1}{ab}+\frac{1}{ac}+\frac{1}{bc}\right)\right]x^4$$
$$+\left[m\left(\frac{z+w}{a}+\frac{y+w}{b}+\frac{z+y}{c}\right)+\frac{m^3}{abc}\right]x^3$$
$$+\left[yz+yw+zw+m^2\left(\frac{w}{ab}+\frac{z}{ac}+\frac{y}{bc}\right)\right]x^2$$
$$+m\left(\frac{zw}{a}+\frac{yw}{b}+\frac{yz}{c}\right)x + yzw = 0.$$

The coefficients of (S) and (T) being equal by hypothesis, and an hypothesis which is *true*, because six quantities are considered, viz.: y, z, w, and $\frac{1}{a}$, $\frac{1}{b}$, and $\frac{1}{c}$, the quantities y, z, w are the quadratic factors of (T), also of (S). It is evident that when y, z, and w become known, that by substituting their values in (T), that $\frac{1}{a}$, $\frac{1}{b}$, and $\frac{1}{c}$ can be obtained. Then, by substituting these values in the quadratics (i.), (ii.), and (iii.), the roots of the general equation (S) can be expressed in terms of its coefficients.

FORMULÆ. GENERAL SOLUTION OF THE SIXTH DEGREE.

$$(U)\begin{cases}\text{(i.) Let } n-\dfrac{m^2}{A}=\left(\dfrac{Ao}{2\,m}-\dfrac{m^2}{2\,A^2}\right)=y+z+w.\\[2ex] \text{(ii.) Let } p-\left(\dfrac{m^2n}{B^2}-\dfrac{m^4}{B^3}\right)=\dfrac{Bt}{m}=yz+yw+zw.\\[2ex] \text{(iii.) Then } \qquad q=yzw.\end{cases}$$

$$\text{i.}=A^3-\frac{2\,mn}{o}A^2+\frac{2\,m^3}{o}A-\frac{m^3}{o}=0.$$

$$\text{ii.}=B^4-\frac{mp}{t}B^3+\frac{m^3n}{t}B-\frac{m^5}{t}=0.$$

When A is obtained from (i.), $y+z+w$ is found from either $n-\frac{m^2}{A}$, or $\frac{Ao}{2\,m}-\frac{m^2}{2\,A^2}$; and when B is obtained from (ii.), $yz+yw+zw$ is found from $p-\left(\frac{m^2n}{B^2}-\frac{m^4}{B^3}\right)$, or $\frac{Bt}{m}$.

When $A=B$, $\frac{1}{a}$, $\frac{1}{b}$, and $\frac{1}{c}$ are equal, while q *in all cases remains permanent, and independent of the values of A or B.*

While A has three values, and B four, a little practice on the part of the reader will enable him to easily determine which value is to be taken. Should the roots of the sixth be all real and unequal, or real and imaginary, the roots, in many instances, will be found in the form of incommensurable roots; *but in all cases the roots thus obtained will clearly indicate whether the root is integral or fractional.*

328. Before proceeding further, we shall now give a few illustrations of the application of the formula in the solution of all kinds and classes of equations of the sixth degree.

Let it be required to find the roots of the following equations:

(1) $x^6 - 8 = 0.$

(2) $x^6 + 7 = 0.$

(3) $x^6 - 7x^2 + 7 = 0.$

(4) $x^6 + 13x^5 + 64x^4 + 154x^2 + 193x + 121x + 30 = 0.$

(5) $x^6 - 21x^5 + 175x^4 - 735x^3 + 1624x^2 - 1764x + 400 = 0.$

(6) $x^6 + 10x^5 + 45\frac{1}{3}x^4 + 117.04x^3 + 162.33x^2 + 96.66x - 27 = 0.$

(7) $x^6 - 60x^5 + 1441x^4 - 17640x^3 + 115099x^2 - 373980x + 467467 = 0.$

(8) $x^6 - 34x^5 + 459x^4 - 3134x^3 + 11348x^2 - 20520x + 14400.$

(9) $x^6 - 6x^5 + 12x^4 - 8x^3 - 13x^2 + 26x - 7 = 0.$

From (1) we have the cubic

(*a*) $$y^3 - 8 = 0.$$

Solving (*a*) we obtain, for the quadratic factors of (1), 2, and $-1 \pm \sqrt{-3}$. The quadratics will be

$$x^2 \pm 0x - 2 = 0,$$
$$x^2 \pm 0x + 1 + \sqrt{-3} = 0,$$
$$x^2 \pm 0x + 1 - \sqrt{-3} = 0,$$

which, solved, will give the roots of the equation.

From (2) we have the cubic

(*b*) $$y^3 + 7 = 0.$$

Solving (*b*), the roots are obtained as in (*a*).

From (3) we have the cubic

(*c*) $$y^3 - 7x + 7 = 0.$$

The roots of (*c*) are all real but unequal (Art. 315).

The roots are found to be 1.3569+, 1.6920+, and − 3.0489+. The quadratics will be

$$x^2 \pm 0x - 1.3569 = 0,$$

$$x^2 \pm 0x - 1.6920 = 0,$$

$$x^2 \pm 0x + 3.0489 = 0,$$

and the solution of which renders the roots of (3).

From (4) we have the cubic

(*d*) $$y^3 + 9.96 + y^2 + 30.99 + y + 30 = 0.$$

The solution of (*d*) gives − 1.99+, − 2.99+, 4.98+ nearly, which clearly indicates that the roots are, or should be, − 2, − 3, and − 5.

The quadratics will then be

$$x^2 + \frac{m}{a}x + 2 = 0,$$

$$x^2 + \frac{m}{b}x + 3 = 0,$$

$$x^2 + \frac{m}{b} + 5 = 0.$$

Substituting for *m* its value 13, and multiplying together the three quadratics, or substituting directly in (*T*) the values of *y*, *z*, and *w*, the quadratics complete will be

$$x^2 + 6x + 5 = 0,$$

$$x^2 + 4x + 3 = 0,$$

$$x^2 + 3x + 2 = 0,$$

which, solved, give the roots of (4).

From (5) we have the cubic

$$(e) \qquad y^3 - 128\,y^2 + 252\,y - 400 = 0.$$

Solving (*e*), we obtain for the quadratic factors of (5), -2, $-13+\sqrt{-31}$, and $-13-\sqrt{-31}$.

A and *B* are found to be equal. Therefore we write the complete quadratics

$$x^2 - 7\,x + 2 = 0,$$

$$x^2 - 7\,x + 13 + \sqrt{-31} = 0,$$

$$x^2 - 7\,x + 13 - \sqrt{-31} = 0,$$

which, solved, render the roots of (5).

From (6) we have the cubic

$$(f) \qquad y^3 + 12\,y^2 + 28.998 + y - 27 = 0.$$

Solving (*f*) the quadratic factors of the difficult equation (6) are obtained. When these factors are obtained, by substituting directly in (*T*), $\frac{1}{a}, \frac{1}{b}, \frac{1}{c}$ are obtained.

From (7) we have the cubic

$$(g) \qquad y^3 - 241\,y^2 + 18699\,y - 459459 = 0,$$

the roots of which are 77, and $82+\sqrt{653}$, $82-\sqrt{653}$.

A and *B* are found to be equal; therefore the complete quadratics will be

$$x^2 - 20\,x + 77 = 0,$$

$$x^2 - 20\,x + 82 + \sqrt{653} = 0,$$

$$x^2 - 20\,x + 82 - \sqrt{653} = 0.$$

Solving these quadratics, the roots of (7) are obtained.

From (8) we have the cubic,

$$(h) \quad y^3 - 73.99 + y^2 + 1799.998 + y - 14400 = 0.$$

Writing the equation

$$y^3 - 74\,y^2 + 1800\,y - 14400 = 0$$

Solving this last equation, we obtain 20, 24, and 30 as the quadratic factors of (8).

A and B being unequal, the quadratics cannot be immediately formed, and we must therefore substitute the values of y, z, and w, which are now found to be 20, 24, and 30, in (T). Having done this, we obtain the complete quadratics, which are

$$x^2 - 12\,x + 20 = 0,$$

$$x^2 - 11\,x + 24 = 0,$$

$$x^2 - 11\,x + 30 = 0.$$

Solving these quadratics, we obtain as the roots of (8), 2, 3, 5, 6, 8, and 10.

From (9) we have the cubic

$$(i) \qquad y^3 \pm 0\,y^2 - 13\,y - 7 = 0.$$

The roots of (i) are all real (Art. 315). A and B being equal, this difficult equation (9) is readily solved, as soon as the roots of (i) are obtained.

329. Leaving the *sixth* for further consideration, we will now turn our attention to the general equation of the fifth degree, which is

$$(V) \qquad x^5 + mx^4 + nx^3 + ox^2 + px + q = 0.$$

The coefficients n and o represent the greatest number of combinations of its roots. The number of combinations represented by n is *ten*. Each combination is the product of two of the roots. With these *ten* combinations as roots, we can build an equation of the *tenth degree*. Such an equation will be, according to Th. V. (Art. 179, Functions of Squares),

$$(W) \quad x^{10} + ny^9 + (mo - p)\,y^8$$
$$+ \{(2\,np - 3\,mq) + (m^2 - 2\,n)p + [o^2 - 2\,(pn - mq)]\}\,y^7$$
$$+ \cdots + oq^3y + q^4 = 0.$$

The coefficient of y^7 represents the sum of one hundred and twenty combinations. If the reader will take the pains to form the coefficient of y^6, he will admit that the task is no easy one, and that it requires much patience and a vast amount of mechanical labor.

Letting the quantities ab, ac, ad, ae, bc, bd, be, cd, ce, de, represent the roots of (W), we may form an equation of the *third degree* from one of the following sets of the given quantities:

(1) $cd + de$,

(2) $ab + ae + ad + ae$,

(3) $bc + bd + be + ce$.

(1) $a(b + c + d + e)$,

(2) $b(c + d + e)$,

(3) $c(d + e) + de$.

Or we may form a quadratic from the following combinations:

(1) $ab + ac + bd + de + ce$,

(2) $ae + ad + bc + be + cd$.

We have carried the investigation far enough to be convinced that the combinations can be made, but the labor will be great and the formula very complex.

330. Changing (V) to another equation of the *fifth* degree, the roots of which will be the products of the roots taken *four* and *four*, the coefficient of x represents the sum of such roots. We may, therefore, write, by the aid of Th. V., the following equation:

$$(X) \qquad x^5 + px^4 + oqx^3 + nq^2x^2 + mq^3x + q^4 = 0.$$

On multiplying (V), Art. 329, and (X) together, we obtain the equation

$$(Y)\quad x^{10}+(m+p)x^9+(n+mp+oq)x^8+(o+np+moq+nq^2)x^7$$
$$+(p+op+noq+mnq^2+mq^3)x^6$$
$$+(q+p^2+o^2q+n^2q^2+m^2q^3+q^4)x^5$$
$$+(pq+poq+onq^2+mnq^3+mq^4)x^4$$
$$+(oq^2+pnq^2+omq^3+nq^4)x^3$$
$$+(nq^3+pmq^3+oq^4)x^2+q^4(m+p)x+q^5=0.$$

The roots of (Y) are evidently the roots of the following five quadratics:

$$x^2+(a+bcde)x+q=0,$$
$$x^2+(b+acde)x+q=0,$$
$$x^2+(c+abde)x+q=0,$$
$$x^2+(d+abce)x+q=0,$$
$$x^2+(e+abcd)x+q=0.$$

Letting, for convenience, the quantities a', b', c', d', e', represent, respectively, the quantities $a+bcde$, $b+acde$, $\cdots$, on substitution *in*, and multiplication *of*, the five preceding quadratics, we obtain the equation,

$$(Z)\quad x^{10}+(a'+b'+c'+d'+e')x^9+(5q+p_2)x^8$$
$$+[4q(a'+b'+c'+d'+e')+p_3]x^7$$
$$+(10q^2+3qp_2+p_4)x^6$$
$$+[6q^2(a'+b'+c'+d'+e')+2qp_3+a'b'c'd'e']x^5$$
$$+\cdots+q^4(a'+b'+c'+d'+e')x+q^5=0.$$

The coefficients of (Y) and (Z) being equal, we may now write the equation of the *fifth* degree, whose roots are the sums of the quantities $(a+bcde)$, $(b+acde)$, $\cdots$. Then, writing y for x, the equation is

$$(A)\quad y^5 + (m+p)y^4 + [(n+mp+oq) - 5q]y^3$$
$$+ [(o+np+moq+nq^2) - 4q(m+p)]y^2$$
$$+ (p+op+noq+mnq^2+mq^3)$$
$$- \{10q^2 + 3q[(n+mp+oq) - 5q]\}y$$
$$+ (q+p^2+o^2q+n^2q^2+m^2q^3+q^4)$$
$$- [6q^2(m+p) + 2q(o+np+moq+nq^2) - 4q(m+p)] = 0.$$

We see that, complex as these combinations are, they can, nevertheless, be formed, and that the sums of the quantities $(a+bcde)$, $(b+acde)$, $\cdots$, can be made the roots of an equation of the *fifth* degree, and that the coefficients of (A) are made up from combinations of the coefficients of the general equation. We shall now leave the *fifth* and take up the *sixth* again.

331. The coefficients of the second term of the *sixth*, like all other equations, represents the sum of the products of the roots, taken two and two. These combinations will form *five* cubic equations, as follows:

$$x^3 + (ab+cd+ef)x^2 + (abcd+abef+cdef)x + q = 0,$$
$$x^3 + (ac+de+bf)x^2 + (acde+abcf+bdef)x + q = 0,$$
$$x^3 + (ad+be+cf)x^2 + (abde+acdf+bcef)x + q = 0,$$
$$x^3 + (ae+bc+df)x^2 + (abce+adef+bcdf)x + q = 0,$$
$$x^3 + (af+bd+ce)x^2 + (abdf+acef+bcde)x + q = 0.$$

Adding these five equations together, and expressing the coefficients in terms of the coefficients of the general equation, we have

$$(B)\qquad 5x^3 + nx^2 + px + 5q = 0.$$

Dividing the equation by 5, we have

$$(C)\qquad x^3 + \frac{n}{5}x^2 + \frac{p}{5}x + q = 0.$$

C is a true cubic, and can be used to advantage when the roots of the sixth are equal, and *real*.

The sixth can also be changed to an equation of the *fifteenth*, *twentieth*, and *twelfth* degrees.

GENERAL SOLUTION OF THE EIGHTH DEGREE.

332. The general equation of the eighth degree is

$$(D) \quad x^8 + mx^7 + nx^6 + ox^5 + px^4 + tx^3 + ux^2 + vx + q = 0.$$

Let (D) be formed by the product of the following quadratics:

$$(1) \quad x^2 + \frac{m}{a}x + e = 0,$$

$$(2) \quad x^2 + \frac{m}{b}x + f = 0,$$

$$(3) \quad x^2 + \frac{m}{c}x + g = 0,$$

$$(4) \quad x^2 + \frac{m}{d}x + h = 0.$$

On multiplying these quadratics together we obtain an equation of the eighth degree, built by the product of four quadratics. e, f, g, and h are the quadratic factors. We are first to consider these factors, and then the quantities $\frac{1}{a}$, $\frac{1}{b}$, $\frac{1}{c}$, and $\frac{1}{d}$.

Formulæ. General Solution of the Eighth Degree.

$$(E)\left\{\begin{array}{l}
\text{(i.) Let } n - \dfrac{3m^2}{2A} = \left[\dfrac{Aa}{3m} - \dfrac{m^2}{3A}\right] = e + f + g + h. \\[2ex]
\text{(ii.) Let } p + \dfrac{9m^4}{8B^2} - \left[\dfrac{3m^2n}{4B} + \dfrac{m^4}{4B^3}\right] = \dfrac{Bt}{2m} + \dfrac{3m^4}{4B^3} - \dfrac{m^2n}{8B} \\[1ex]
\qquad\qquad = ef + eg + eh + fg + fh + gh. \\[2ex]
\text{(iii.) Let } u - \left[\dfrac{Ct}{2} + \dfrac{3m^5}{4C^3} - \dfrac{m^3n}{8C}\right] = \dfrac{Cv}{m} \\[1ex]
\qquad\qquad = efg + efh + egh + fgh. \\[2ex]
\text{(iv.) Then} \qquad q = efgh.
\end{array}\right.$$

When A, B, and C are found, we may readily form the biquadratic, which can be changed to a cubic by formula (K), Art. 318. When A, B, and C are equal, the sum of the roots of the quadratics that build the eighth are equal, in which case the roots may be equal; but if the sum of the roots of the quadratics is equal, it does not necessarily follow that the roots are equal. When the roots of any equation (numerical) are equal, it can be easily detected by Art. 138 (Absolute Theorems).

333. We will now give a few practical illustrations of the formulæ (E) in the solution of equations of the *eighth degree.*

Let it be required to find the roots of the following equations:

(1) $x^8 + 2x^6 - 17x^4 - 18x^2 + 73 = 0.$

(2) $x^8 - 17x^6 + 67x^5 + 5x^4 - 595x^3 + 1736x^2 - 2215x + 1711 = 0.$

(3) $x^8 - 12x^7 + 65x^6 - 207x^5 + 371x^4 - 255x^3 - 458x^2 + 1185x - 1211 = 0.$

. . . .

From (1) we have the biquadratic

$$(a) \qquad y^4 + y^3 - 17y^2 - 18y + 73 = 0.$$

By formula (K), Art. 318, (a) reduces to the cubic

$$(b) \qquad z^3 - 17z^2 - 300z + 5361 = 0.$$

The odd powers of (1) being wanting, the coefficient of x in the quadratics must be 0.

From (2) we have the biquadratic

$$(c) \qquad y^4 + y^3 - 67y^2 + 5y + 1711 = 0.$$

We may now reduce (c) to a cubic.

From (3) we have the biquadratic

$$(d) \qquad y^4 + 11y^3 + 13y^2 - 395y - 1211 = 0.$$

Find the values for y in (d), and substitute in the product of the four preceding quadratics (1), (2), (3), and (4), and, solving by quadratics the roots of the difficult equation (3) are obtained.

But, in determining (d), we find that A, B, and C, of the formulæ (E), are equal. We may, therefore, write for the first two terms of such quadratics,

$$\text{(i.)}\ x^2 - 3x,$$

$$\text{(ii.)}\ x^2 - 3x,$$

$$\text{(iii.)}\ x^2 - 3x,$$

$$\text{(iv.)}\ x^2 - 3x.$$

When the roots of (d) are obtained, by substituting their values in the quadratics, (i.), (ii.), (iii.), (iv.), which, solved, renders the roots of equation (3).

MISCELLANEOUS SUBJECTS.

334. The term, general solution, applied to equations, means a method for the solution of equations that proves to be true in the major. It has been used, however, in a much broader sense. Thus, when we speak of a general solution of the *fourth* degree, the meaning conveyed by the term (general solution) is that the method applies alike to all equations of the *fourth degree*. It is presumed that a general solution of any degree equation will render the roots of all kinds and classes of such equations. This has been the accepted meaning in the past. We now question the universality of the term as heretofore applied to the solution of equations. Not in the major, nor in the minor-major cases, will the methods which have been offered for a general solution of the fourth degree render the roots. They are not *general*, much less *universal;* and, therefore, cannot be relied upon. It is time that such methods (presumed to be true in all cases) should be questioned. We now question them; and, *with reason.* They will appear in the order of their importance.

335. The general equation of the fourth degree is

(i.) $$x^4 + mx^3 + nx^2 + ox + q = 0.$$

(ii.) Assume that

$$\left(x^2 + \frac{m}{2}x + A\right)^2 - (Bx + C)^2 = x^4 + mx^3 + nx^2 + ox + q.$$

This is the most pleasing and polished artifice ever offered for a general solution of the *fourth* degree; and it has to recommend it that distinguished scholar and mathematician of whom all Englishmen are proud, and to whom all mankind are indebted for his valuable and scholarly arrangement and compilation of mathematical works. It requires, however, but little probing to expose its compassed application.

(1) It has for its object a general solution of the fourth degree.

(2) It is, therefore, not to be regarded as a special solution, applicable to only certain classes of equations of the fourth degree. Were it to be so regarded, its author would have so designated it.

(3) By performing the indicated operations in (i.), and equating homogeneous terms in (ii.) and (i.), we have for consideration the quantities A, B, and C, which are the only quantities to be considered, and which it is proposed to find in terms of the coefficients of the general equation.

What has become of the fourth quantity under consideration? The equation being of the fourth degree, we unquestionably have for consideration its four coefficients m, n, o, q, which are functions of its four roots, which the equation is known to contain. A glance at the formula (ii.)

reveals the fact that the relation of the roots to one of these coefficients is known, or assumed to be known. That is, the sum of the roots of each quadratic that enters into the formation of the biquadratic is known or assumed to be known.

To make the foregoing statements plain, let us perform the indicated operations in (ii.).

$$(1)\quad \left(x^2+\frac{m}{2}x+A\right)^2=x^4+mx^3+\left(2A+\frac{m^2}{4}\right)x^2+Amx+A^2.$$

$$(2)\qquad (Bx+C)^2=B^2x^2+2BCx+C^2.$$

Taking (2) from (1), we have

$$(\text{iii.})\quad x^4+mx^3+\left(2A+\frac{m^2}{4}-B^2\right)x^2+(Am-2BC)x+A^2-C^2.$$

By comparing (iii.) with (i.), we see that the only coefficients affected by $(Bx+C)^2$ is n, o, and q. It is, therefore, assumed that the sum of the roots in each quadratic that enters into the formation of (i.) is numerically or algebraically the same. It cannot, therefore, be classed as a general solution; and by no means universal in its application to the solution of all kinds and classes of equations of the fourth degree. It is a desperate effort to form a cubic from a biquadratic by the consideration of only three coefficients of the general equation.

Let us assume that

$$(\text{iv.})\quad \left(x^2+\frac{m}{a}x+B\right)\left(x^2+\frac{m}{b}x+C\right)=x^4+mx^3+nx^2+ox+q.$$

This is a true hypothesis, because four quantities are considered, viz.: $\frac{m}{b}$, $\frac{m}{a}$, B, and C. The functions of these quantities form the coefficients of the general equation.

Again, assume that

$$(\text{v.})\quad \left(x^2+\frac{m}{2}x+B\right)\left(x^2+\frac{m}{2}x+C\right)=x^4+mx^3+nx^2+ox+q.$$

(v.) cannot be true in all cases; and can only be applied when $n - \frac{m^2}{4} = \frac{2o}{m}$ (Art. 261, Functions of Squares).

336. All methods requiring the removal of the second term, in order to obtain a general solution of the given equation, are erroneous. This applies to equations of all degrees. Any attempt to destroy, by artifice, the natural relation of the roots to the coefficients will end in failure, and produce naught but unsatisfactory results. Therefore, *to evolve a general solution for an equation of the mth degree m quantities must be considered; and no more, no less.*

www.ingramcontent.com/pod-product-compliance
Lightning Source LLC
LaVergne TN
LVHW010602110826
845149LV00003B/746

* 9 7 8 1 4 1 8 1 8 0 6 7 6 *